SEX CRIMINALS

TWO WORLDS, ONE COP

MATT FRACTION
CHIP ZDARSKY

THOMAS K
EDITING

DREW GILL
PRODUCTION

IMAGE COMICS, INC.
Robert Kirkman – Chief Operating Officer
Erik Larsen – Chief Financial Officer
Todd McFarlane – President
Marc Silvestri – Chief Executive Officer
Jim Valentino – Vice-President

Eric Stephenson – Publisher
Ron Richards – Director of Business Development
Jennifer de Guzman – Director of Trade Book Sales
Kat Salazar – Director of PR & Marketing
Corey Murphy – Director of Retail Sales
Jeremy Sullivan – Director of Digital Sales
Emilio Bautista – Sales Assistant
Branwyn Bigglestone – Senior Accounts Manager
Emily Miller – Accounts Manager
Jessica Ambriz – Administrative Assistant
Tyler Shainline – Events Coordinator
David Brothers – Content Manager
Jonathan Chan – Production Manager
Drew Gill – Art Director
Meredith Wallace – Print Manager
Addison Duke – Production Artist
Vincent Kukua – Production Artist
Tricia Ramos – Production Assistant
IMAGECOMICS.COM

To Chip's mom and dad
Thank you for fucking
And making my Chipper
He is my everything

MATT

To mommy and daddy.
I got my above-average peener
size from daddy, my insatiable
sexual curiosity from mommy, and
my innate sense of right and
wrong from both. See you at
Thanksgiving.

CHIP

6
COMING ON

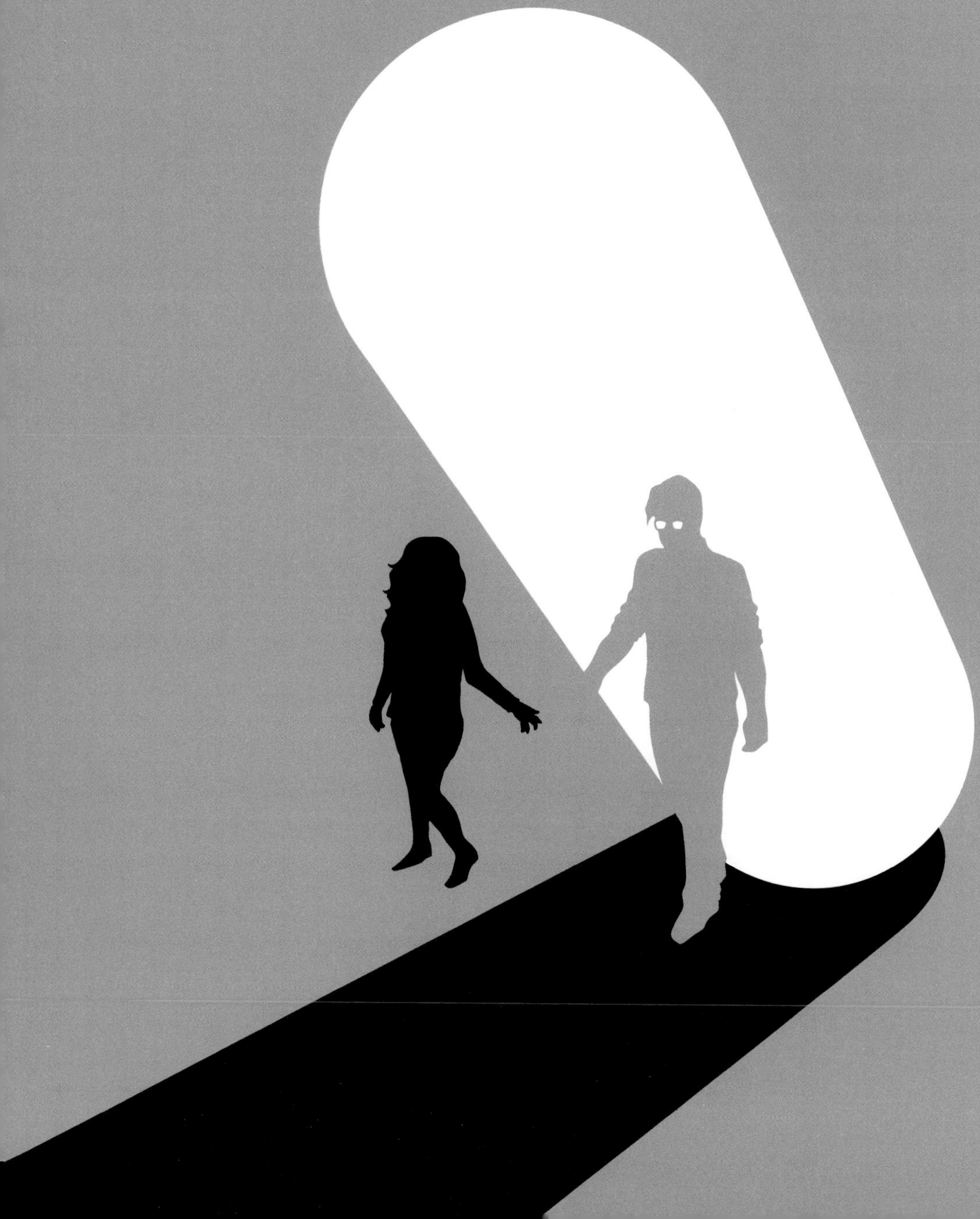

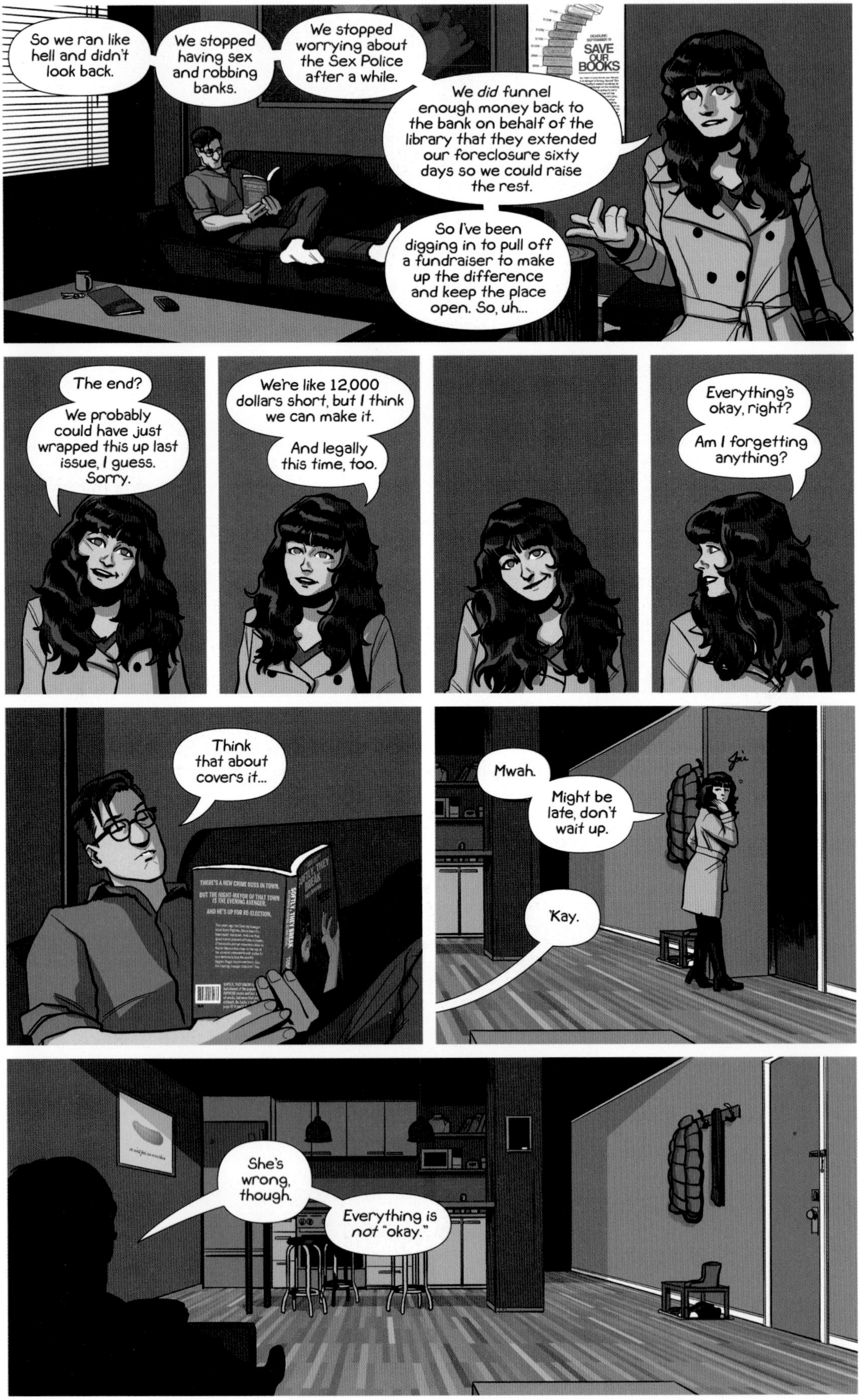
So we ran like hell and didn't look back.
We stopped having sex and robbing banks.
We stopped worrying about the Sex Police after a while.
SAVE OUR BOOKS
We *did* funnel enough money back to the bank on behalf of the library that they extended our foreclosure sixty days so we could raise the rest.
So I've been digging in to pull off a fundraiser to make up the difference and keep the place open. So, uh...
The end?
We probably could have just wrapped this up last issue, I guess. Sorry.
We're like 12,000 dollars short, but I think we can make it.
And legally this time, too.
Everything's okay, right?
Am I forgetting anything?
Think that about covers it...
THERE'S A NEW CRIME BOSS IN TOWN.
BUT THE NIGHT-MAYOR OF THAT TOWN IS THE EVENING AVENGER.
AND HE'S UP FOR RE-ELECTION.
SOFTLY, THEY BREAK
Mwah.
Might be late, don't wait up.
'Kay.
She's wrong, though.
Everything is *not* "okay."

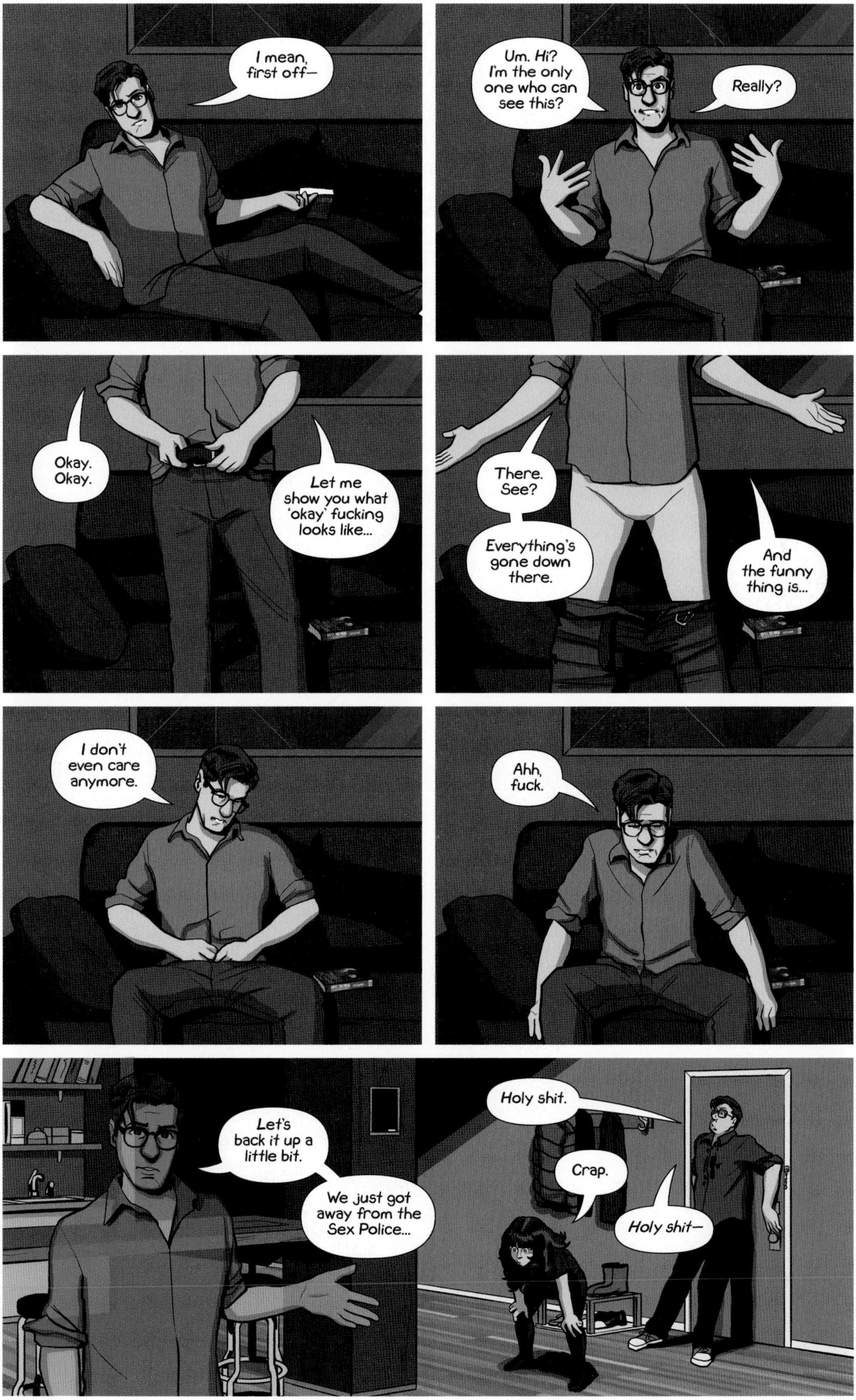
I mean, first off—
Um. Hi? I'm the only one who can see this?
Really?
Okay. Okay.
Let me show you what 'okay' fucking looks like...
There. See?
Everything's gone down there.
And the funny thing is...
I don't even care anymore.
Ahh, fuck.
Let's back it up a little bit.
We just got away from the Sex Police...
Holy shit.
Crap.
Holy shit—

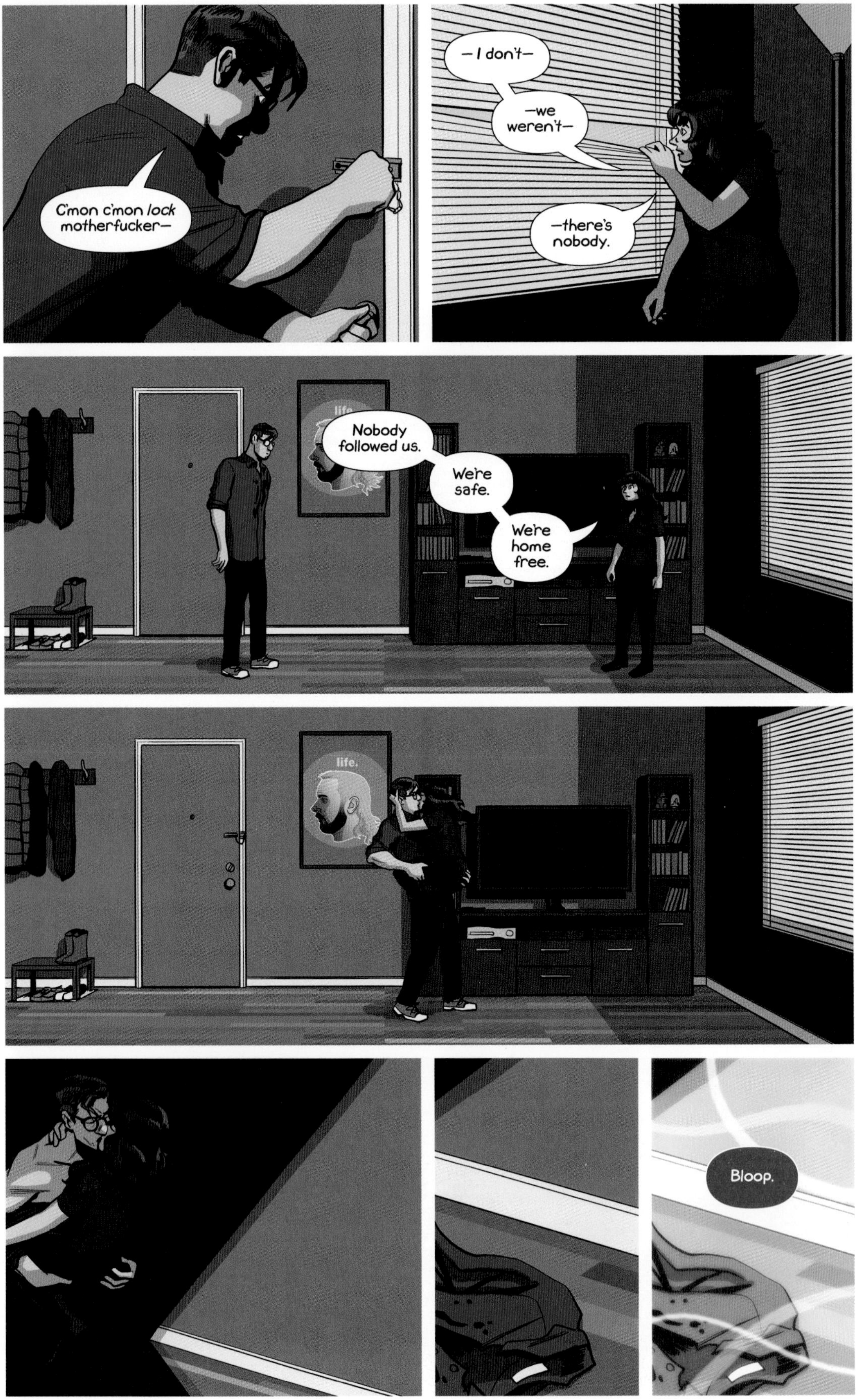
C'mon c'mon *lock* motherfucker—
—I don't—
—we weren't—
—there's nobody.
Nobody followed us.
We're safe.
We're home free.
Bloop.

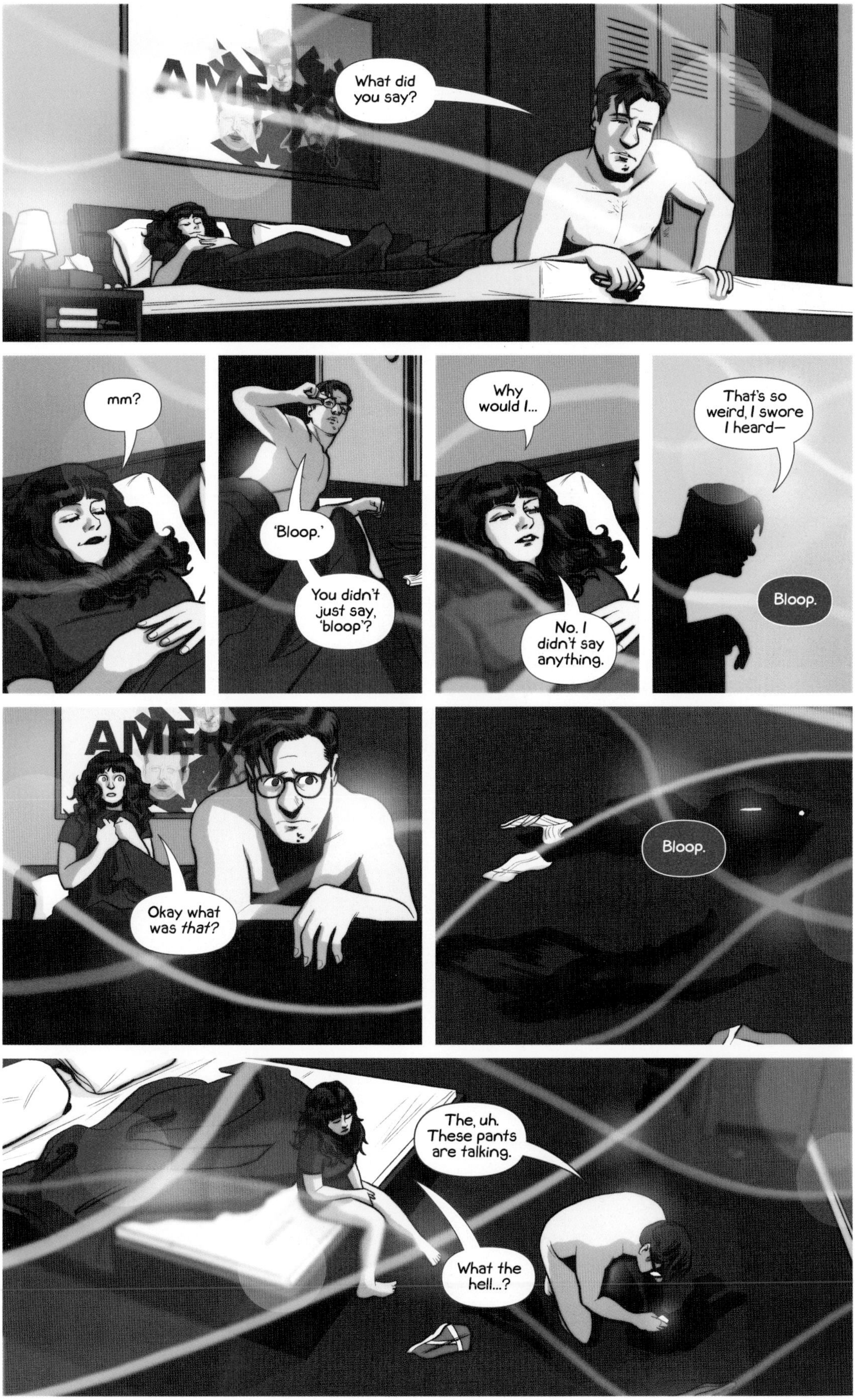
What did you say?
mm?
'Bloop.'
You didn't just say, 'bloop'?
Why would I...
No. I didn't say anything.
That's so weird, I swore I heard—
Bloop.
Okay what was *that*?
Bloop.
The, uh. These pants are talking.
What the hell...?

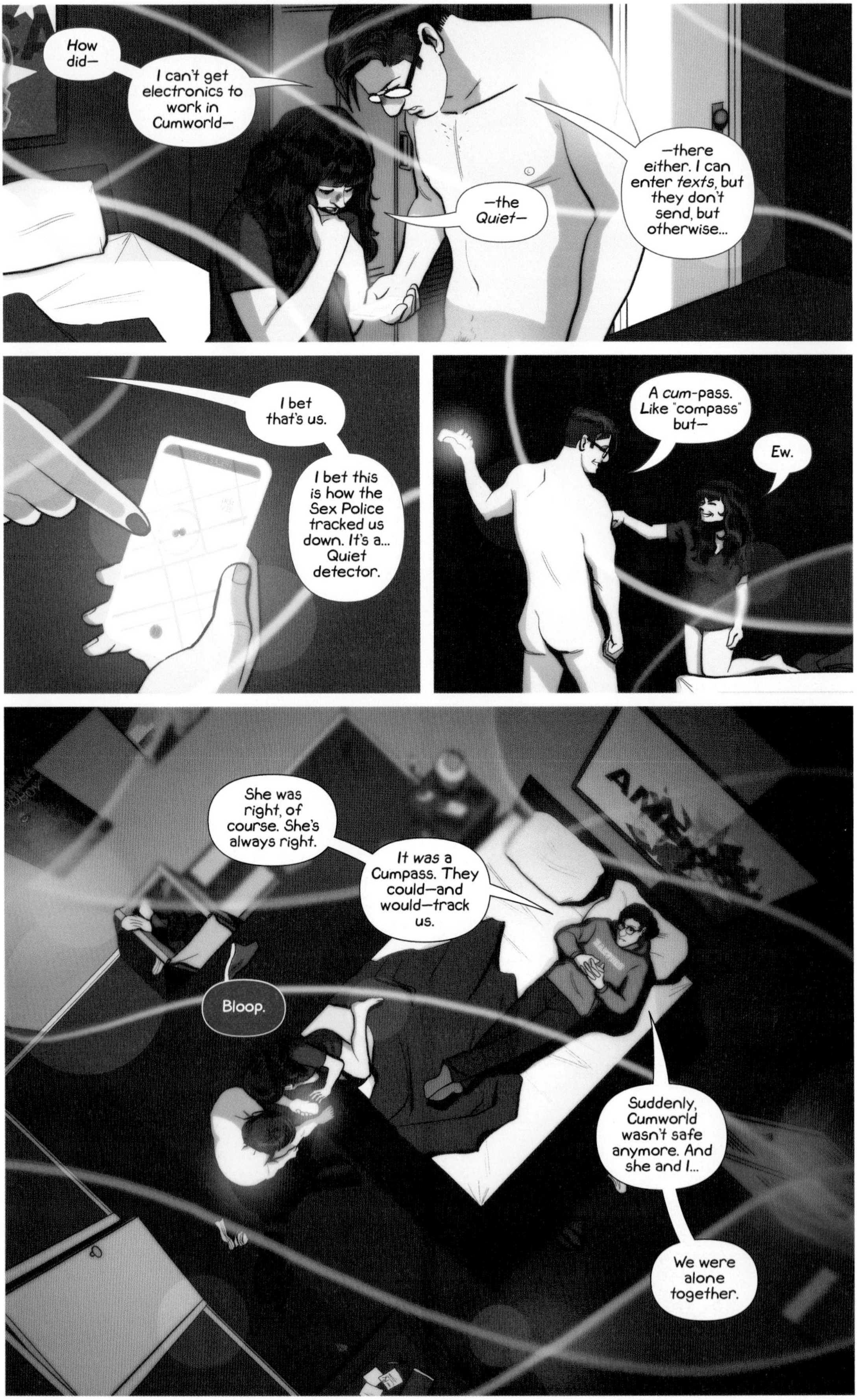
How did—
I can't get electronics to work in Cumworld—
—the *Quiet*—
—there either. I can enter *texts*, but they don't send, but otherwise...
I bet that's us.
I bet this is how the Sex Police tracked us down. It's a... Quiet detector.
A *cum*-pass. Like "compass" but—
Ew.
She was right, of course. She's always right.
It *was* a Cumpass. They could—and would—track us.
Bloop.
Suddenly, Cumworld wasn't safe anymore. And she and I...
We were alone together.

Okay so... so, see, before we get to that extension, we have to get to the dickless ghost thing, and to get to that we needed the Cumpass.

Okay, so:

LIFE GOES ON

Bloop.

TH
"all the news th
in the paper"

Park

attraction in Ellis Park was
finally put out on Monday
morning over th
quick-think

minutes firefighters
on the scene and sp
non-flammable wat

thanks

Whoa—she rubbed one out.

Mm.

Maybe she doesn't even need to rub anymore. Maybe she can just, like—squeeeeeze into Cum—

—the Quiet.

Mm.

Hey, speaking of—

Ehn—

—kinda need to get this done for the bank presentation thing.

Yeah, sure, no, of course.

...

Let me know if I can help or—

Uh oh.

Honeymoon's over.

Hey, if I go rub one out in the shower, that thing'll go off, huh.

Who invented this, anyway? I mean—where did it come from?

It's not like you can just go to the Tronic Barn and buy one. I bet they're expensive to make, too.

Shit, everything's expensive when you're a grown-up.

We are grown-ups, Jon....

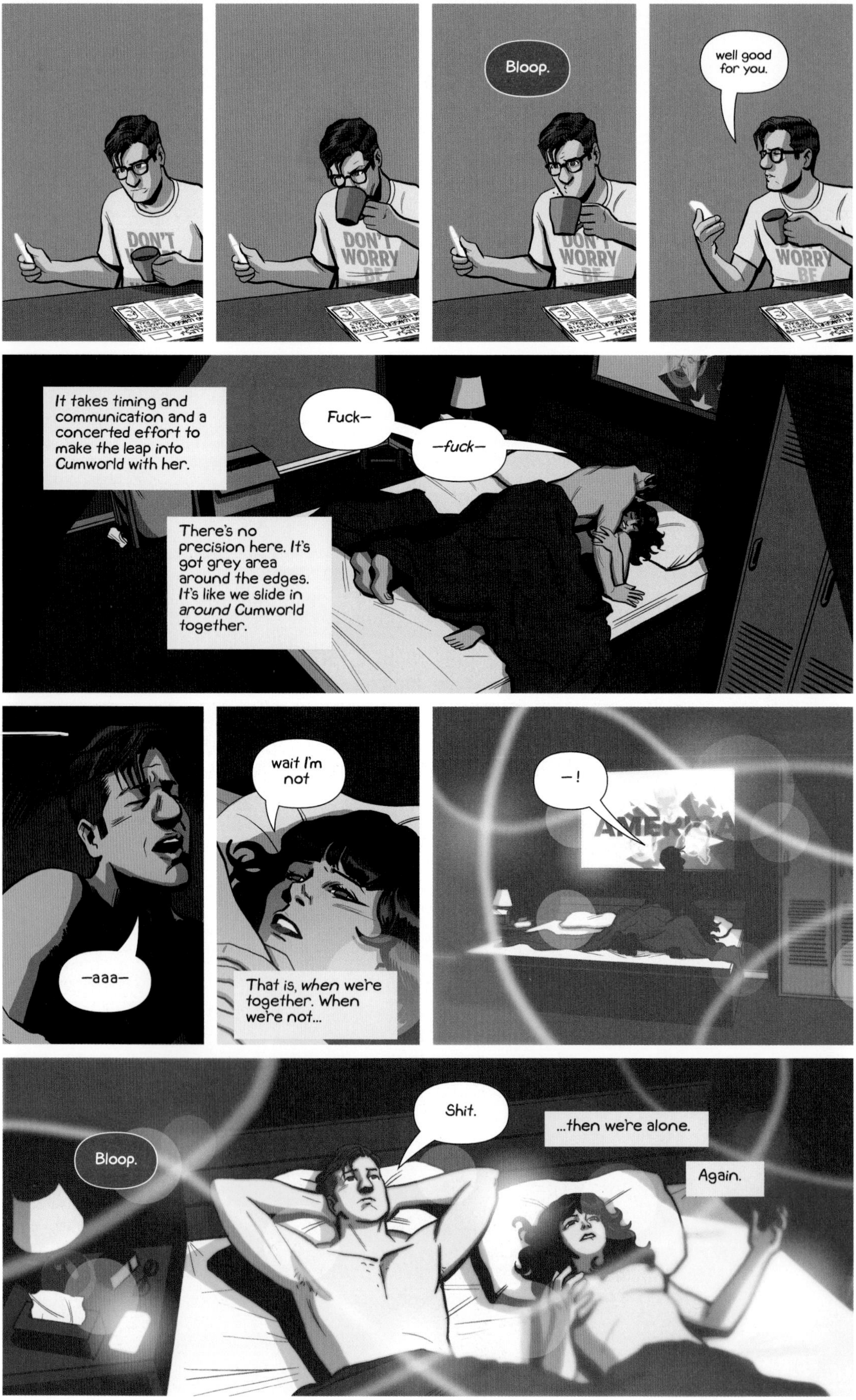
Bloop.
well good for you.
It takes timing and communication and a concerted effort to make the leap into Cumworld with her.
Fuck—
—fuck—
There's no precision here. It's got grey area around the edges. It's like we slide in *around* Cumworld together.
—aaa—
wait I'm not
That is, *when* we're together. When we're not...
—!
Bloop.
Shit.
...then we're alone.
Again.

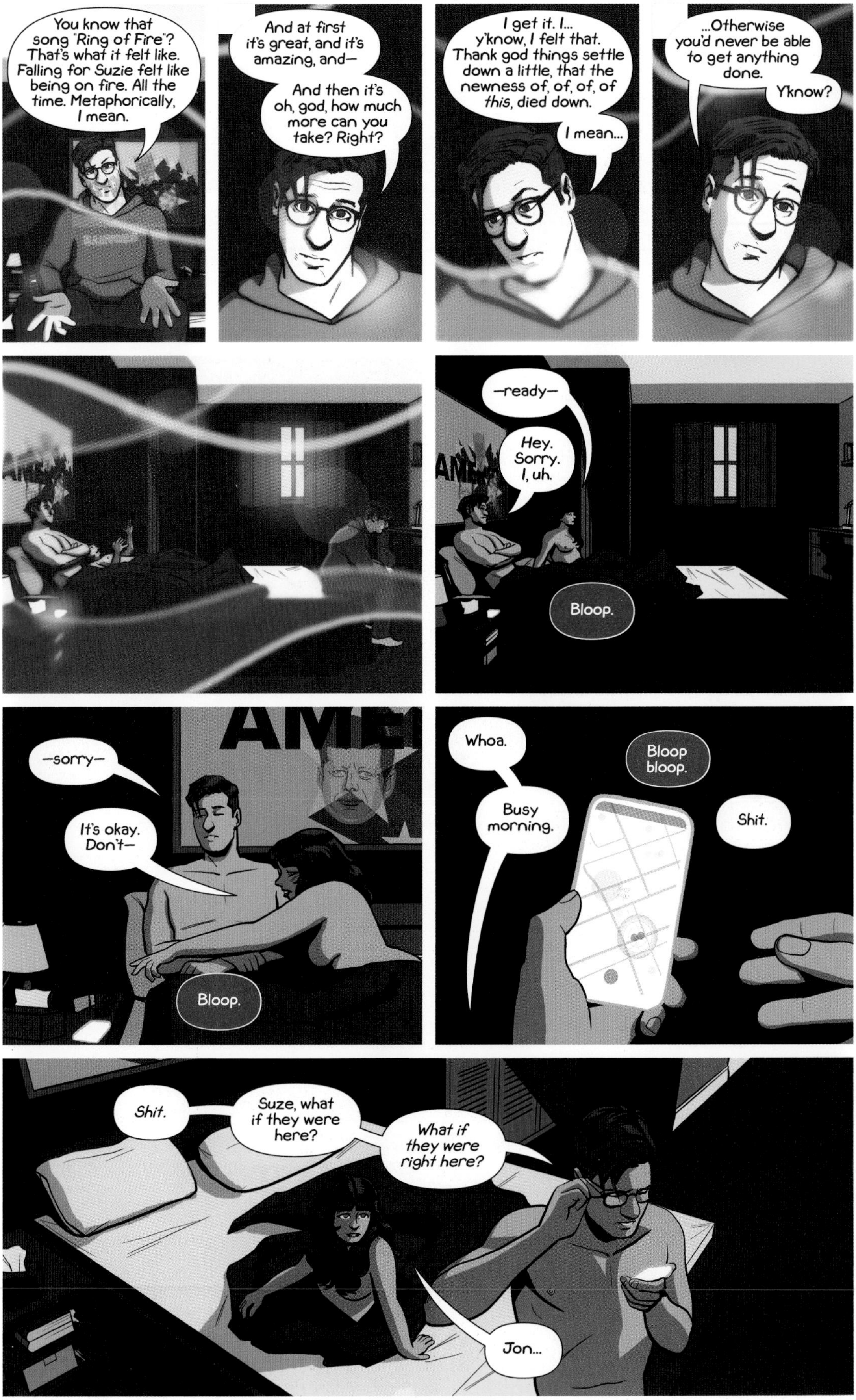
You know that song "Ring of Fire"? That's what it felt like. Falling for Suzie felt like being on fire. All the time. Metaphorically, I mean.
HARVARD
And at first it's great, and it's amazing, and—
And then it's oh, god, how much more can you take? Right?
I get it. I... y'know, I felt that. Thank god things settle down a little, that the newness of, of, of, of *this*, died down.
I mean...
...Otherwise you'd never be able to get anything done.
Y'know?
—ready—
Hey. Sorry. I, uh.
Bloop.
—sorry—
It's okay. Don't—
Bloop.
Whoa.
Busy morning.
Bloop bloop.
Shit.
Shit.
Suze, what if they were here?
What if they were right here?
Jon...

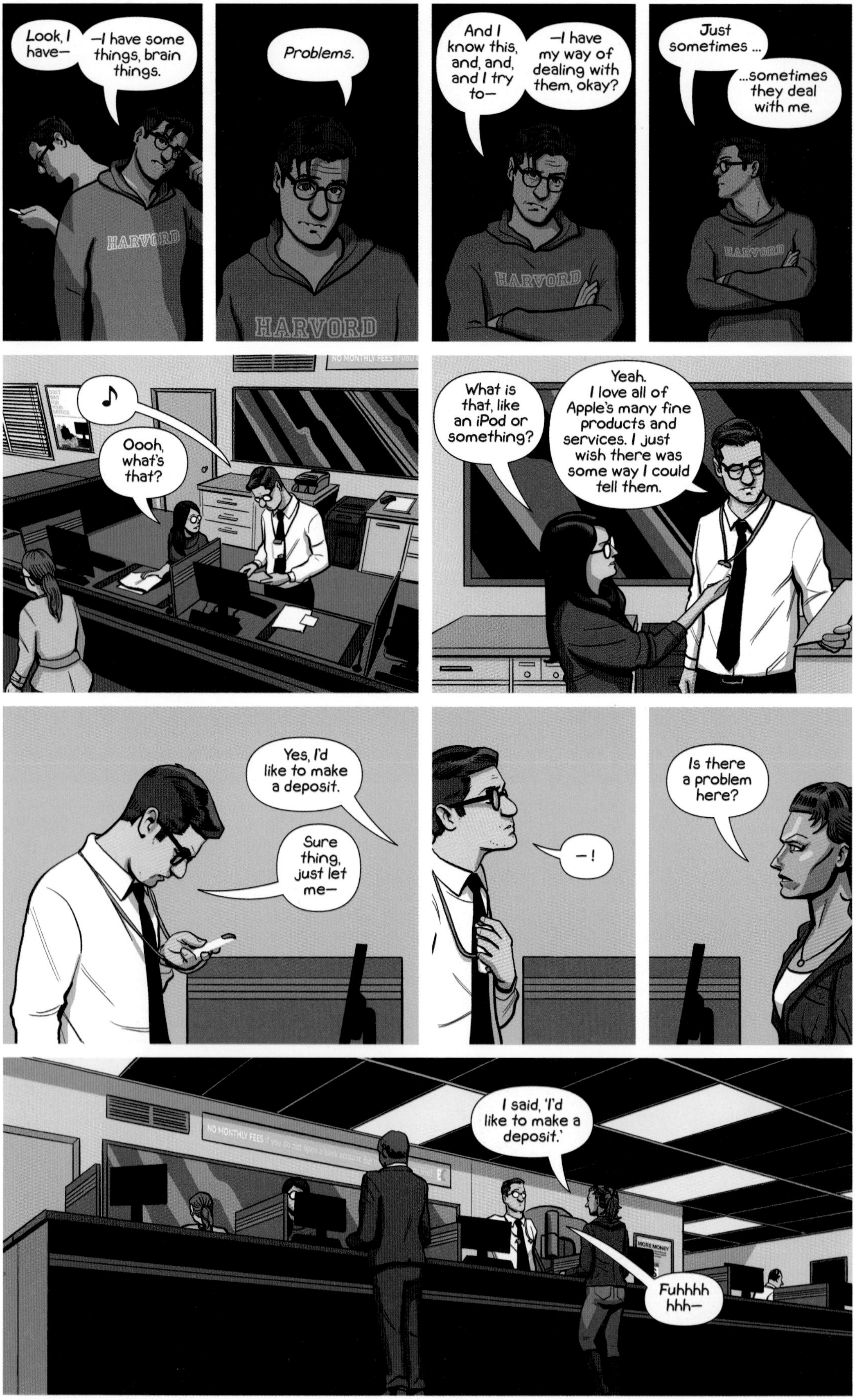
Look, I have—
—I have some things, brain things.
HARVORD
Problems.
HARVORD
And I know this, and, and, and I try to—
—I have my way of dealing with them, okay?
HARVORD
Just sometimes ...
...sometimes they deal with me.
HARVORD
NO MONTHLY FEES
♪
Oooh, what's that?
What is that, like an iPod or something?
Yeah. I love all of Apple's many fine products and services. I just wish there was some way I could tell them.
Yes, I'd like to make a deposit.
Sure thing, just let me—
—!
Is there a problem here?
NO MONTHLY FEES
MORE MONEY
I said, 'I'd like to make a deposit.'
Fuhhhh hhh—

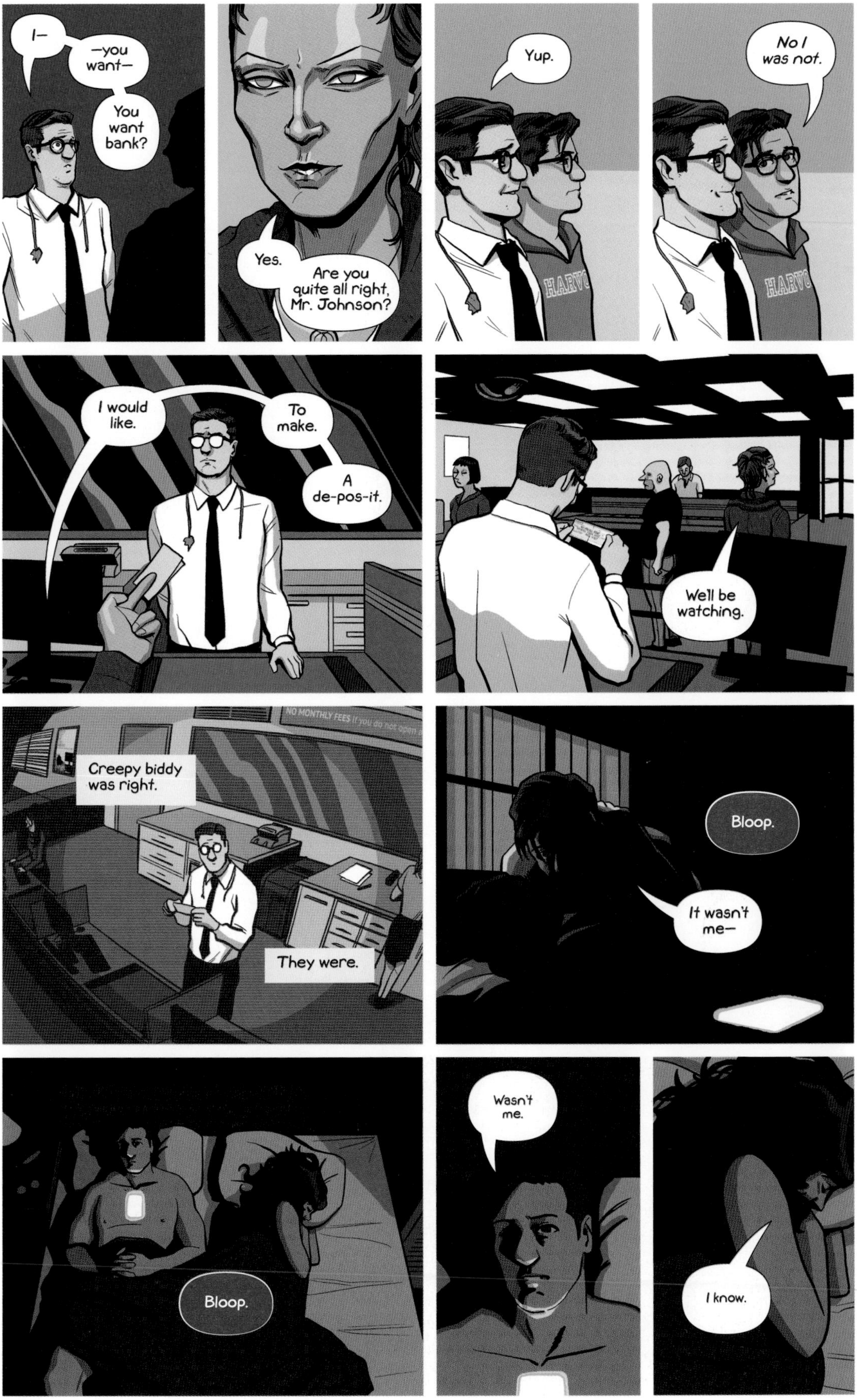
I—
—you want—
You want bank?
Yes.
Are you quite all right, Mr. Johnson?
Yup.
No I was not.
HARVO
HARVO
I would like.
To make.
A de-pos-it.
We'll be watching.
NO MONTHLY FEES
Creepy biddy was right.
They were.
Bloop.
It wasn't me—
Bloop.
Wasn't me.
I know.

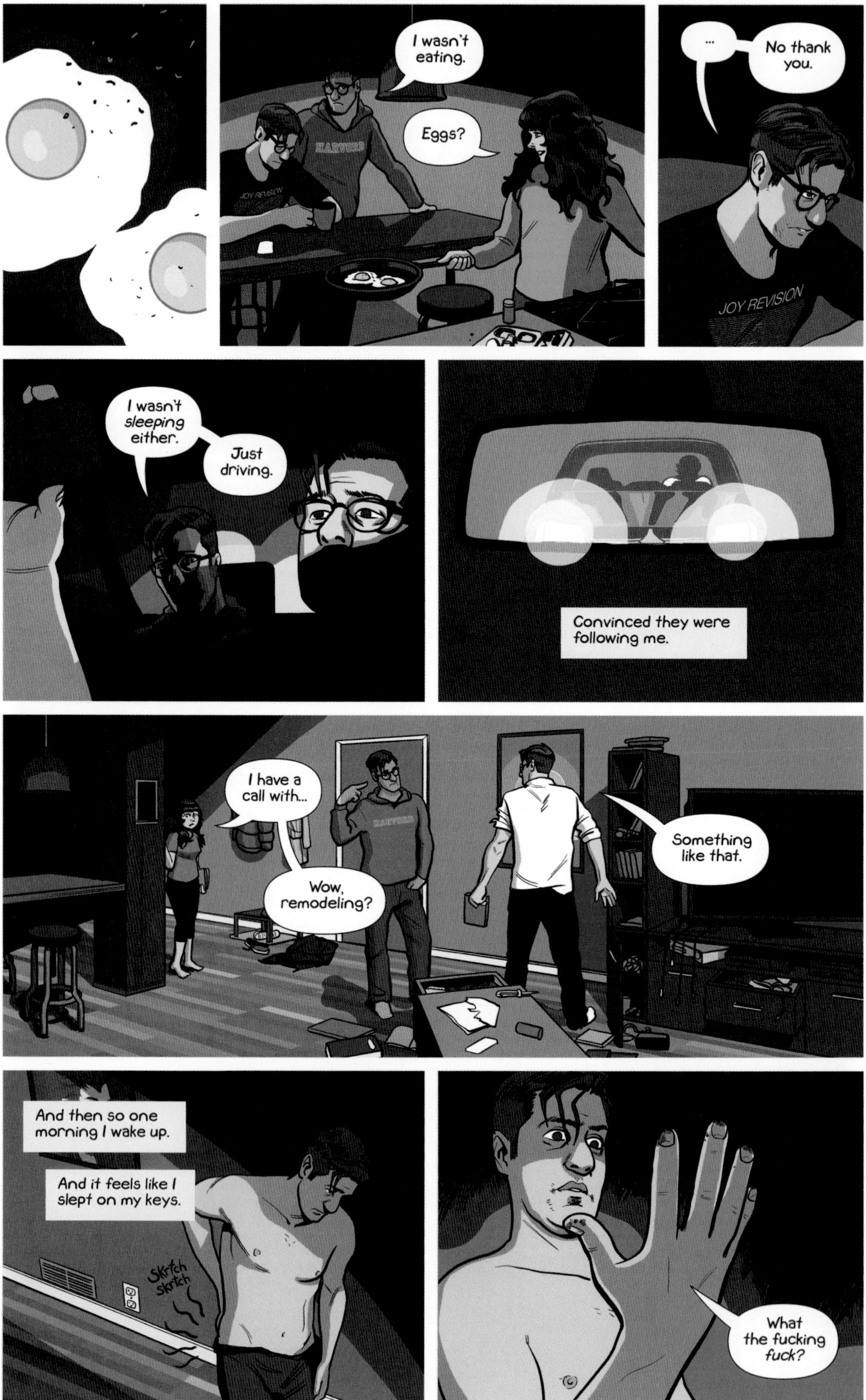

I wasn't eating.
Eggs?
...
No thank you.
I wasn't sleeping either.
Just driving.
Convinced they were following me.
I have a call with...
Wow, remodeling?
Something like that.
And then so one morning I wake up.
And it feels like I slept on my keys.
Skrtch skrtch
What the fucking fuck?

Fuck... the...

What?

OW OW OW OW OW OW OW OW

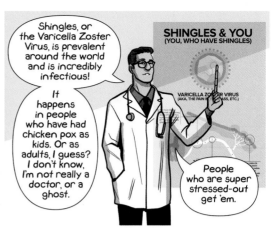

SHINGLES & YOU
(YOU, WHO HAVE SHINGLES)

Shingles, or the Varicella Zoster Virus, is prevalent around the world and is incredibly infectious!

It happens in people who have had chicken pox as kids. Or as adults, I guess? I don't know, I'm not really a doctor, or a ghost.

VARICELLA ZOSTER VIRUS (AKA, THE PAIN IN THE ASS, ETC.)

People who are super stressed-out get 'em.

Or maybe, say, *immunocompromised* people. With diseases liiiiike... H.I.V.

And anybody can ask Jeeves what swollen lumps in your middle mean.

Oh my fuck I have cancer.

Oh god I have AIDS too.

Nailed it!

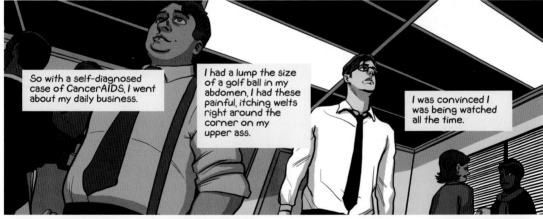

So with a self-diagnosed case of CancerAIDS, I went about my daily business.

I had a lump the size of a golf ball in my abdomen, I had these painful, itching welts right around the corner on my upper ass.

I was convinced I was being watched all the time.

Maybe I wasn't all crazy.

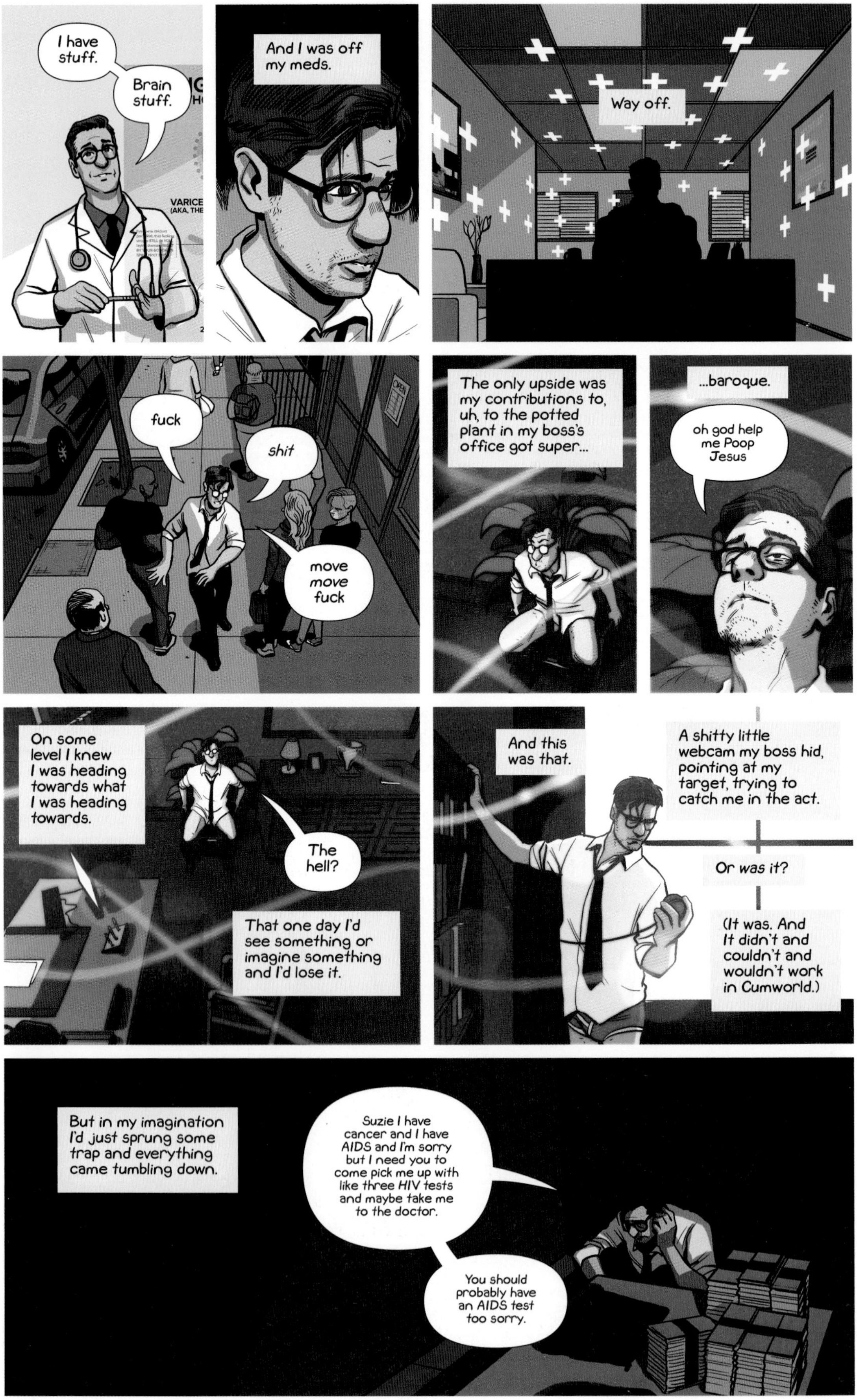
I have stuff.
Brain stuff.
And I was off my meds.
Way off.
fuck
shit
move move fuck
The only upside was my contributions to, uh, to the potted plant in my boss's office got super...
...baroque.
oh god help me Poop Jesus
On some level I knew I was heading towards what I was heading towards.
The hell?
That one day I'd see something or imagine something and I'd lose it.
And this was that.
A shitty little webcam my boss hid, pointing at my target, trying to catch me in the act.
Or was it?
(It was. And It didn't and couldn't and wouldn't work in Cumworld.)
But in my imagination I'd just sprung some trap and everything came tumbling down.
Suzie I have cancer and I have AIDS and I'm sorry but I need you to come pick me up with like three HIV tests and maybe take me to the doctor.
You should probably have an AIDS test too sorry.

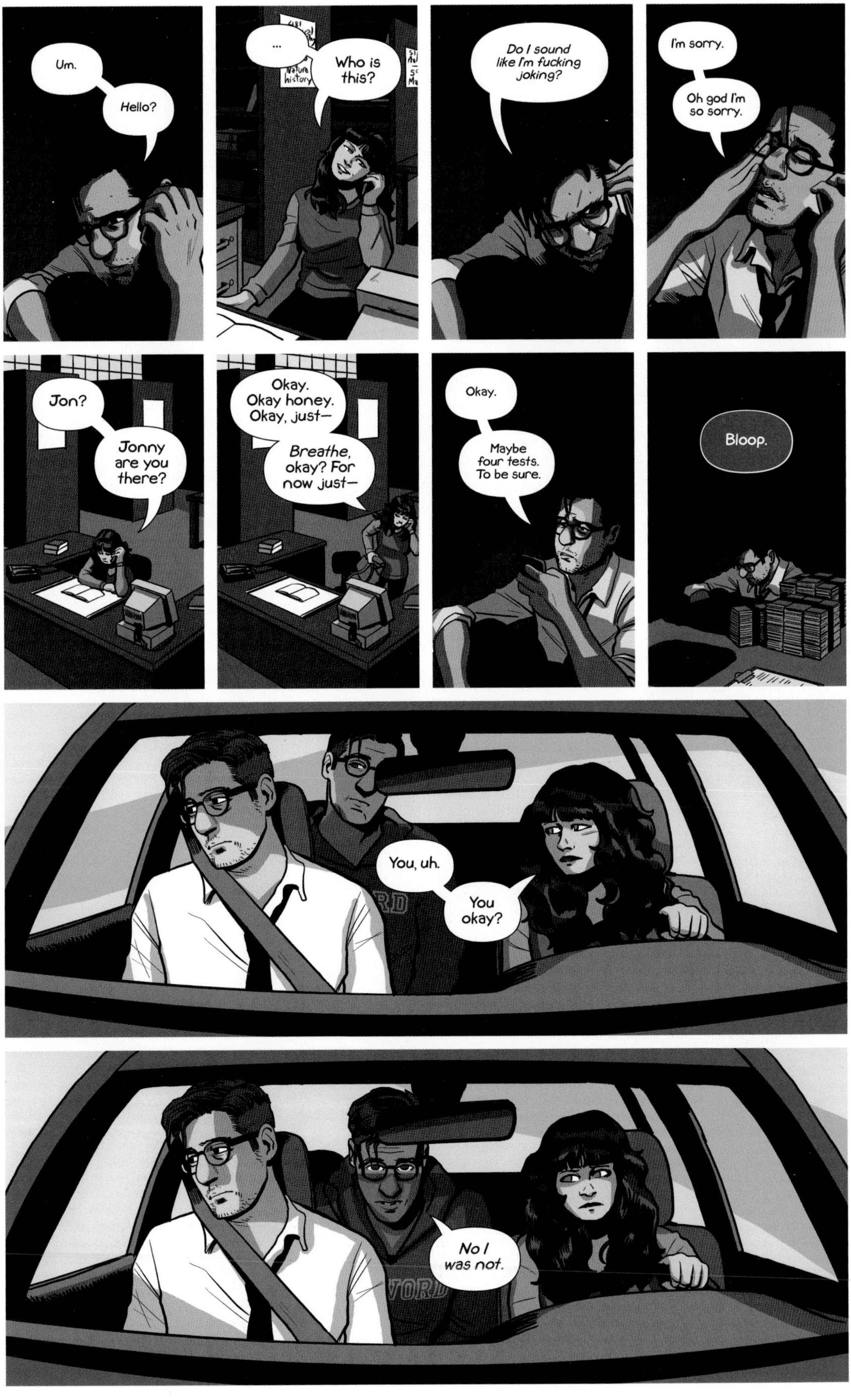
Um.
Hello?
...
Who is this?
Do I sound like I'm fucking joking?
I'm sorry.
Oh god I'm so sorry.
Jon?
Jonny are you there?
Okay. Okay honey. Okay, just—
Breathe, okay? For now just—
Okay.
Maybe four tests. To be sure.
Bloop.
You, uh.
You okay?
No I was not.

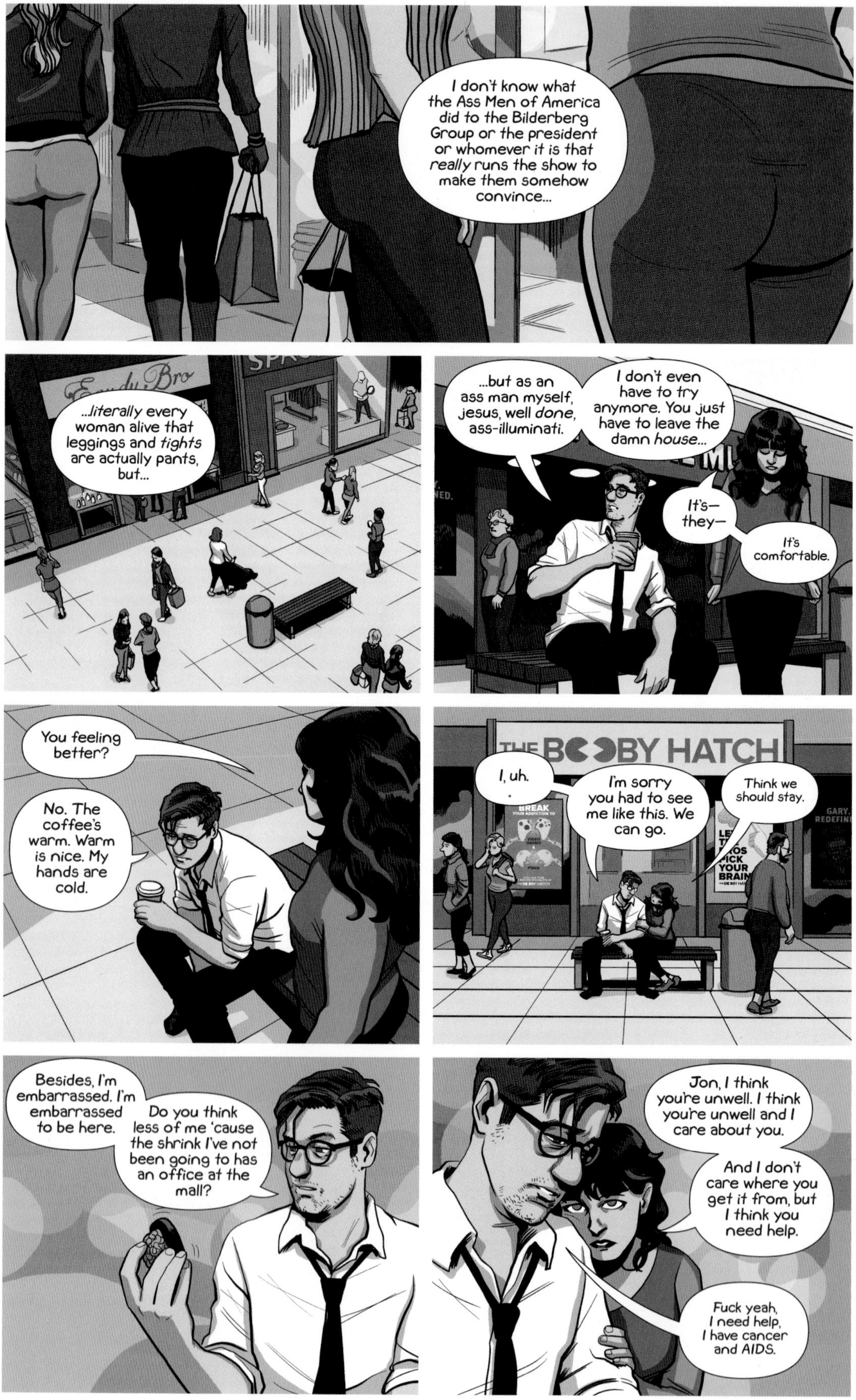
I don't know what the Ass Men of America did to the Bilderberg Group or the president or whomever it is that *really* runs the show to make them somehow convince...
...*literally* every woman alive that leggings and *tights* are actually pants, but...
...but as an ass man myself, jesus, well *done*, ass-illuminati.
I don't even have to try anymore. You just have to leave the damn *house*...
It's— they—
It's comfortable.
You feeling better?
No. The coffee's warm. Warm is nice. My hands are cold.
THE BOOBY HATCH
BREAK
I, uh.
I'm sorry you had to see me like this. We can go.
Think we should stay.
Besides, I'm embarrassed. I'm embarrassed to be here.
Do you think less of me 'cause the shrink I've not been going to has an office at the mall?
Jon, I think you're unwell. I think you're unwell and I care about you.
And I don't care where you get it from, but I think you need help.
Fuck yeah, I need help, I have cancer and AIDS.

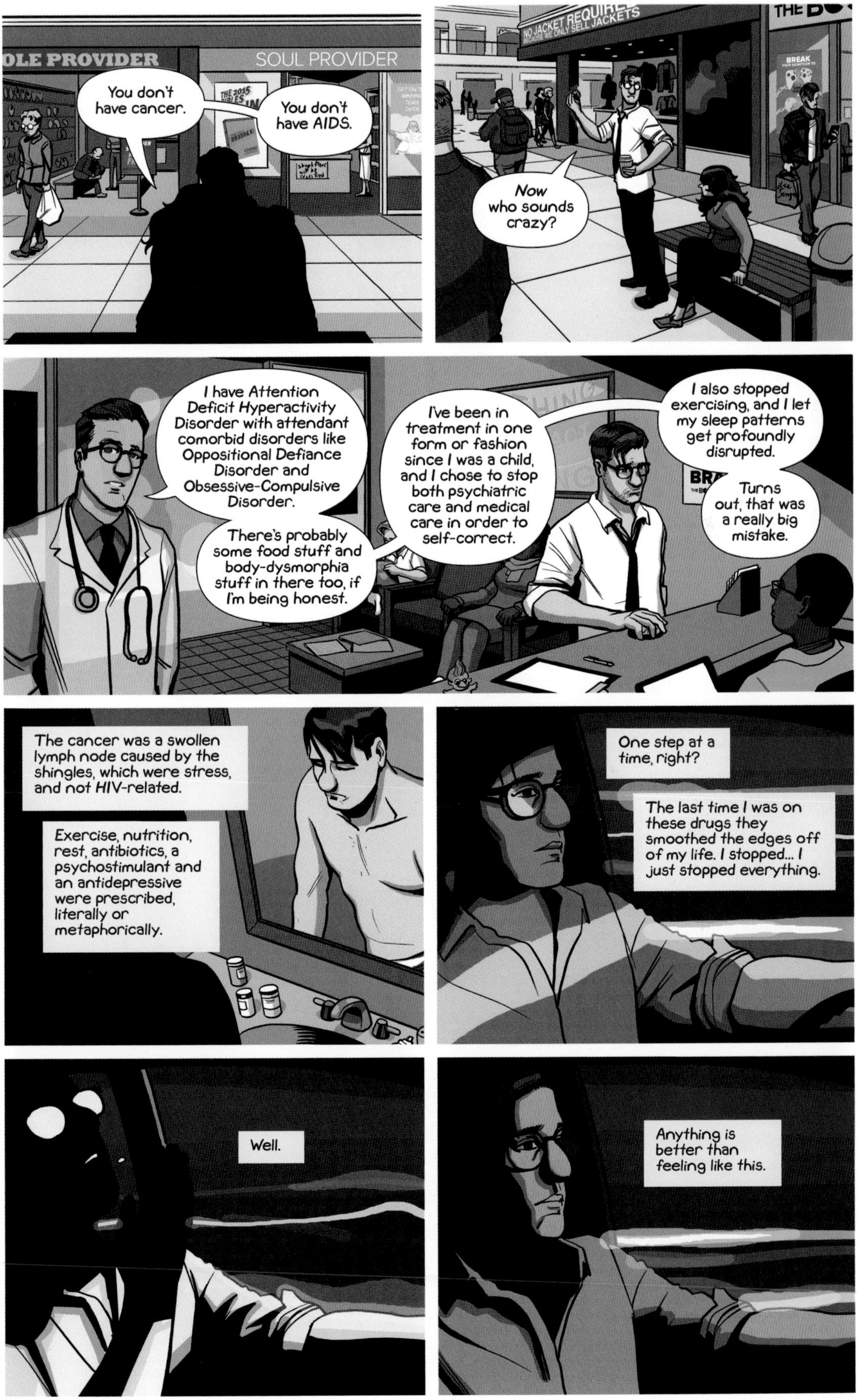
OLE PROVIDER
SOUL PROVIDER
You don't have cancer.
You don't have AIDS.
NO JACKET REQUIRED
BECAUSE WE ONLY SELL JACKETS
Now who sounds crazy?
I have Attention Deficit Hyperactivity Disorder with attendant comorbid disorders like Oppositional Defiance Disorder and Obsessive-Compulsive Disorder.
There's probably some food stuff and body-dysmorphia stuff in there too, if I'm being honest.
I've been in treatment in one form or fashion since I was a child, and I chose to stop both psychiatric care and medical care in order to self-correct.
I also stopped exercising, and I let my sleep patterns get profoundly disrupted.
Turns out, that was a really big mistake.
The cancer was a swollen lymph node caused by the shingles, which were stress, and not HIV-related.
Exercise, nutrition, rest, antibiotics, a psychostimulant and an antidepressive were prescribed, literally or metaphorically.
One step at a time, right?
The last time I was on these drugs they smoothed the edges off of my life. I stopped... I just stopped everything.
Well.
Anything is better than feeling like this.

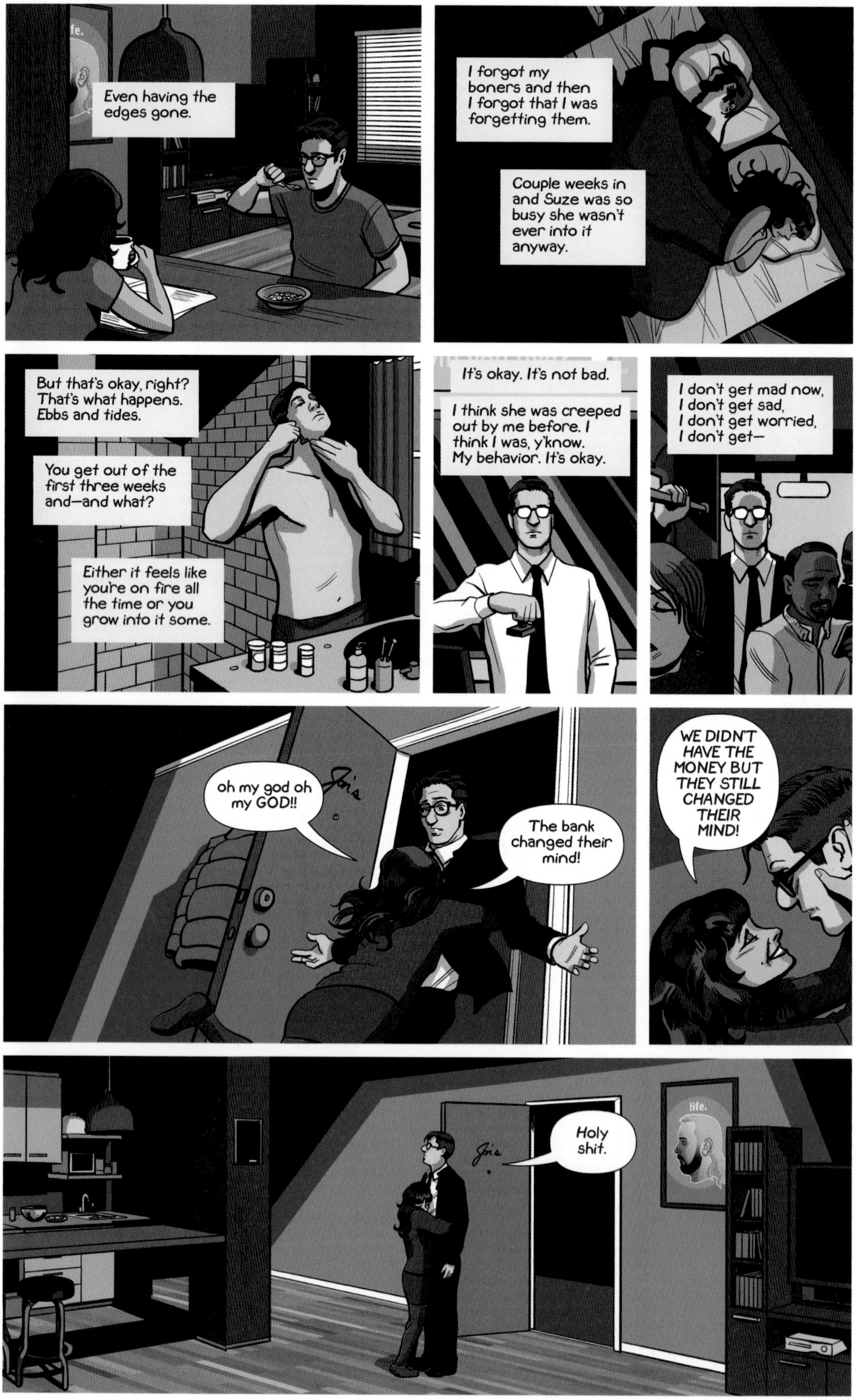
Even having the edges gone.
I forgot my boners and then I forgot that I was forgetting them.
Couple weeks in and Suze was so busy she wasn't ever into it anyway.
But that's okay, right? That's what happens. Ebbs and tides.
You get out of the first three weeks and—and what?
Either it feels like you're on fire all the time or you grow into it some.
It's okay. It's not bad.
I think she was creeped out by me before. I think I was, y'know. My behavior. It's okay.
I don't get mad now, I don't get sad, I don't get worried, I don't get—
oh my god oh my GOD!!
The bank changed their mind!
WE DIDN'T HAVE THE MONEY BUT THEY STILL CHANGED THEIR MIND!
Holy shit.

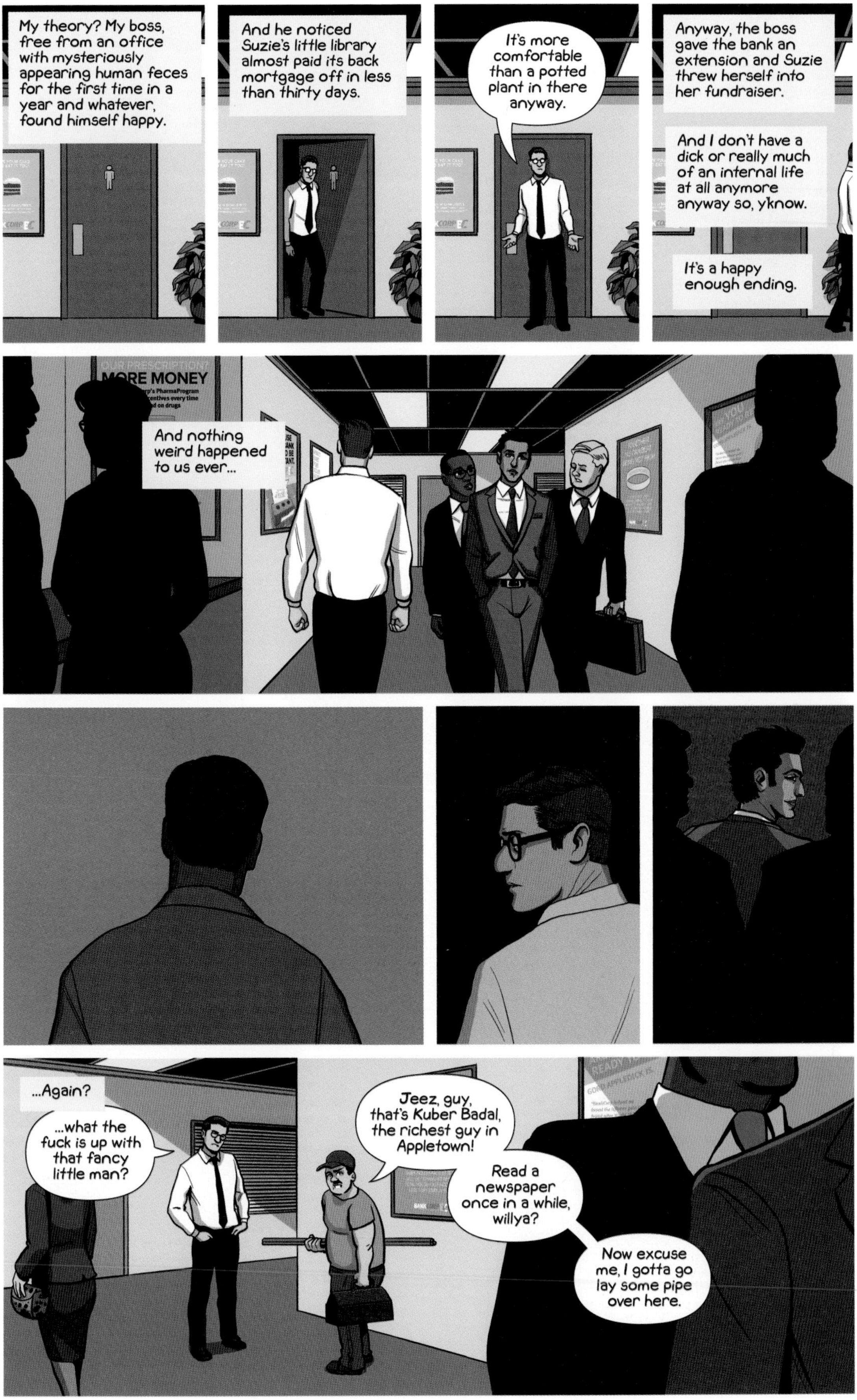
My theory? My boss, free from an office with mysteriously appearing human feces for the first time in a year and whatever, found himself happy.
And he noticed Suzie's little library almost paid its back mortgage off in less than thirty days.
It's more comfortable than a potted plant in there anyway.
Anyway, the boss gave the bank an extension and Suzie threw herself into her fundraiser.
And I don't have a dick or really much of an internal life at all anymore anyway so, y'know.
It's a happy enough ending.
OUR PRESCRIPTION?
MORE MONEY
And nothing weird happened to us ever...
...Again?
...what the fuck is up with that fancy little man?
Jeez, guy, that's Kuber Badal, the richest guy in Appletown!
Read a newspaper once in a while, willya?
Now excuse me, I gotta go lay some pipe over here.

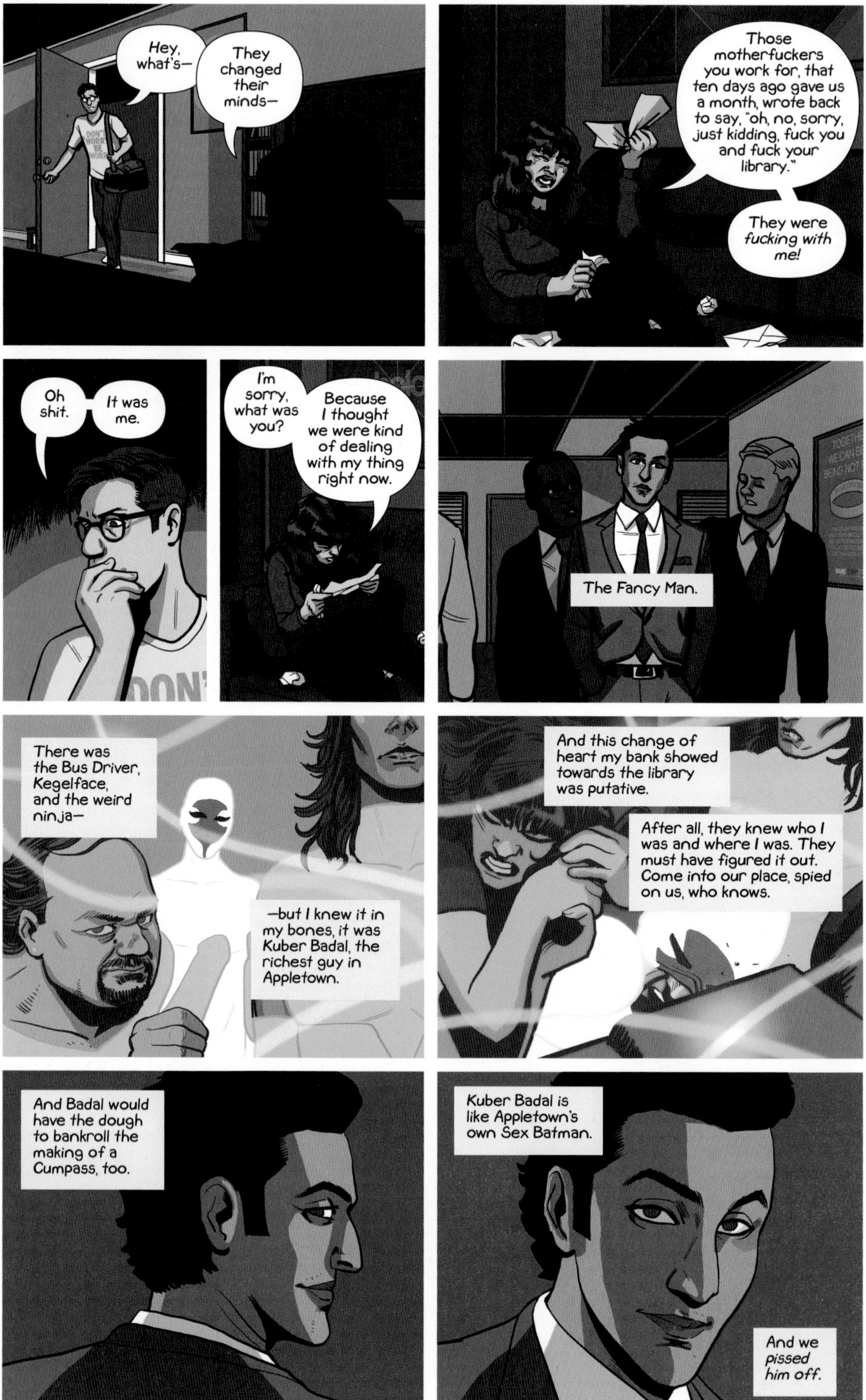
Hey, what's—
They changed their minds—
Those motherfuckers you work for, that ten days ago gave us a month, wrote back to say, "oh, no, sorry, just kidding, fuck you and fuck your library."
They were fucking with me!
Oh shit.
It was me.
I'm sorry, what was you?
Because I thought we were kind of dealing with my thing right now.
The Fancy Man.
There was the Bus Driver, Kegelface, and the weird ninja—
—but I knew it in my bones, it was Kuber Badal, the richest guy in Appletown.
And this change of heart my bank showed towards the library was putative.
After all, they knew who I was and where I was. They must have figured it out. Come into our place, spied on us, who knows.
And Badal would have the dough to bankroll the making of a Cumpass, too.
Kuber Badal is like Appletown's own Sex Batman.
And we pissed him off.

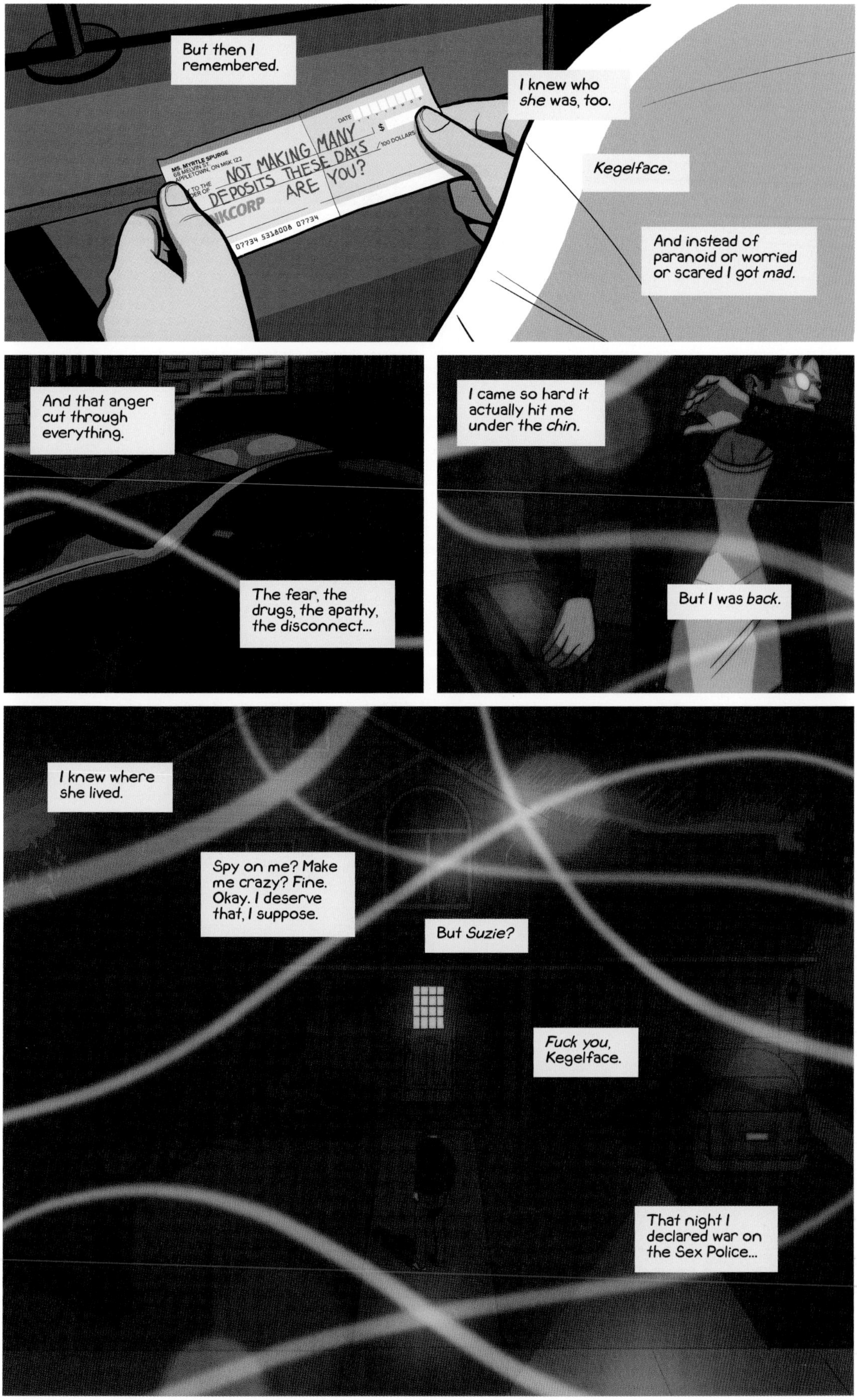
But then I remembered.
MS. MYRTLE SPURGE
68 MELVIN ST.
APPLETOWN, ON M6K 1Z2
NOT MAKING MANY DEPOSITS THESE DAYS ARE YOU?
07734 5318008 07734
I knew who *she* was, too.
Kegelface.
And instead of paranoid or worried or scared I got *mad.*
And that anger cut through everything.
The fear, the drugs, the apathy, the disconnect...
I came so hard it actually hit me under the *chin.*
But I was *back.*
I knew where she lived.
Spy on me? Make me crazy? Fine. Okay. I deserve that, I suppose.
But *Suzie?*
Fuck you, Kegelface.
That night I declared war on the Sex Police...

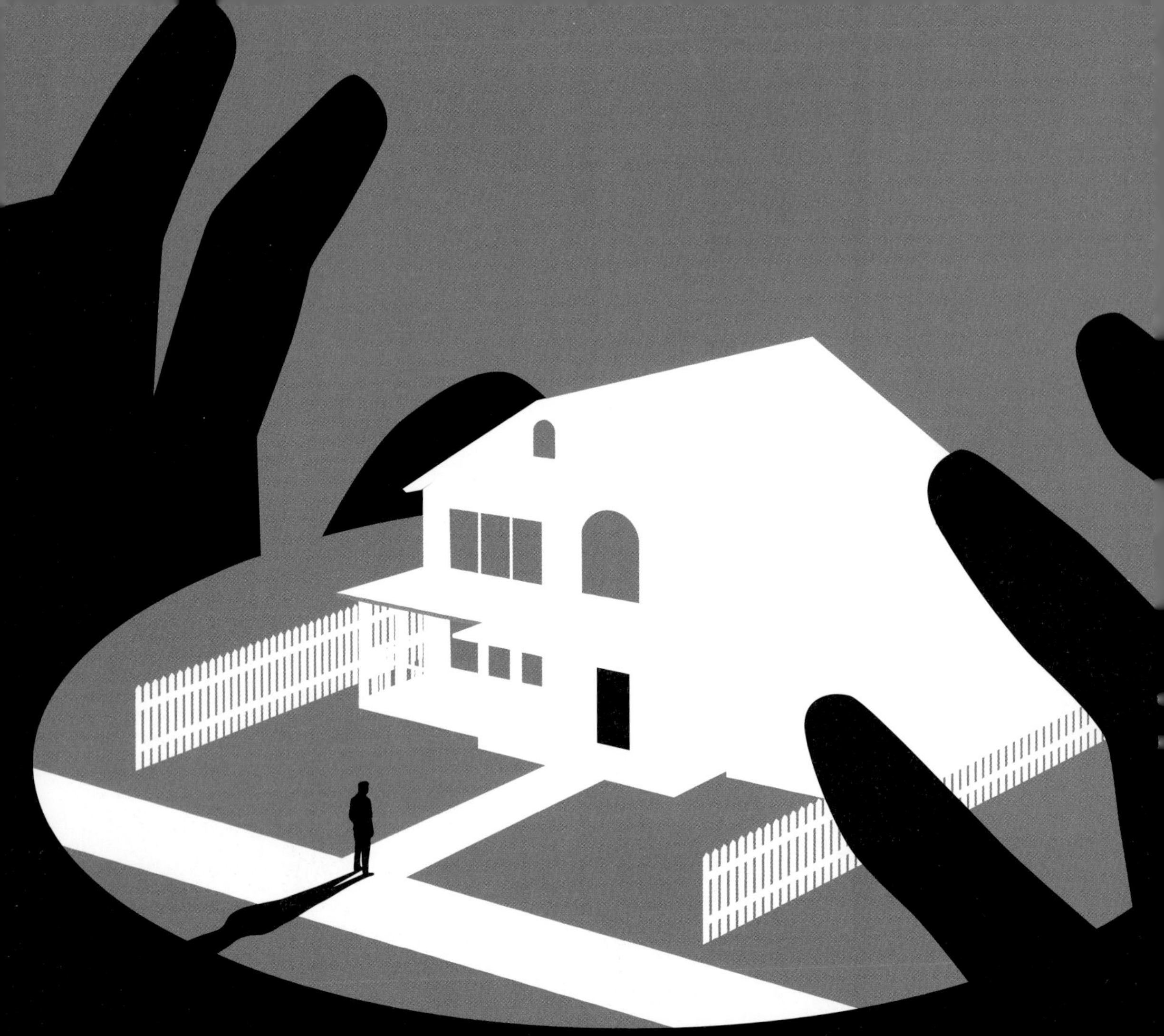

7
BREAK, ENTER

SUZIE
GETTING
IT BACK

My body hates me.

Seriously, I look like a boiled *Hulk*.

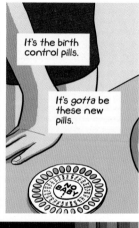

It's the birth control pills.

It's *gotta* be these new pills.

It's been just a couple weeks. As things with *Jon* and I headed toward, y'know, a regular thing, I thought, well, why not go back on The Pill.

It hadn't sat right with me in the past but I thought, well, maybe there's new drugs, new things to try.

I'm retaining so much water I'm peeing sand and my skin is so splotchy I look like a freshly-spanked *Hellraiser* monster.

Jon would know what those are called I bet.

These pills make me want to un-have every sex I ever had, so I suppose as birth control it's a success.

Birth?

Controlled.

I was wondering if I could get another appointment, maybe get so*MY MUFFIN!*

Well, the pills he prescribed kind of make me feel like garbage?

no no my muffin i need you come ba—

—my *TIGHTS*—

Rip

SHIT!

FUCK EVERYTHING this is the worst—

Five second rule, right?

Three for heavily-trafficked sidewalks?

Oh great.

A witness for my shame.

Hey hobo.

You gonna finish that?

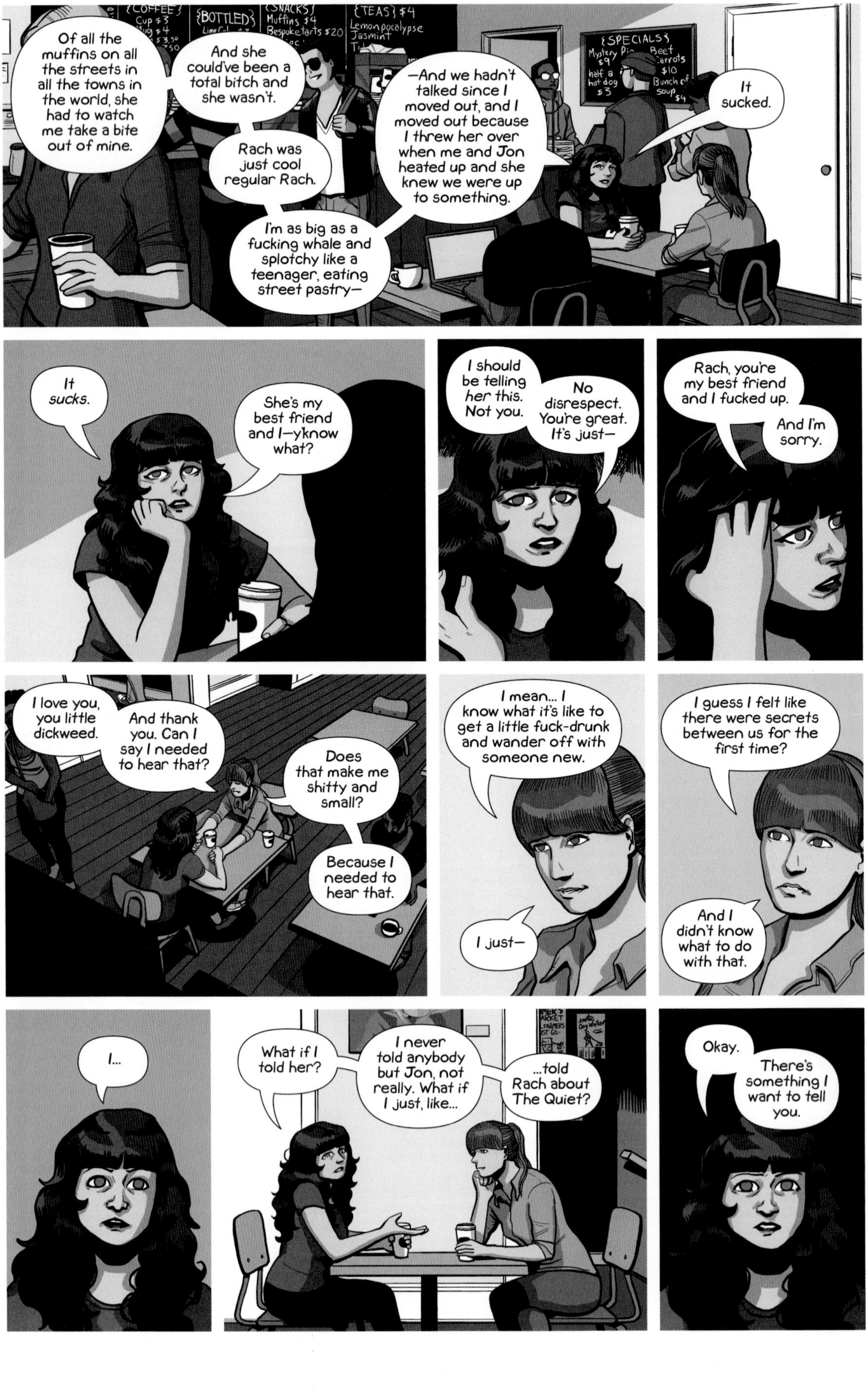
{COFFEE} Cup $3 Mug $4
{BOTTLED}
{SNACKS} Muffins $4 Bespoke tarts $20
{TEAS} $4 Lemonpocalypse Jasmint
{SPECIALS} Mystery Pie $9 Beef Carrots $10 half a hot dog $3 Bunch of soup $4
Of all the muffins on all the streets in all the towns in the world, she had to watch me take a bite out of mine.
And she could've been a total bitch and she wasn't.
Rach was just cool regular Rach.
I'm as big as a fucking whale and splotchy like a teenager, eating street pastry—
—And we hadn't talked since I moved out, and I moved out because I threw her over when me and Jon heated up and she knew we were up to something.
It sucked.
It *sucks*.
She's my best friend and I—y'know what?
I should be telling *her* this. Not you.
No disrespect. You're great. It's just—
Rach, you're my best friend and I fucked up.
And I'm sorry.
I love you, you little dickweed.
And thank you. Can I say I needed to hear that?
Does that make me shitty and small?
Because I needed to hear that.
I mean... I know what it's like to get a little fuck-drunk and wander off with someone new.
I just—
I guess I felt like there were secrets between us for the first time?
And I didn't know what to do with that.
I...
What if I told her?
I never told anybody but Jon, not really. What if I just, like...
...told Rach about The Quiet?
Okay.
There's something I want to tell you.

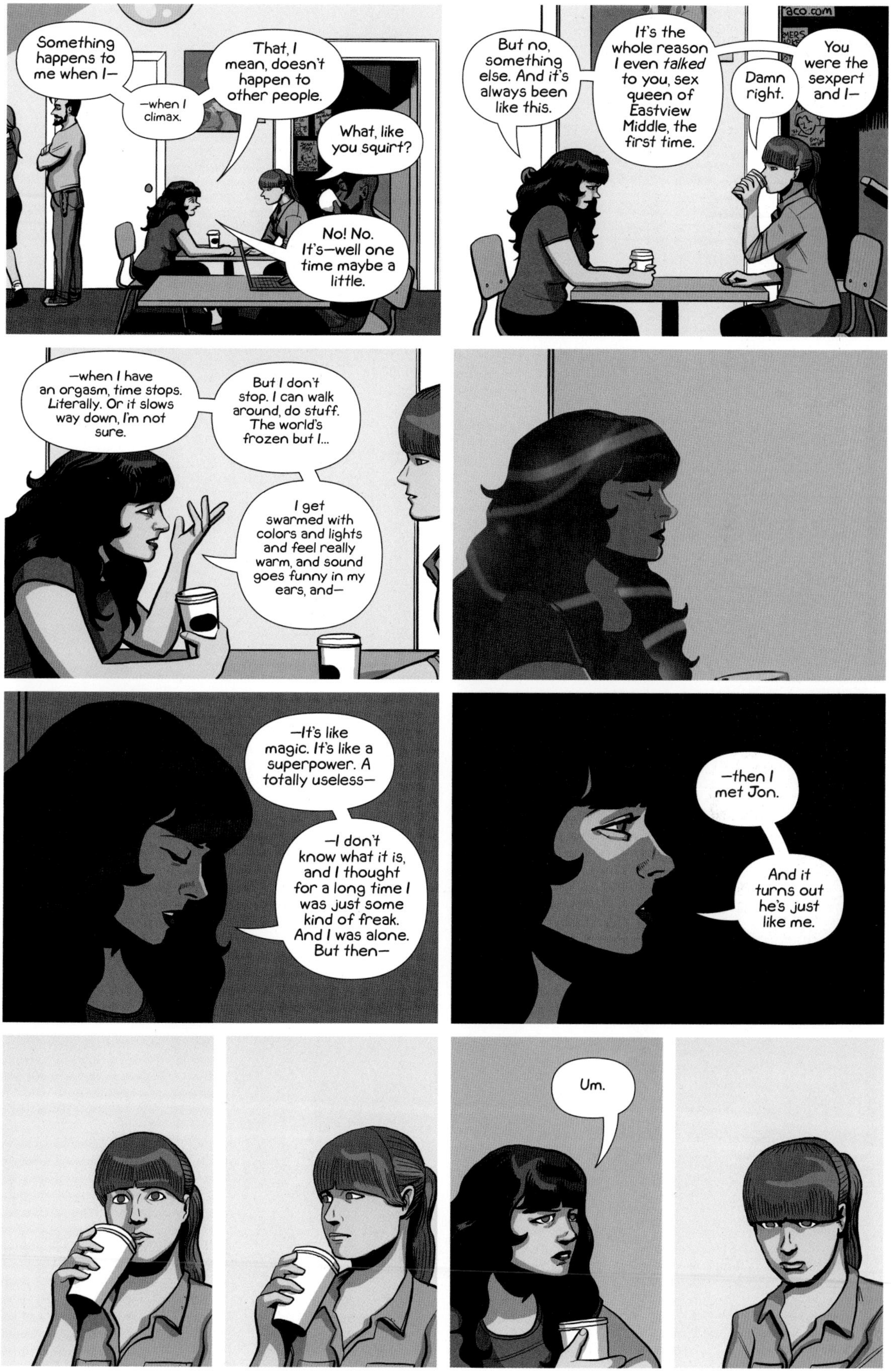
Something happens to me when I—
—when I climax.
That, I mean, doesn't happen to other people.
What, like you squirt?
No! No. It's—well one time maybe a little.
But no, something else. And it's always been like this.
It's the whole reason I even *talked* to you, sex queen of Eastview Middle, the first time.
You were the sexpert and I—
Damn right.
—when I have an orgasm, time stops. Literally. Or it slows way down, I'm not sure.
But I don't stop. I can walk around, do stuff. The world's frozen but I...
I get swarmed with colors and lights and feel really warm, and sound goes funny in my ears, and—
—It's like magic. It's like a superpower. A totally useless—
—I don't know what it is, and I thought for a long time I was just some kind of freak. And I was alone. But then—
—then I met Jon.
And it turns out he's just like me.
Um.

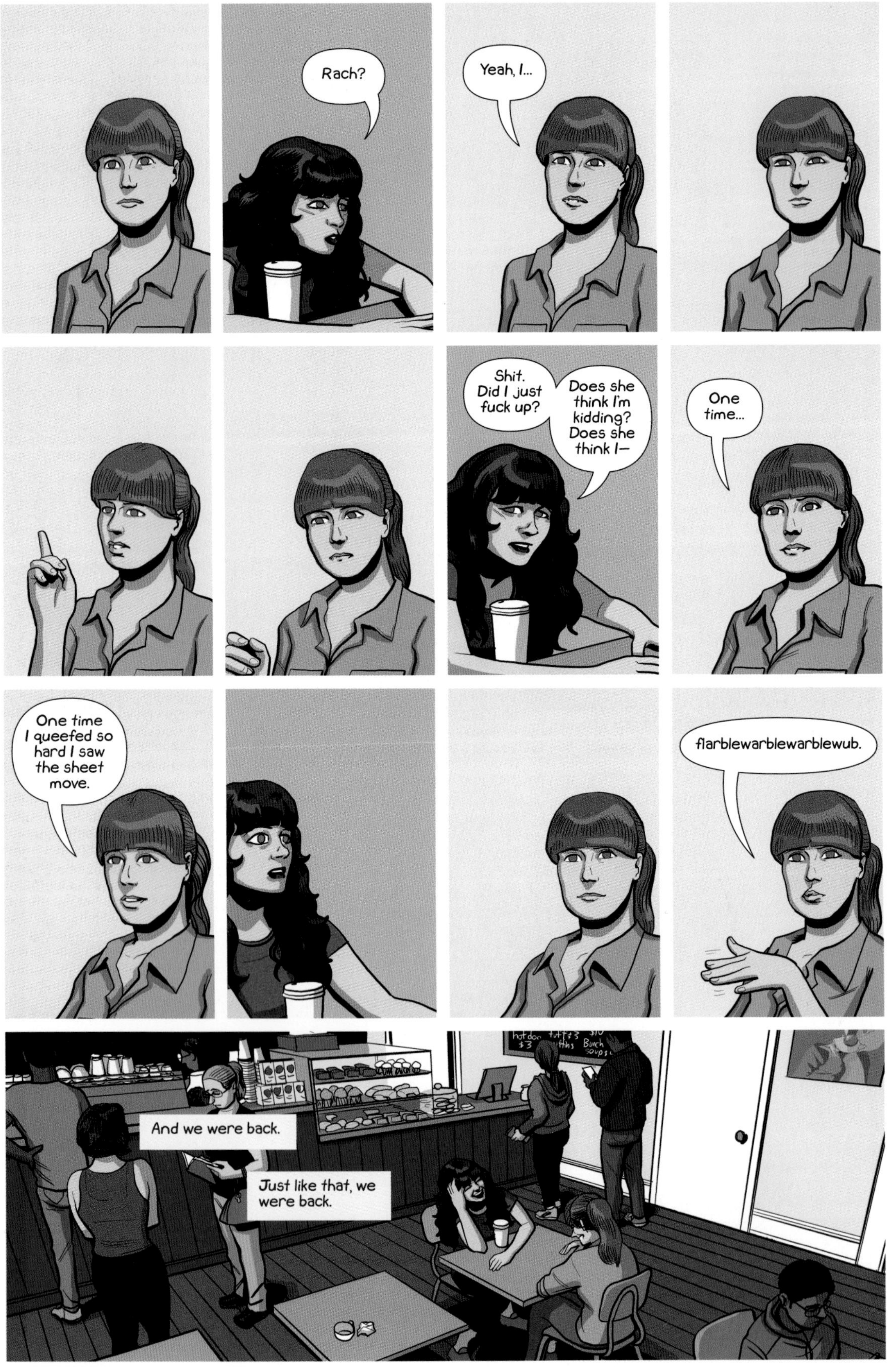
Rach?
Yeah, I...
Shit. Did I just fuck up?
Does she think I'm kidding? Does she think I—
One time...
One time I queefed so hard I saw the sheet move.
flarblewarblewarblewub.
And we were back.
Just like that, we were back.

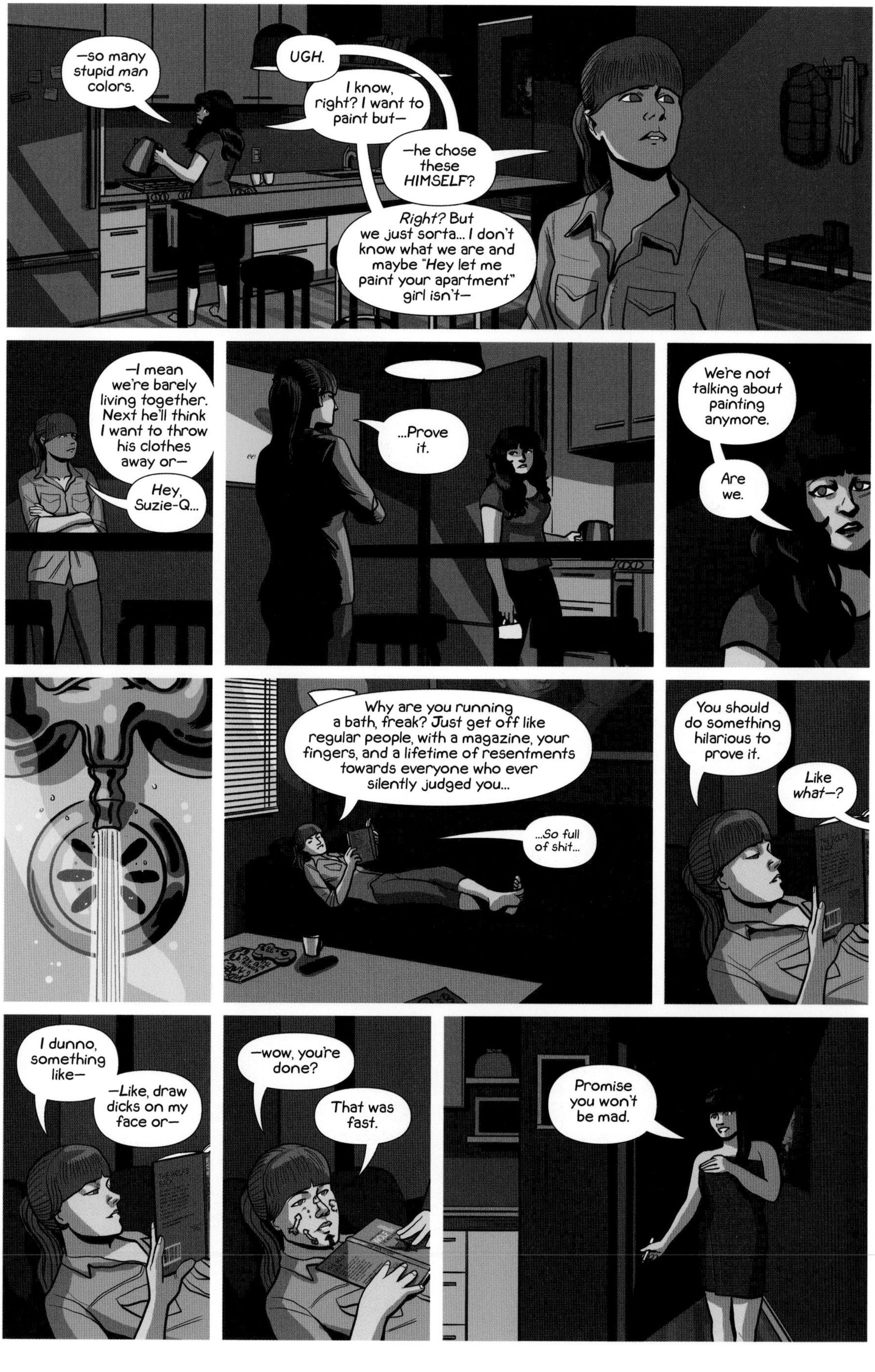
—so many stupid *man* colors.
UGH.
I know, right? I want to paint but—
—he chose these *HIMSELF*?
Right? But we just sorta... I don't know what we are and maybe "Hey let me paint your apartment" girl isn't—
—I mean we're barely living together. Next he'll think I want to throw his clothes away or—
Hey, Suzie-Q...
...Prove it.
We're not talking about painting anymore.
Are we.
Why are you running a bath, freak? Just get off like regular people, with a magazine, your fingers, and a lifetime of resentments towards everyone who ever silently judged you...
...So full of shit...
You should do something hilarious to prove it.
Like *what*—?
I dunno, something like—
—Like, draw dicks on my face or—
—wow, you're done?
That was fast.
Promise you won't be mad.

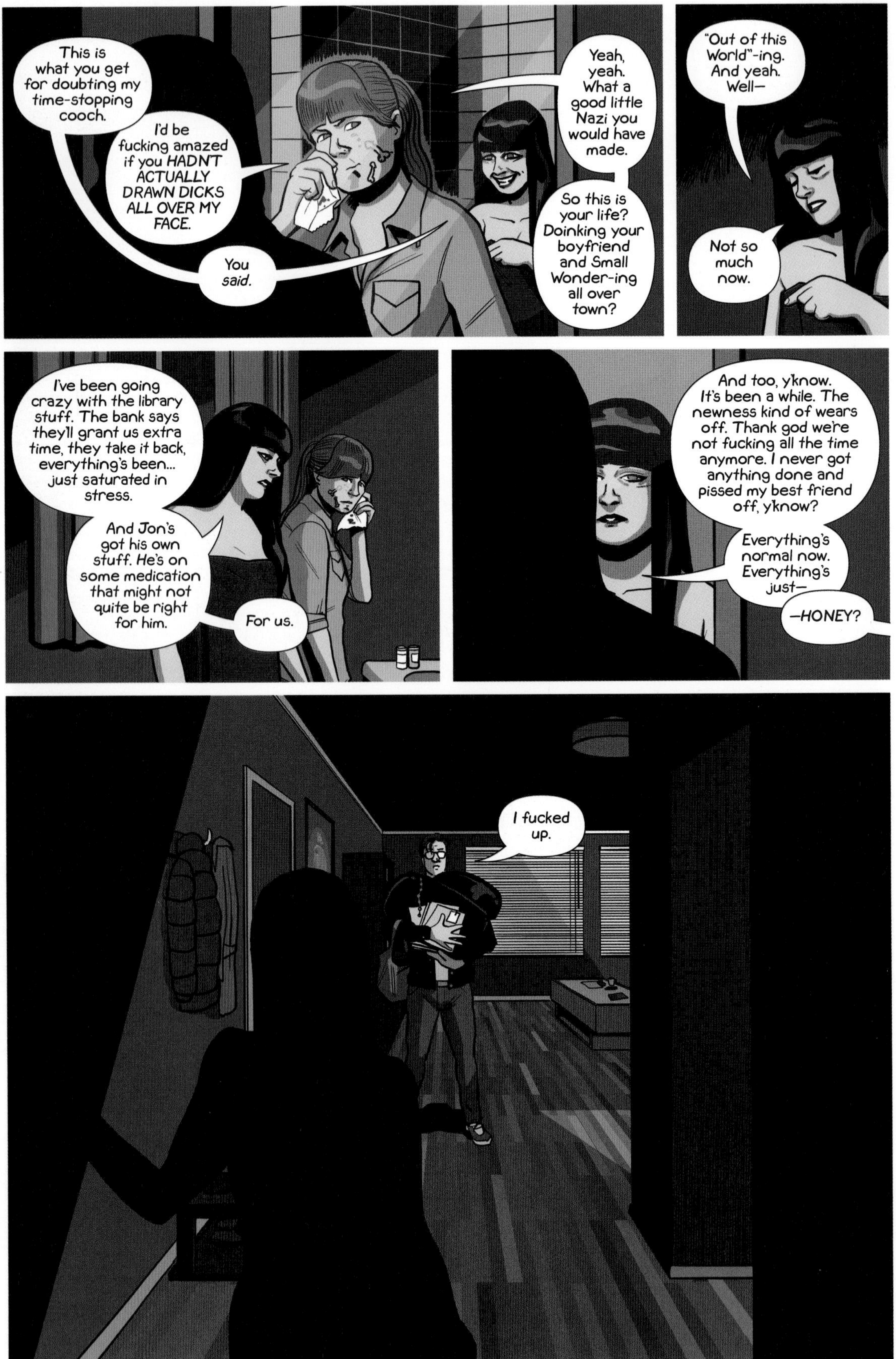
This is what you get for doubting my time-stopping cooch.
I'd be fucking amazed if you HADN'T ACTUALLY DRAWN DICKS ALL OVER MY FACE.
You said.
Yeah, yeah. What a good little Nazi you would have made.
So this is your life? Doinking your boyfriend and Small Wonder-ing all over town?
"Out of this World"-ing. And yeah. Well—
Not so much now.
I've been going crazy with the library stuff. The bank says they'll grant us extra time, they take it back, everything's been... just saturated in stress.
And Jon's got his own stuff. He's on some medication that might not quite be right for him.
For us.
And too, y'know. It's been a while. The newness kind of wears off. Thank god we're not fucking all the time anymore. I never got anything done and pissed my best friend off, y'know?
Everything's normal now. Everything's just—
—HONEY?
I fucked up.

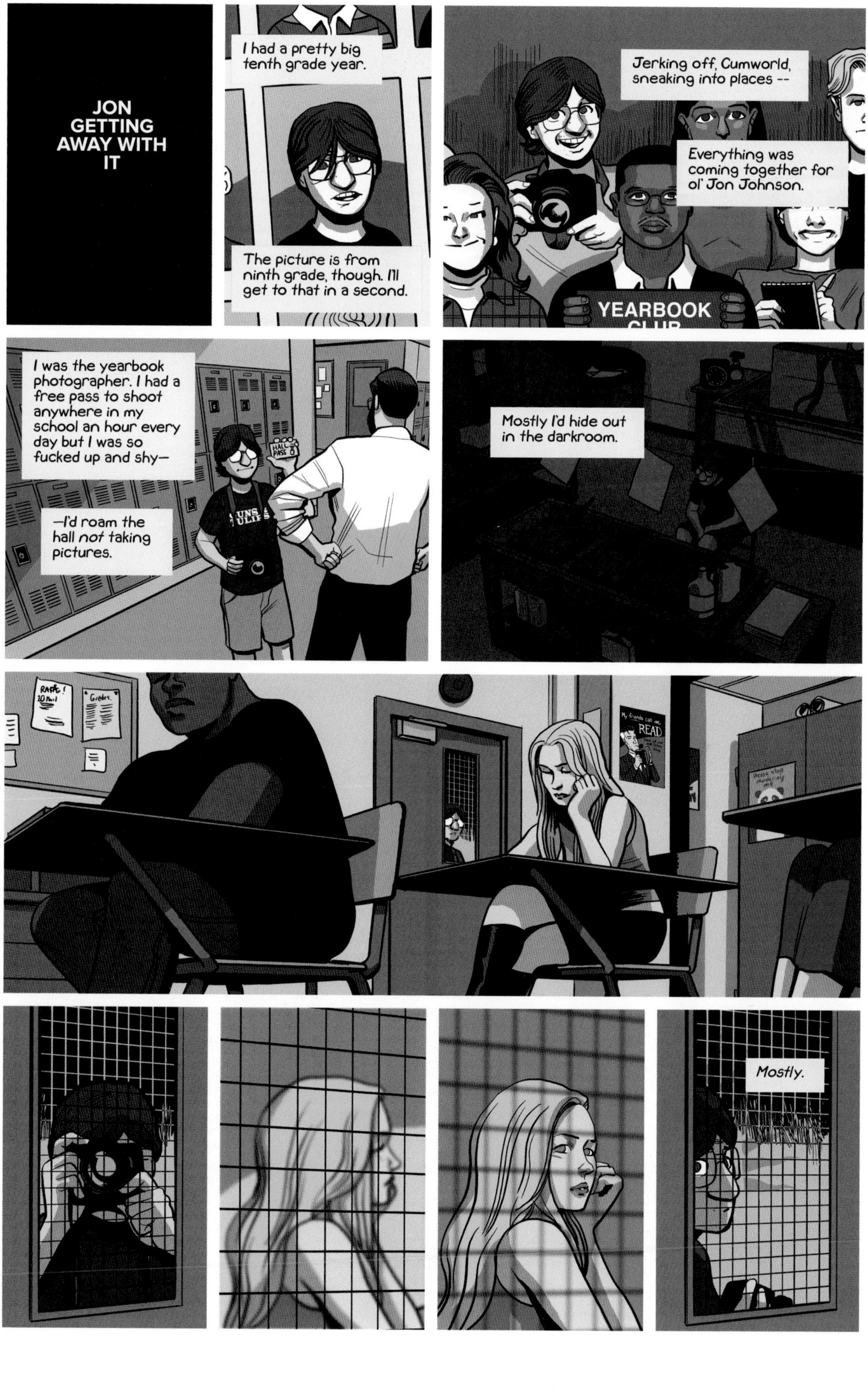
JON GETTING AWAY WITH IT
I had a pretty big tenth grade year.
The picture is from ninth grade, though. I'll get to that in a second.
Jerking off, Cumworld, sneaking into places --
Everything was coming together for ol' Jon Johnson.
YEARBOOK CLUB
I was the yearbook photographer. I had a free pass to shoot anywhere in my school an hour every day but I was so fucked up and shy—
HALL PASS
—I'd roam the hall *not* taking pictures.
Mostly I'd hide out in the darkroom.
READ
Mostly.

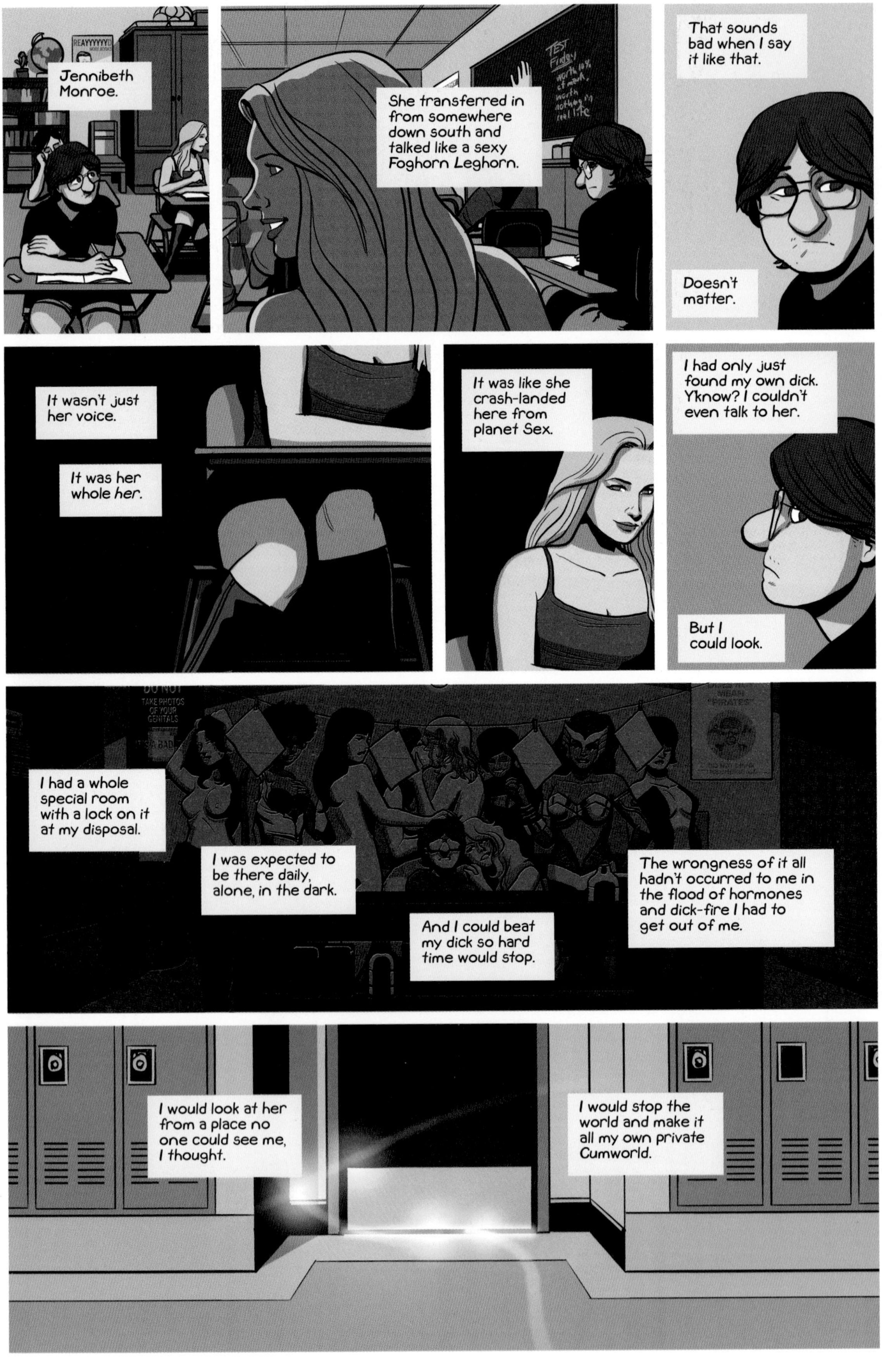
Jennibeth Monroe.
She transferred in from somewhere down south and talked like a sexy Foghorn Leghorn.
That sounds bad when I say it like that.
Doesn't matter.
It wasn't just her voice.
It was her whole *her*.
It was like she crash-landed here from planet Sex.
I had only just found my own dick. Y'know? I couldn't even talk to her.
But I could look.
DO NOT TAKE PHOTOS OF YOUR GENITALS
I had a whole special room with a lock on it at my disposal.
I was expected to be there daily, alone, in the dark.
And I could beat my dick so hard time would stop.
The wrongness of it all hadn't occurred to me in the flood of hormones and dick-fire I had to get out of me.
I would look at her from a place no one could see me, I thought.
I would stop the world and make it all my own private Cumworld.

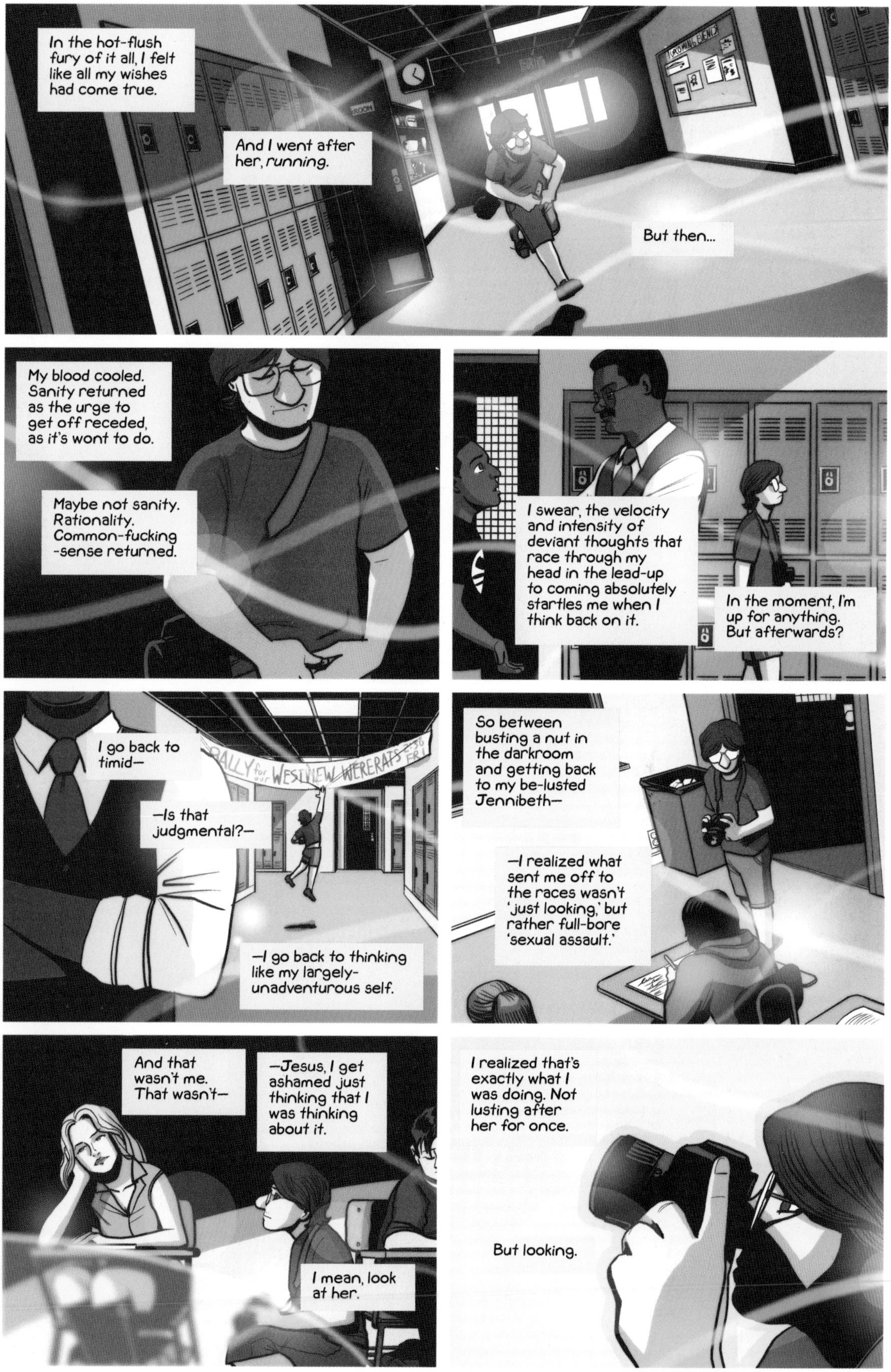

In the hot-flush fury of it all, I felt like all my wishes had come true.
And I went after her, *running.*
But then...
My blood cooled. Sanity returned as the urge to get off receded, as it's wont to do.
Maybe not sanity. Rationality. Common-fucking -sense returned.
I swear, the velocity and intensity of deviant thoughts that race through my head in the lead-up to coming absolutely startles me when I think back on it.
In the moment, I'm up for anything. But afterwards?
I go back to timid—
RALLY for our WESTVIEW WERERATS
—Is that judgmental?—
—I go back to thinking like my largely-unadventurous self.
So between busting a nut in the darkroom and getting back to my be-lusted Jennibeth—
—I realized what sent me off to the races wasn't 'just looking,' but rather full-bore 'sexual assault.'
And that wasn't me. That wasn't—
—Jesus, I get ashamed just thinking that I was thinking about it.
I mean, look at her.
I realized that's exactly what I was doing. Not lusting after her for once.
But looking.

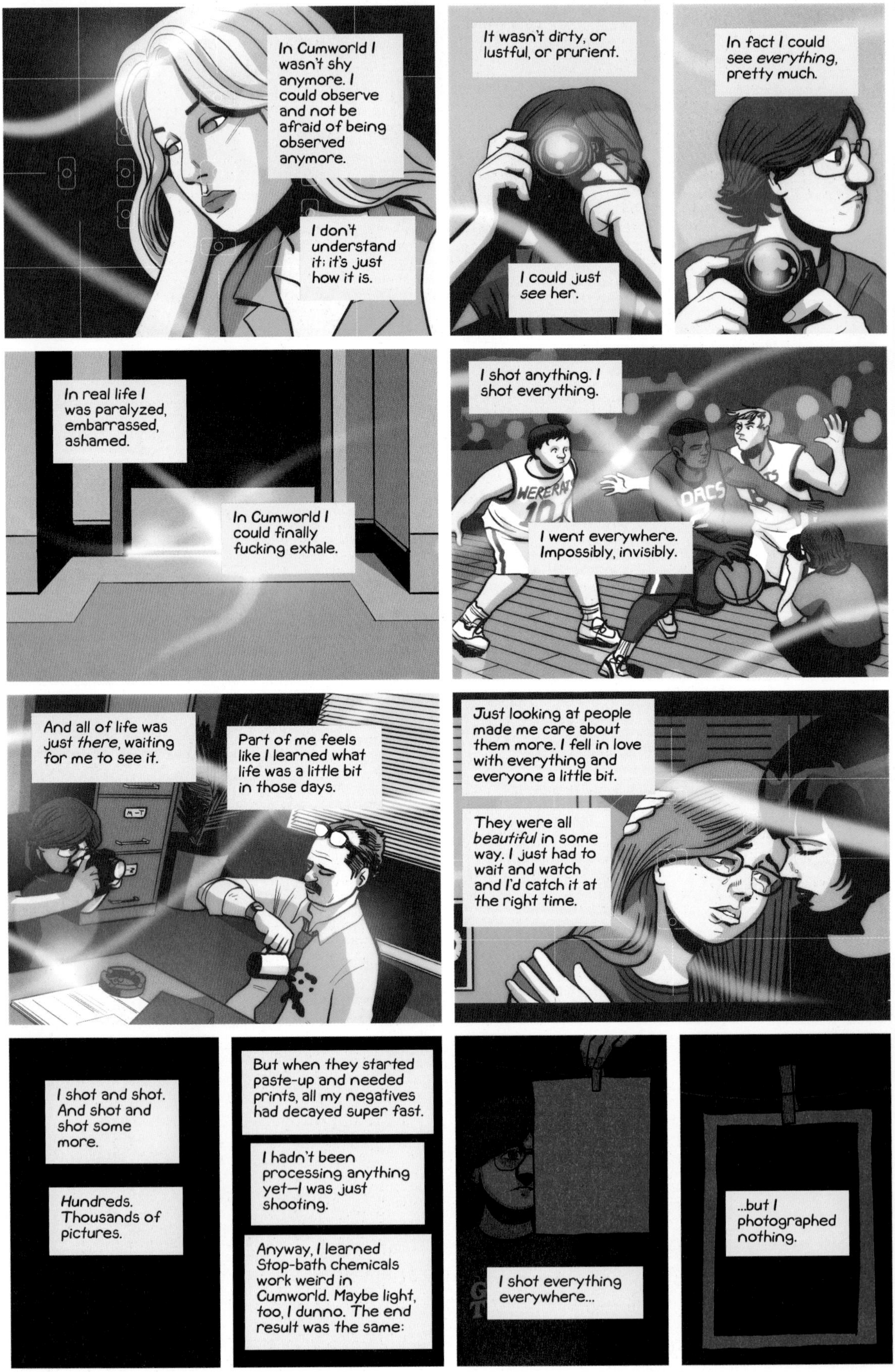
In Cumworld I wasn't shy anymore. I could observe and not be afraid of being observed anymore.
I don't understand it; it's just how it is.
It wasn't dirty, or lustful, or prurient.
I could just *see* her.
In fact I could see *everything*, pretty much.
In real life I was paralyzed, embarrassed, ashamed.
In Cumworld I could finally fucking exhale.
I shot anything. I shot everything.
I went everywhere. Impossibly, invisibly.
And all of life was just *there*, waiting for me to see it.
Part of me feels like I learned what life was a little bit in those days.
Just looking at people made me care about them more. I fell in love with everything and everyone a little bit.
They were all *beautiful* in some way. I just had to wait and watch and I'd catch it at the right time.
I shot and shot. And shot and shot some more.
Hundreds. Thousands of pictures.
But when they started paste-up and needed prints, all my negatives had decayed super fast.
I hadn't been processing anything yet—I was just shooting.
Anyway, I learned Stop-bath chemicals work weird in Cumworld. Maybe light, too, I dunno. The end result was the same:
I shot everything everywhere...
...but I photographed nothing.

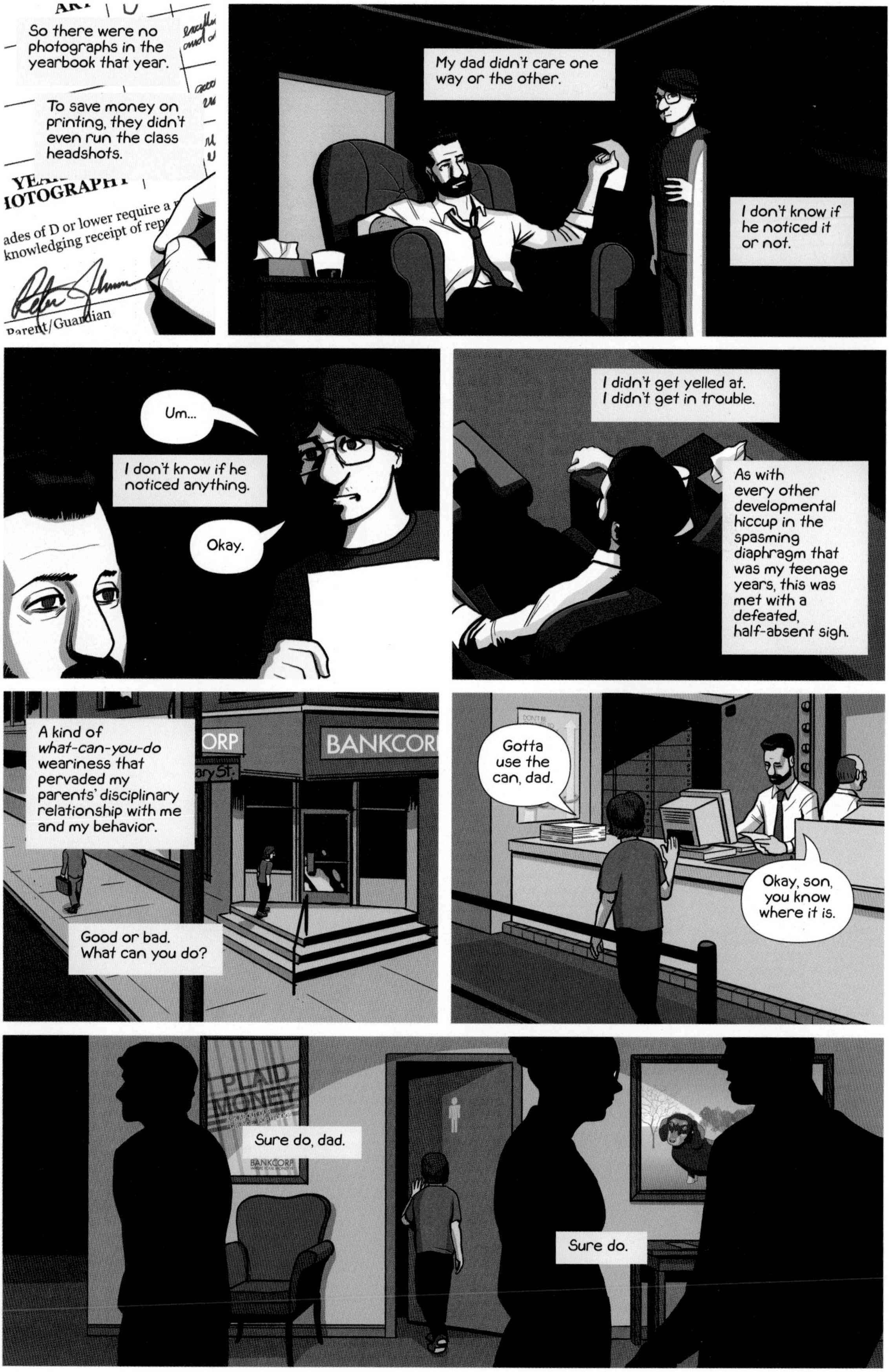
So there were no photographs in the yearbook that year.
To save money on printing, they didn't even run the class headshots.
Parent/Guardian
My dad didn't care one way or the other.
I don't know if he noticed it or not.
Um...
I don't know if he noticed anything.
Okay.
I didn't get yelled at. I didn't get in trouble.
As with every other developmental hiccup in the spasming diaphragm that was my teenage years, this was met with a defeated, half-absent sigh.
A kind of *what-can-you-do* weariness that pervaded my parents' disciplinary relationship with me and my behavior.
BANKCORP
Good or bad. What can you do?
Gotta use the can, dad.
Okay, son, you know where it is.
PLAID MONEY
BANKCORP
Sure do, dad.
Sure do.

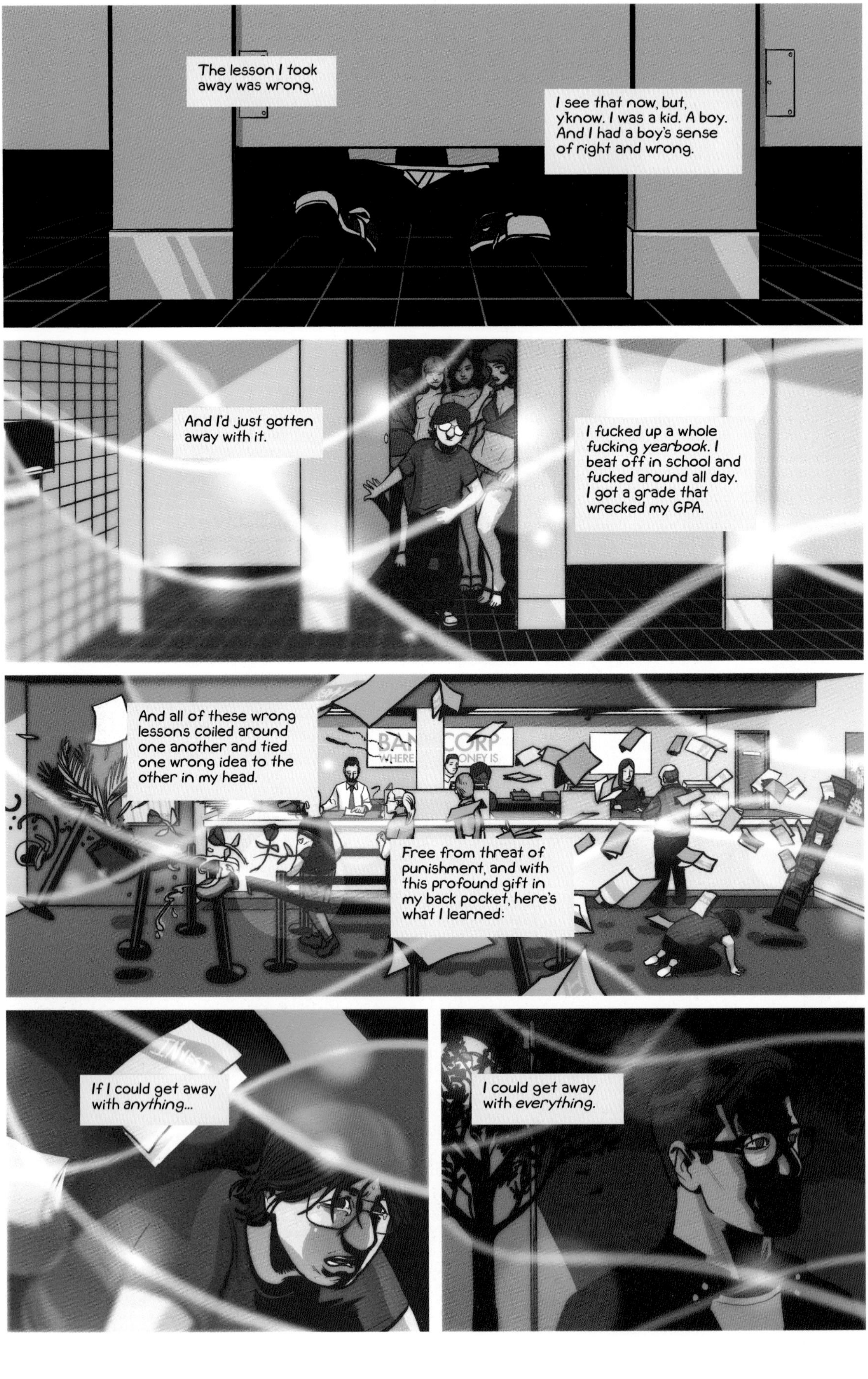
The lesson I took away was wrong.
I see that now, but, y'know. I was a kid. A boy. And I had a boy's sense of right and wrong.
And I'd just gotten away with it.
I fucked up a whole fucking *yearbook*. I beat off in school and fucked around all day. I got a grade that wrecked my GPA.
And all of these wrong lessons coiled around one another and tied one wrong idea to the other in my head.
Free from threat of punishment, and with this profound gift in my back pocket, here's what I learned:
If I could get away with *anything*...
I could get away with *everything*.

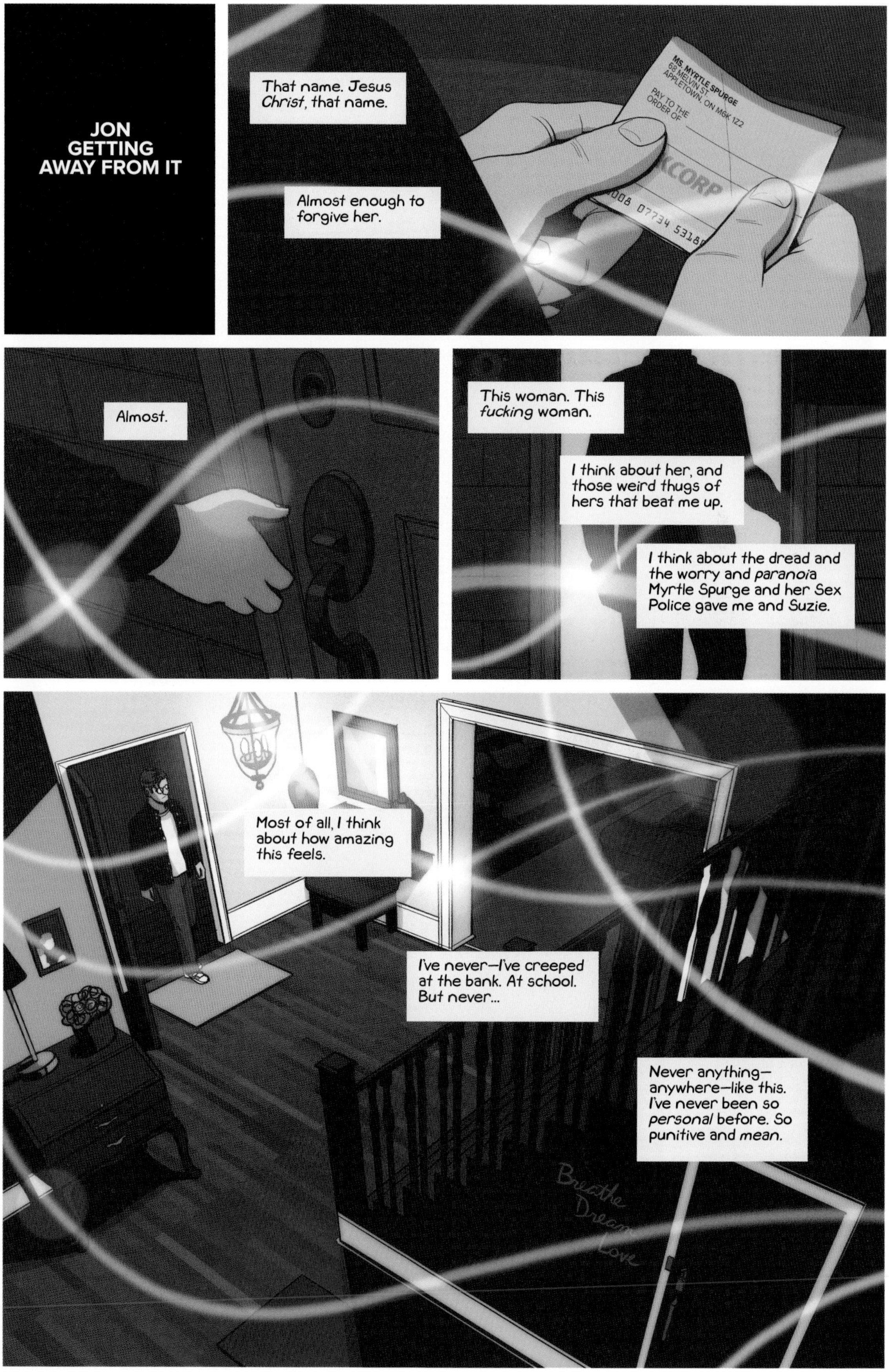
JON GETTING AWAY FROM IT
That name. Jesus *Christ*, that name.
MS. MYRTLE SPURGE
68 MELVIN ST.
APPLETOWN, ON M6K 1Z2
PAY TO THE ORDER OF
Almost enough to forgive her.
Almost.
This woman. This *fucking* woman.
I think about her, and those weird thugs of hers that beat me up.
I think about the dread and the worry and *paranoia* Myrtle Spurge and her Sex Police gave me and Suzie.
Most of all, I think about how amazing this feels.
I've never—I've creeped at the bank. At school. But never...
Never anything—anywhere—like this. I've never been so *personal* before. So punitive and *mean*.
Breathe
Dream
Love

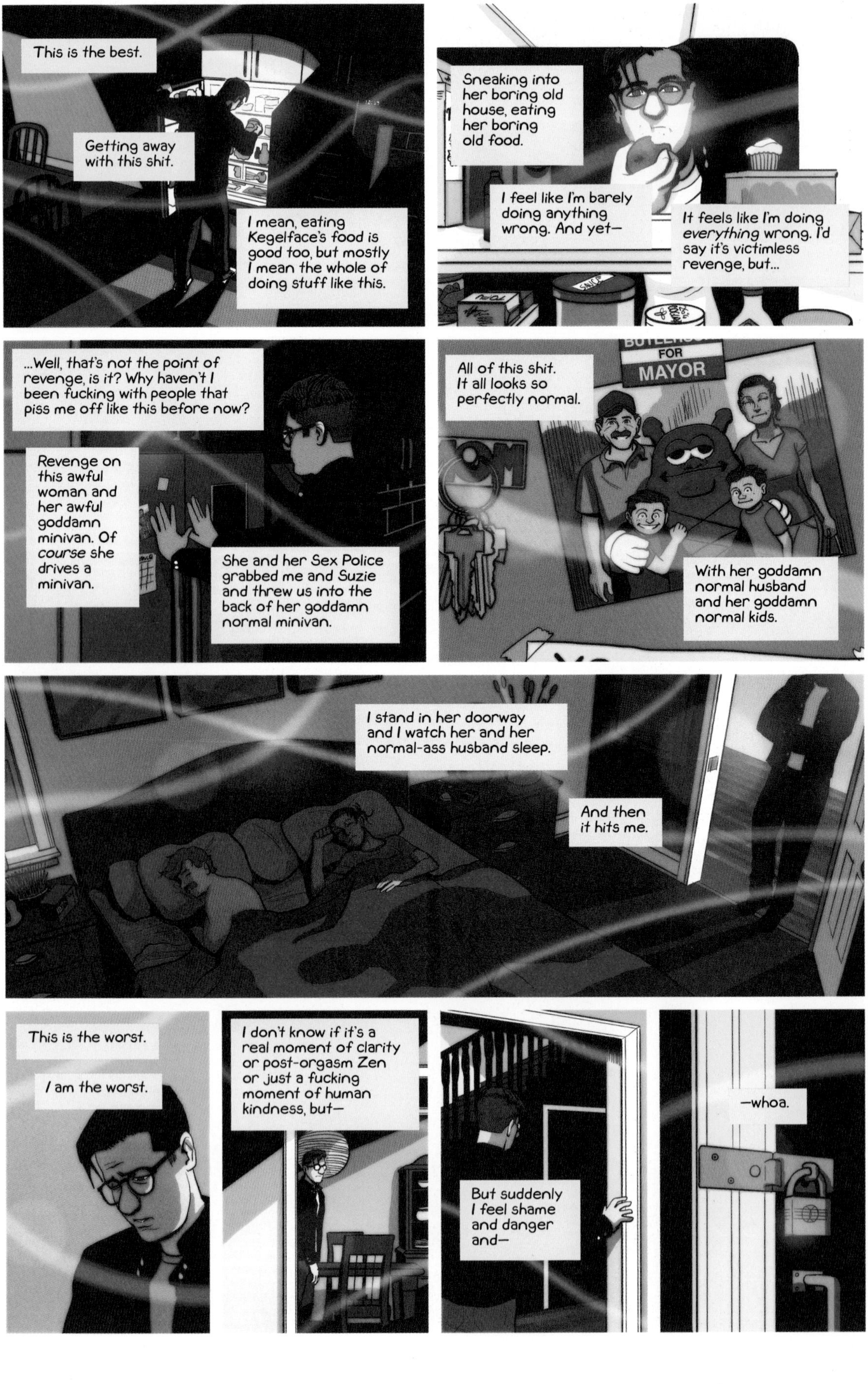
This is the best.
Getting away with this shit.
I mean, eating Kegelface's food is good too, but mostly I mean the whole of doing stuff like this.
Sneaking into her boring old house, eating her boring old food.
I feel like I'm barely doing anything wrong. And yet—
It feels like I'm doing *everything* wrong. I'd say it's victimless revenge, but...
...Well, that's not the point of revenge, is it? Why haven't I been fucking with people that piss me off like this before now?
Revenge on this awful woman and her awful goddamn minivan. Of *course* she drives a minivan.
She and her Sex Police grabbed me and Suzie and threw us into the back of her goddamn normal minivan.
All of this shit. It all looks so perfectly normal.
FOR
MAYOR
With her goddamn normal husband and her goddamn normal kids.
I stand in her doorway and I watch her and her normal-ass husband sleep.
And then it hits me.
This is the worst.
I am the worst.
I don't know if it's a real moment of clarity or post-orgasm Zen or just a fucking moment of human kindness, but—
But suddenly I feel shame and danger and—
—whoa.

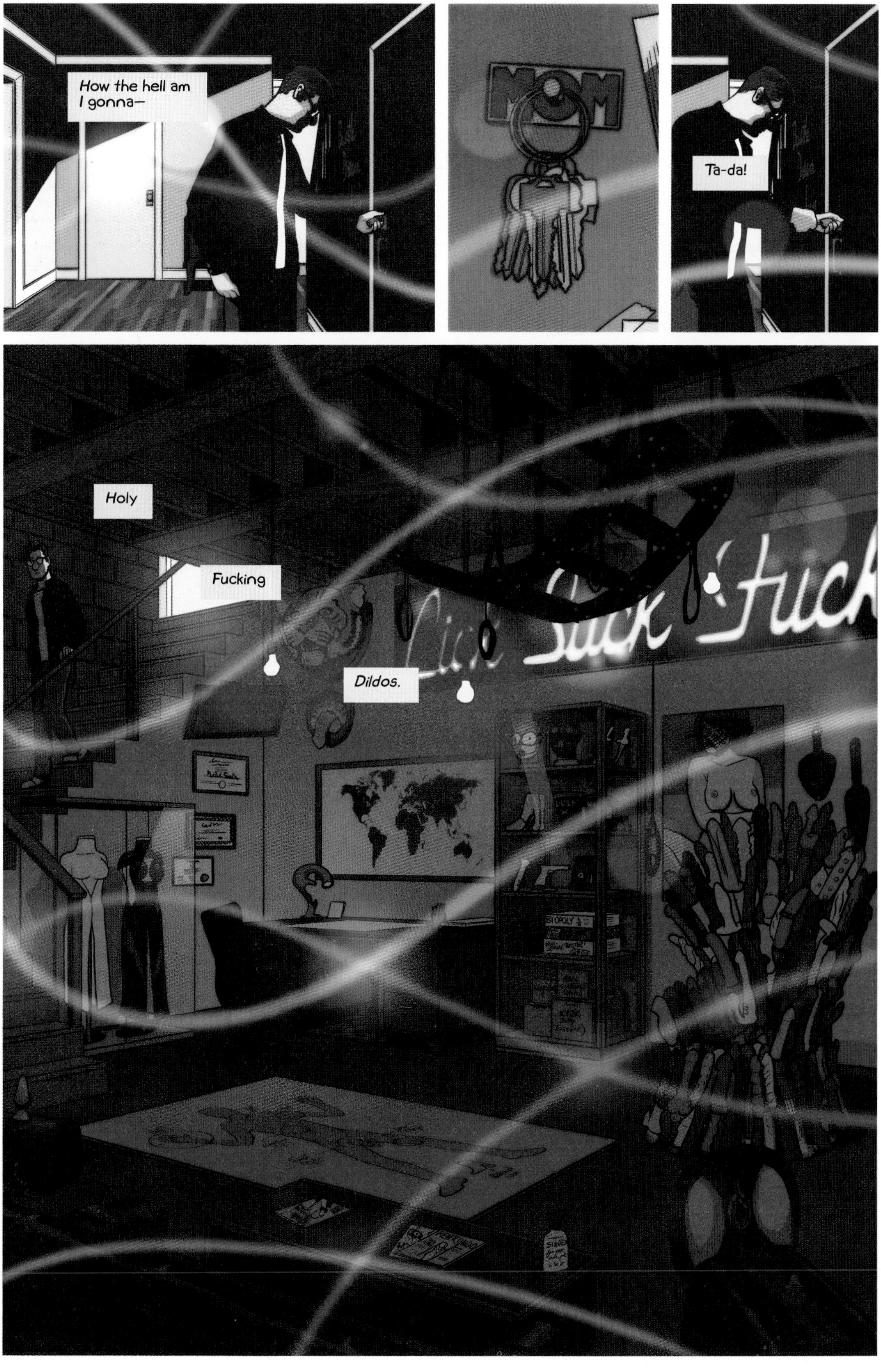
How the hell am I gonna—
MOM
Ta-da!
Holy
Fucking
Dildos.

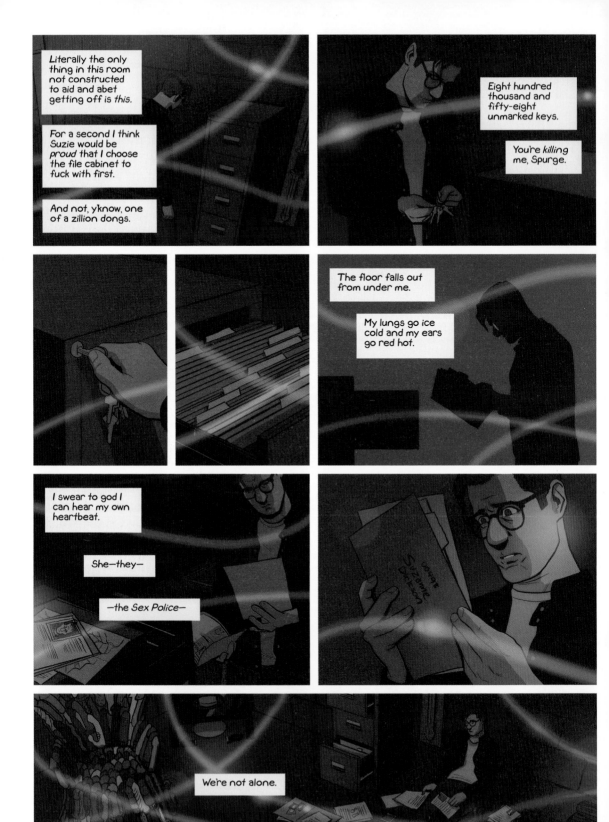

Literally the only thing in this room not constructed to aid and abet getting off is *this*.

For a second I think Suzie would be *proud* that I choose the file cabinet to fuck with first.

And not, yknow, one of a zillion dongs.

Eight hundred thousand and fifty-eight unmarked keys.

You're *killing* me, Spurge.

The floor falls out from under me.

My lungs go ice cold and my ears go red hot.

I swear to god I can hear my own heartbeat.

She—they—

—the *Sex Police*—

We're not alone.

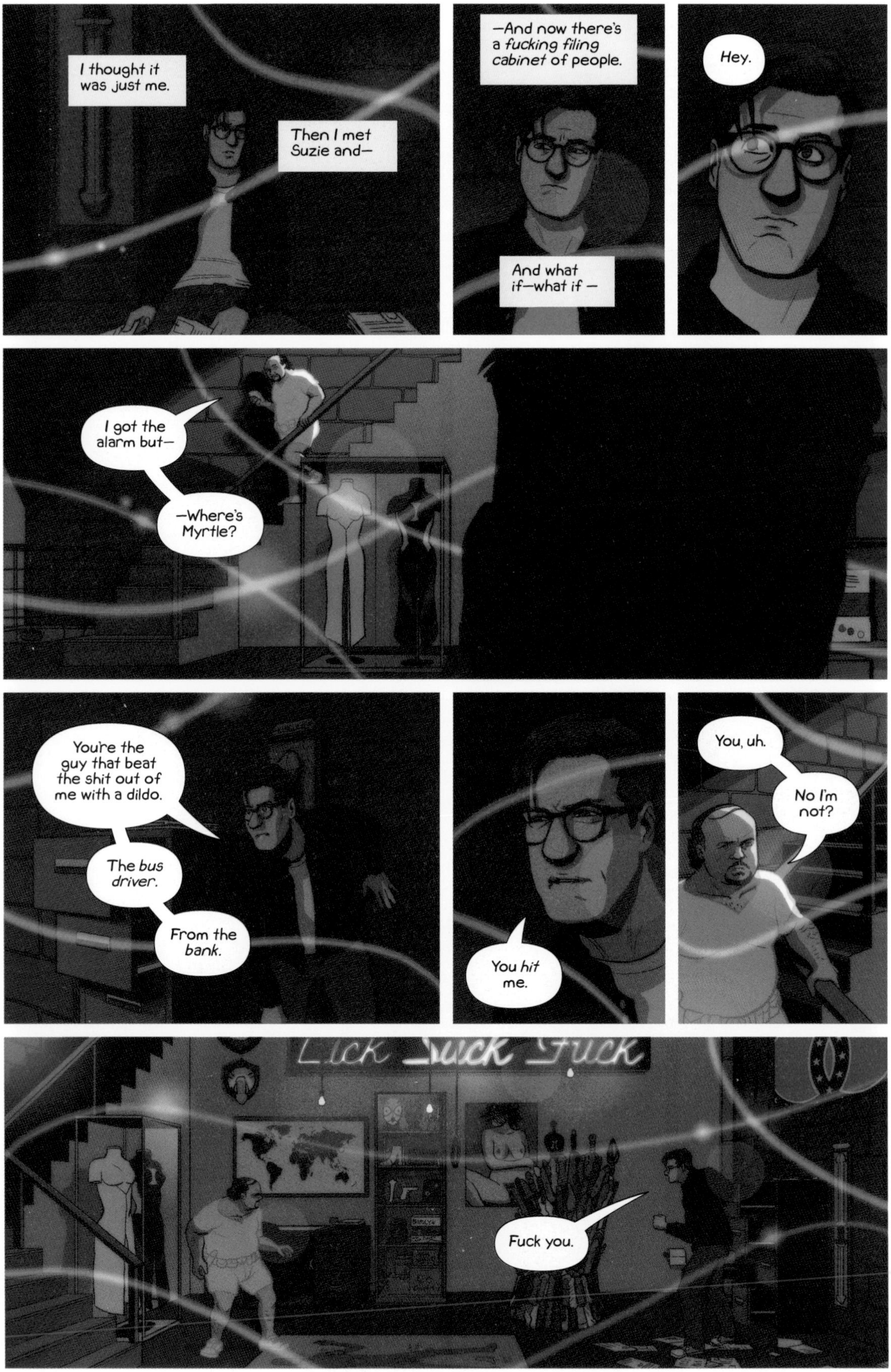
I thought it was just me.
Then I met Suzie and—
—And now there's a *fucking filing cabinet* of people.
And what if—what if —
Hey.
I got the alarm but—
—Where's Myrtle?
You're the guy that beat the shit out of me with a dildo.
The *bus driver*.
From the *bank*.
You *hit* me.
You, uh.
No I'm not?
Lick Suck Fuck
Fuck you.

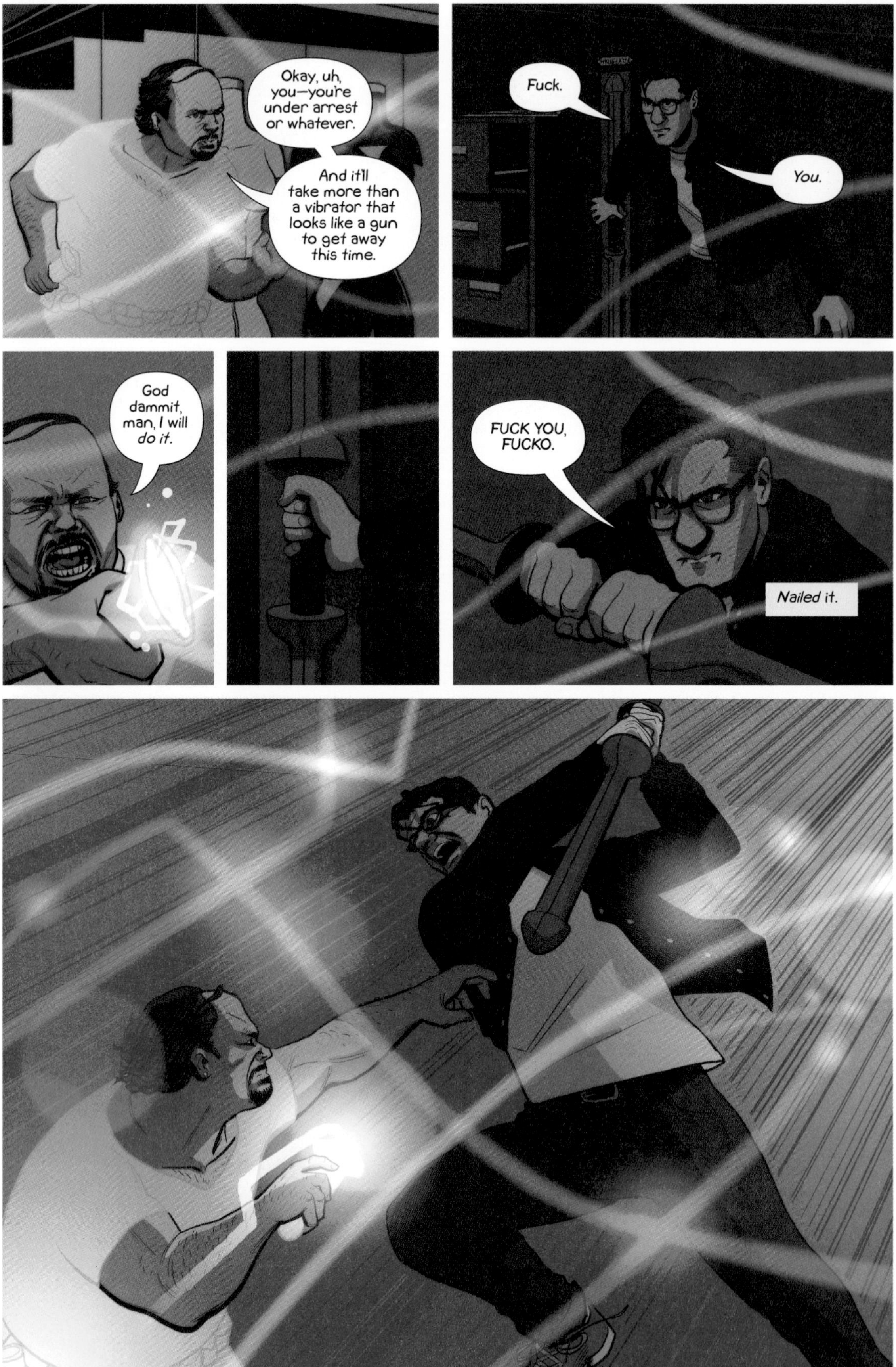
Okay, uh, you—you're under arrest or whatever.
And it'll take more than a vibrator that looks like a gun to get away this time.
Fuck.
You.
God dammit, man, I will *do it*.
FUCK YOU, FUCKO.
Nailed it.

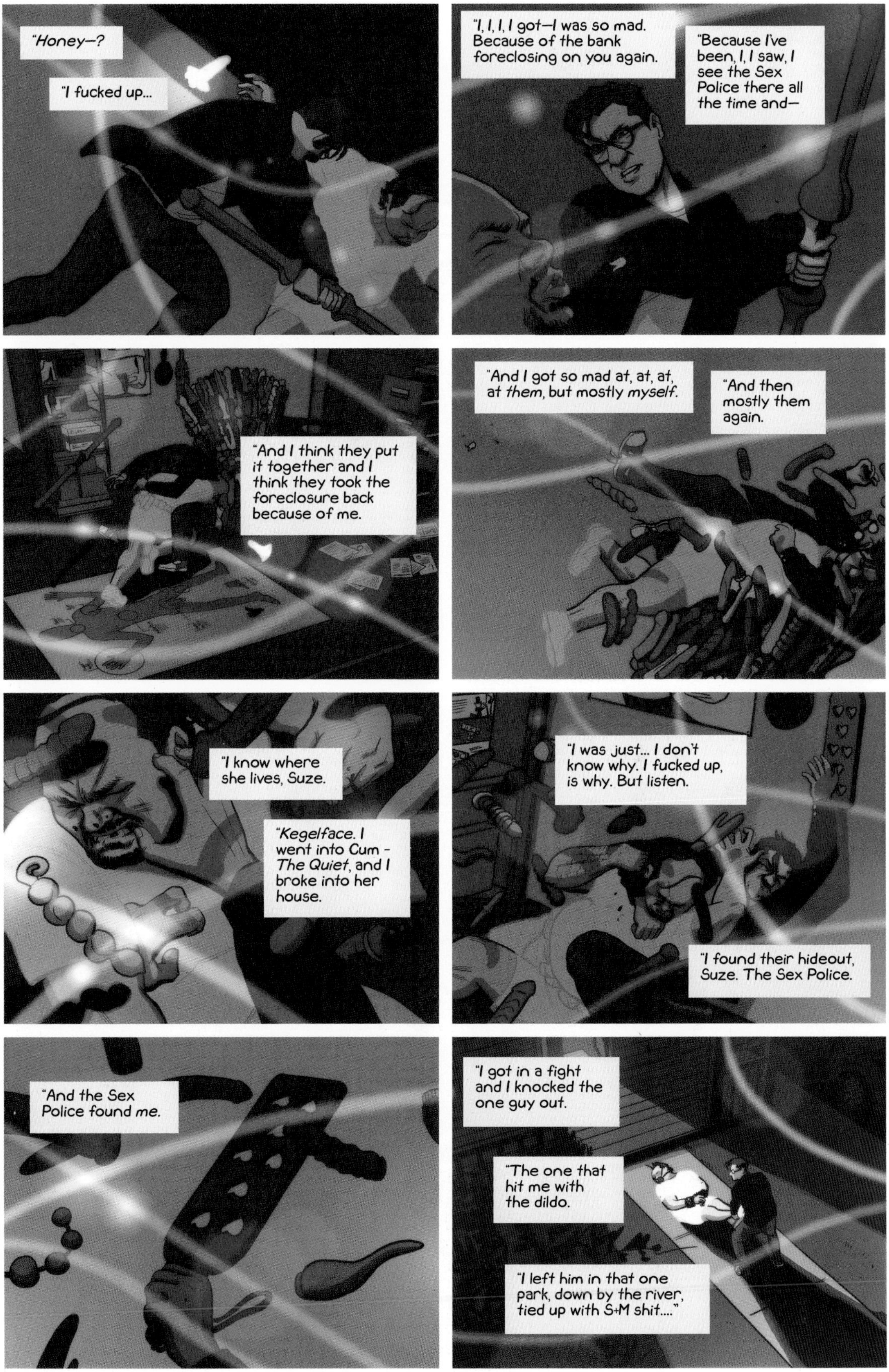
"Honey—?
"I fucked up...
"I, I, I, I got—I was so mad. Because of the bank foreclosing on you again.
"Because I've been, I, I saw, I see the Sex Police there all the time and—
"And I think they put it together and I think they took the foreclosure back because of me.
"And I got so mad at, at, at, at *them*, but mostly *myself*.
"And then mostly them again.
"I know where she lives, Suze.
"*Kegelface*. I went into Cum - *The Quiet*, and I broke into her house.
"I was just... I don't know why. I fucked up, is why. But listen.
"I found their hideout, Suze. The Sex Police.
"And the Sex Police found *me*.
"I got in a fight and I knocked the one guy out.
"The one that hit me with the dildo.
"I left him in that one park, down by the river, tied up with S+M shit...."

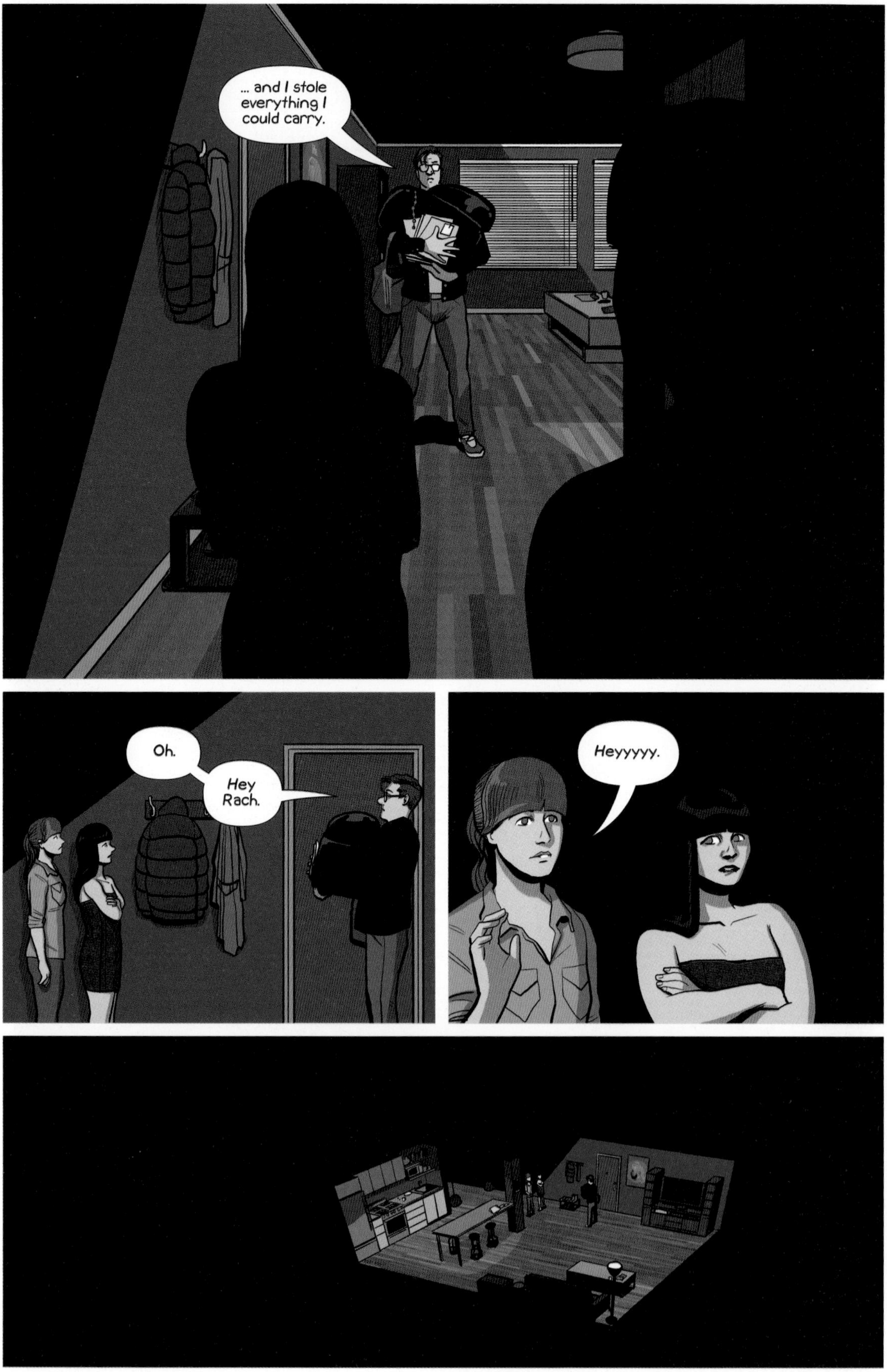
... and I stole everything I could carry.
Oh.
Hey Rach.
Heyyyyy.

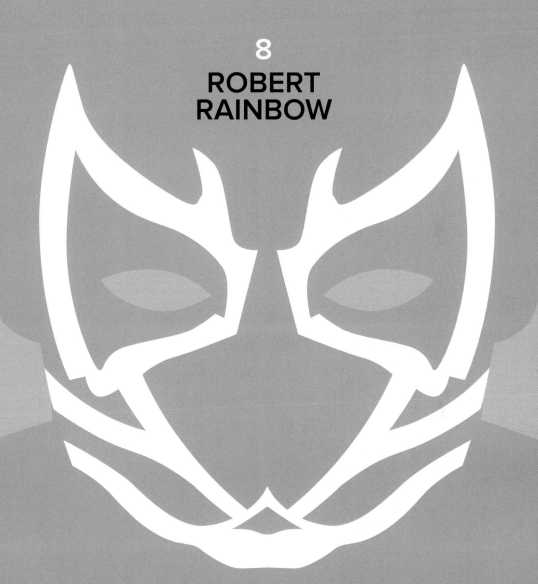

8
ROBERT
RAINBOW

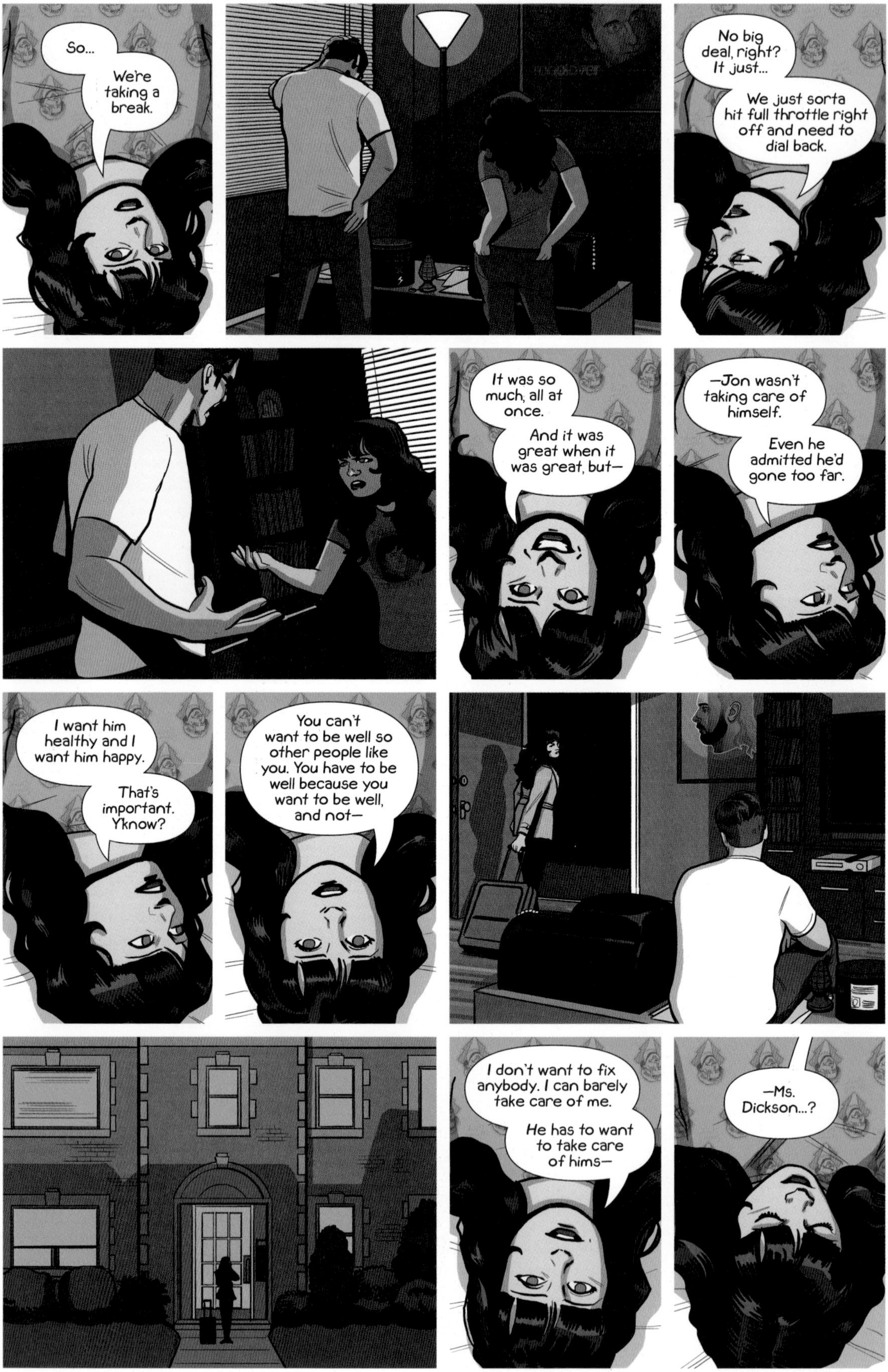
So...
We're taking a break.
No big deal, right? It just...
We just sorta hit full throttle right off and need to dial back.
It was so much, all at once.
And it was great when it was great, but—
—Jon wasn't taking care of himself.
Even he admitted he'd gone too far.
I want him healthy and I want him happy.
That's important. Y'know?
You can't want to be well so other people like you. You have to be well because you want to be well, and not—
I don't want to fix anybody. I can barely take care of me.
He has to want to take care of hims—
—Ms. Dickson...?

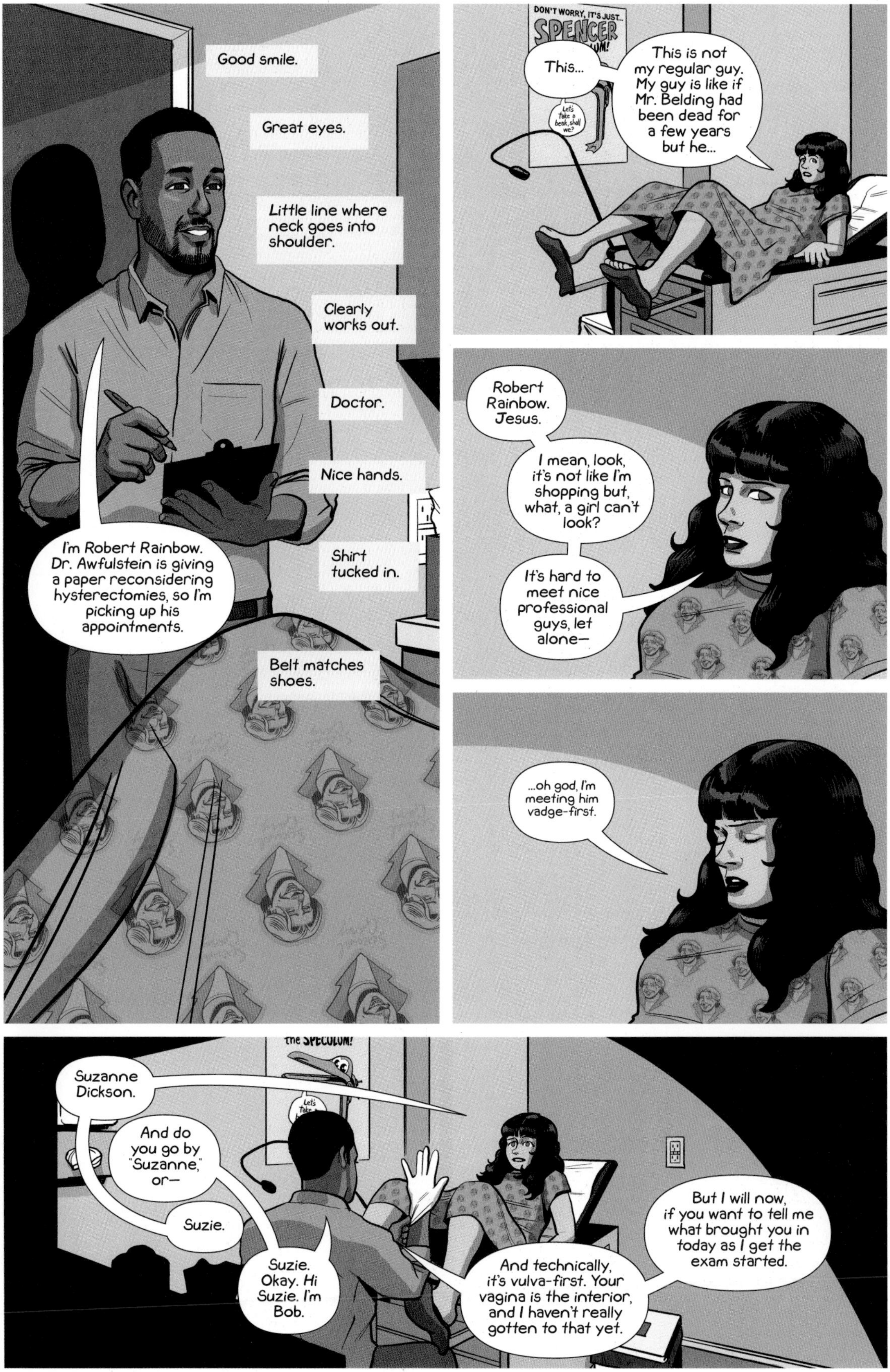
Good smile.
Great eyes.
Little line where neck goes into shoulder.
Clearly works out.
Doctor.
Nice hands.
Shirt tucked in.
I'm Robert Rainbow. Dr. Awfulstein is giving a paper reconsidering hysterectomies, so I'm picking up his appointments.
Belt matches shoes.
DON'T WORRY, IT'S JUST... SPENCER
This...
This is not my regular guy. My guy is like if Mr. Belding had been dead for a few years but he...
Let's take a beak, shall we?
Robert Rainbow. Jesus.
I mean, look, it's not like I'm shopping but, what, a girl can't look?
It's hard to meet nice professional guys, let alone—
...oh god, I'm meeting him vadge-first.
the SPECULUM!
Suzanne Dickson.
And do you go by "Suzanne," or—
Suzie.
Suzie. Okay. Hi Suzie. I'm Bob.
And technically, it's vulva-first. Your vagina is the interior, and I haven't really gotten to that yet.
But I will now, if you want to tell me what brought you in today as I get the exam started.

Might feel a little cold—

Ahh, the art of having a nonsexual conversation with someone while they poke around inside you:

I ahh I feel awful?

My birth control pills make me feel awful?

Okay. Awful-how?

Like a monster? Like a boiled, bloated, dried-up, barren-wombed, desert hag?

With weird, rock-hard tits?

A "hag" is more representative of nature's ugly side.

Sounds to me more like you're experiencing Manticore-like symptoms, or maybe something Efreet-esque.

DON'T WORRY, IT'S JUST... SPENCED the

Let's take a break, shall

I don't know what those are.

That's why I get to be the doctor, Suzie.

I had to dick around through years of medical school to know my Dracolichs from my Shambling Mounds.

Why don't you tell me what your birth control needs are.

Beyond, yknow. Controlling birth.

No, well, that's—that's the big one.

I'm not sure what you mean?

Do you feel you need a kind of all-day, every-day option?

Do you want to explore surgical solutions? What about barrier-based contraception?

Let's start with this—

Are you in a sexually-active relationship?

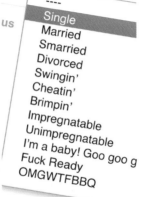

----
us   Single
Married
Smarried
Divorced
Swingin'
Cheatin'
Brimpin'
Impregnatable
Unimpregnatable
I'm a baby! Goo goo g
Fuck Ready
OMGWTFBBQ

I don't really know.

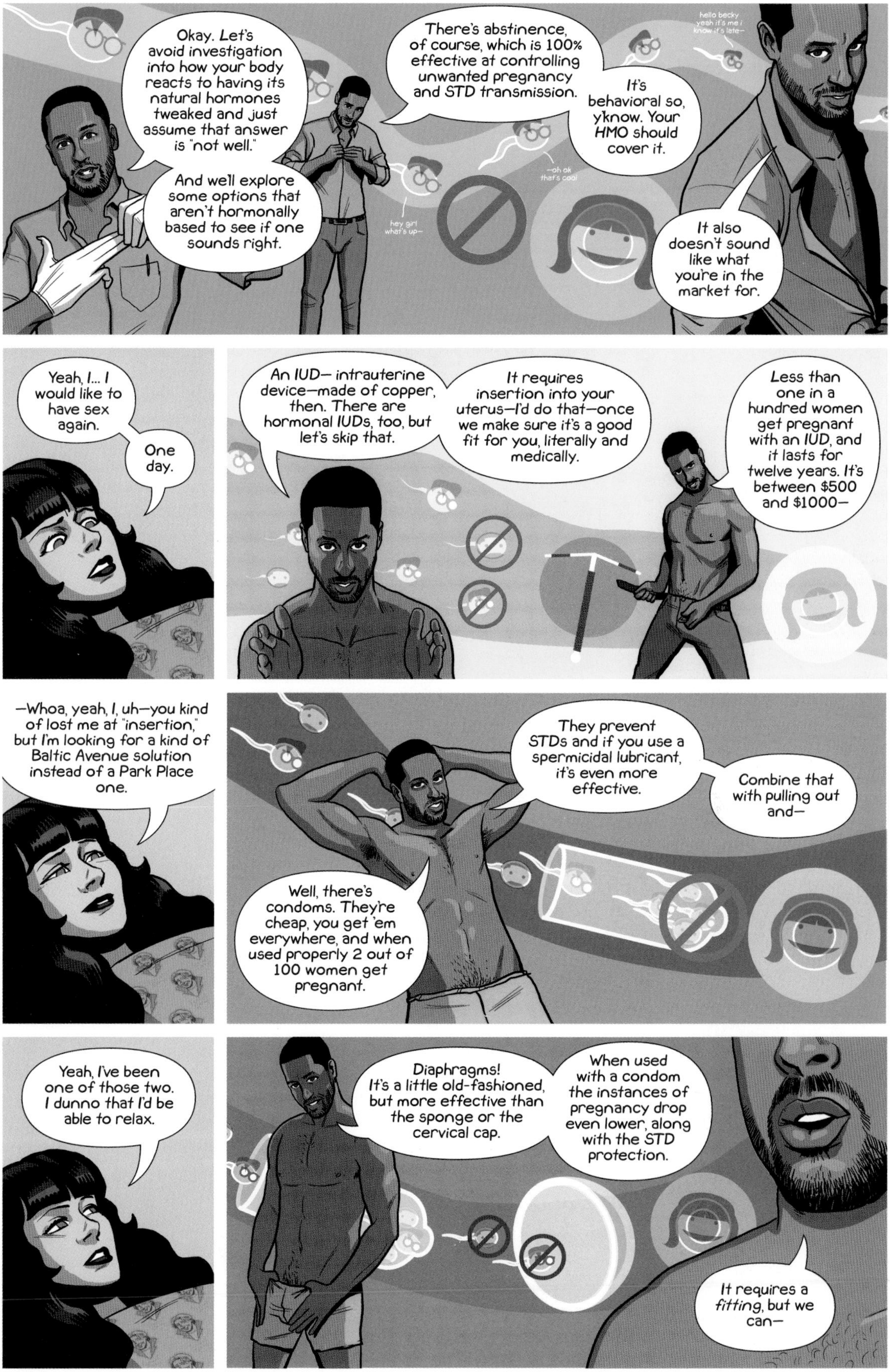
Okay. Let's avoid investigation into how your body reacts to having its natural hormones tweaked and just assume that answer is "not well."
And we'll explore some options that aren't hormonally based to see if one sounds right.
There's abstinence, of course, which is 100% effective at controlling unwanted pregnancy and STD transmission.
hey girl what's up—
—oh ok that's cool
hello becky yeah it's me i know it's late—
It's behavioral so, y'know. Your HMO should cover it.
It also doesn't sound like what you're in the market for.
Yeah, I... I would like to have sex again.
One day.
An IUD— intrauterine device—made of copper, then. There are hormonal IUDs, too, but let's skip that.
It requires insertion into your uterus—I'd do that—once we make sure it's a good fit for you, literally and medically.
Less than one in a hundred women get pregnant with an IUD, and it lasts for twelve years. It's between $500 and $1000—
—Whoa, yeah, I, uh—you kind of lost me at "insertion," but I'm looking for a kind of Baltic Avenue solution instead of a Park Place one.
Well, there's condoms. They're cheap, you get 'em everywhere, and when used properly 2 out of 100 women get pregnant.
They prevent STDs and if you use a spermicidal lubricant, it's even more effective.
Combine that with pulling out and—
Yeah, I've been one of those two. I dunno that I'd be able to relax.
Diaphragms! It's a little old-fashioned, but more effective than the sponge or the cervical cap.
When used with a condom the instances of pregnancy drop even lower, along with the STD protection.
It requires a fitting, but we can—

* *All facts and statistics taken from http://www.plannedparenthood.org/health-info/birth-control*
Come on! Plan your parenthood!

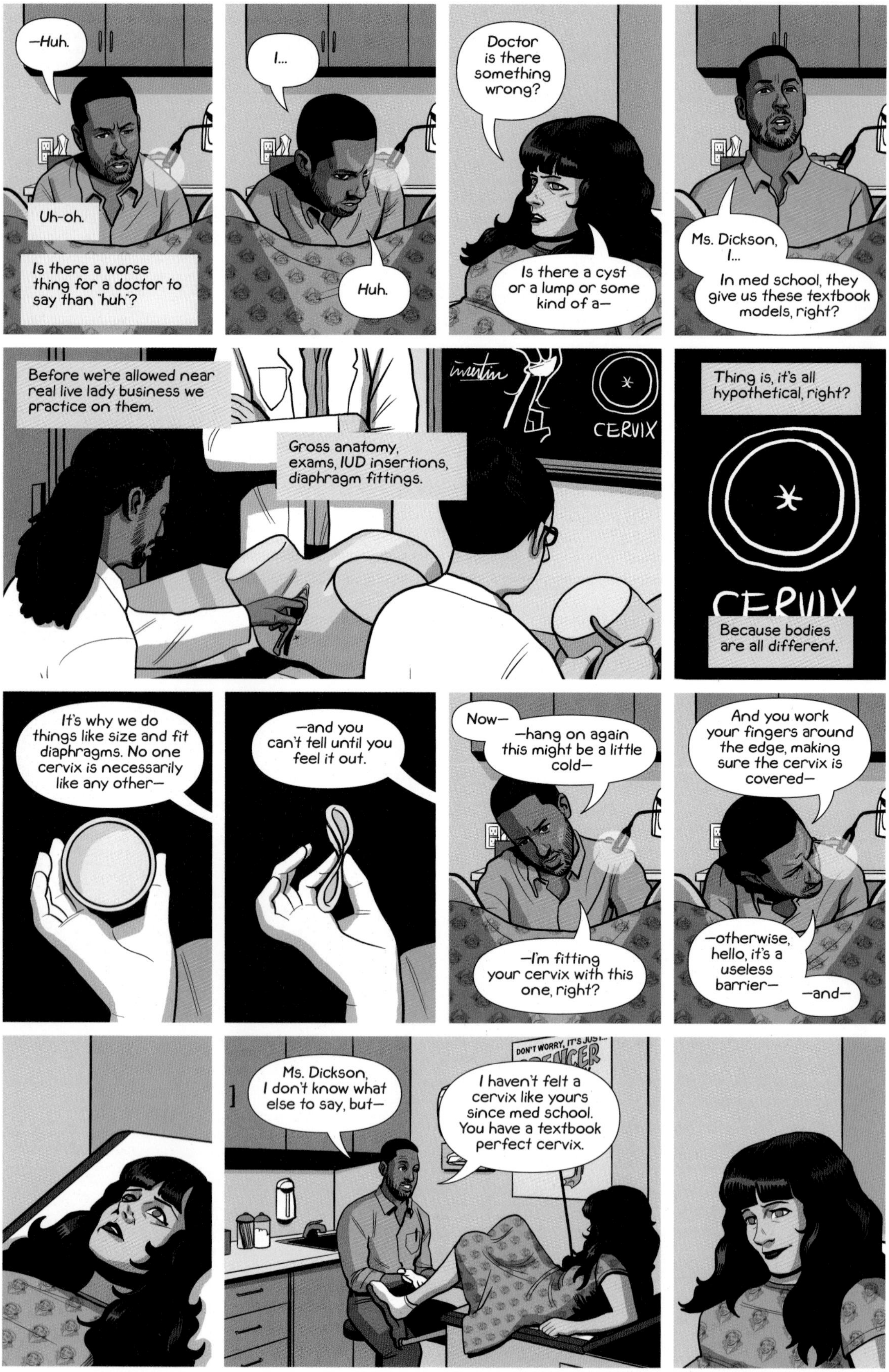
—Huh.
Uh-oh.
Is there a worse thing for a doctor to say than "huh"?
I...
Huh.
Doctor is there something wrong?
Is there a cyst or a lump or some kind of a—
Ms. Dickson, I...
In med school, they give us these textbook models, right?
Before we're allowed near real live lady business we practice on them.
Gross anatomy, exams, IUD insertions, diaphragm fittings.
CERVIX
Thing is, it's all hypothetical, right?
CERVIX
Because bodies are all different.
It's why we do things like size and fit diaphragms. No one cervix is necessarily like any other—
—and you can't tell until you feel it out.
Now—
—hang on again this might be a little cold—
—I'm fitting your cervix with this one, right?
And you work your fingers around the edge, making sure the cervix is covered—
—otherwise, hello, it's a useless barrier—
—and—
Ms. Dickson, I don't know what else to say, but—
I haven't felt a cervix like yours since med school. You have a textbook perfect cervix.

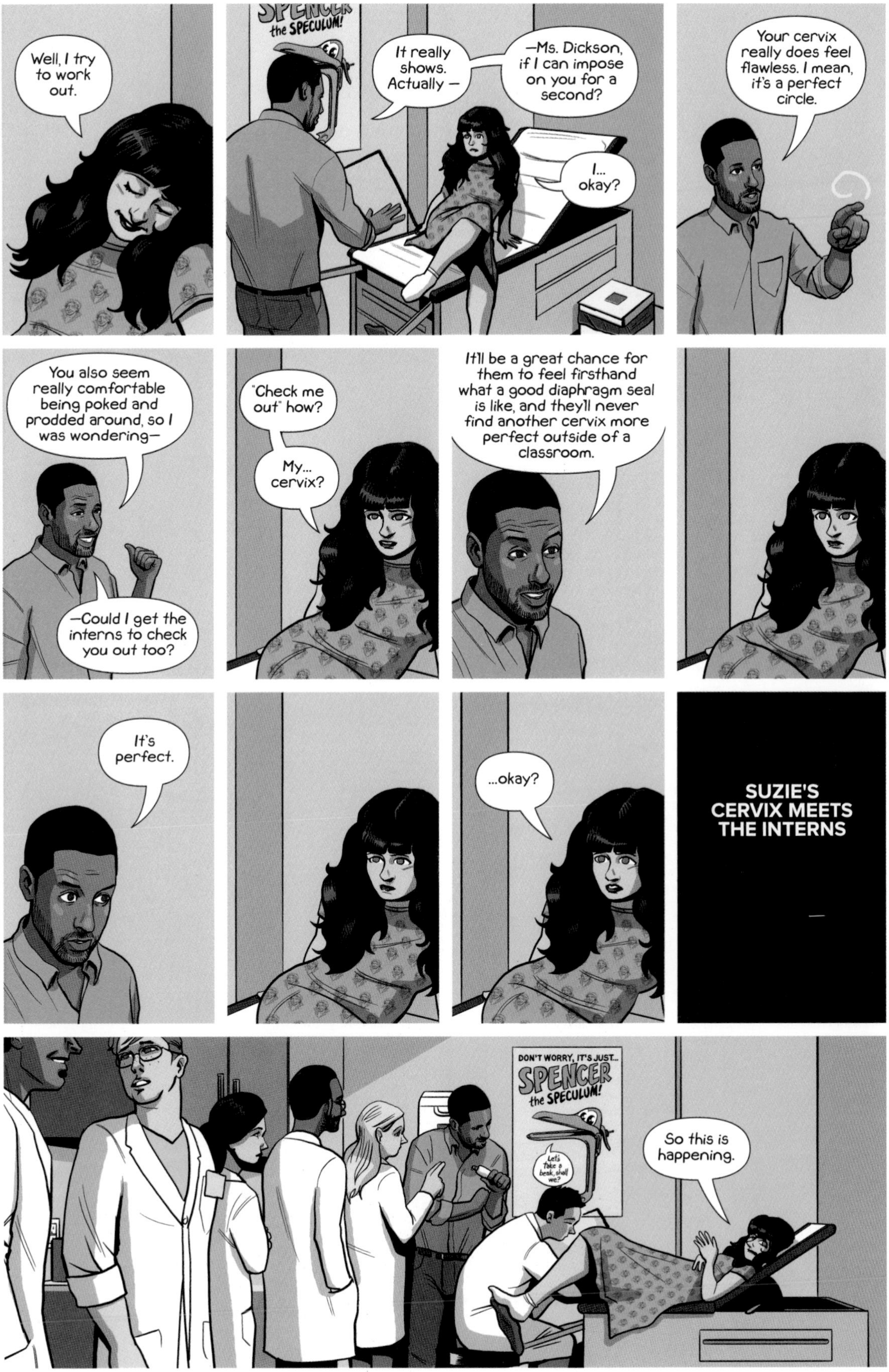
Well, I try to work out.
the SPECULUM!
It really shows. Actually —
—Ms. Dickson, if I can impose on you for a second?
I... okay?
Your cervix really does feel flawless. I mean, it's a perfect circle.
You also seem really comfortable being poked and prodded around, so I was wondering—
—Could I get the interns to check you out too?
"Check me out" how?
My... cervix?
It'll be a great chance for them to feel firsthand what a good diaphragm seal is like, and they'll never find another cervix more perfect outside of a classroom.
It's perfect.
...okay?
SUZIE'S CERVIX MEETS THE INTERNS
DON'T WORRY, IT'S JUST...
SPENCER the SPECULUM!
Let's take a beak, shall we?
So this is happening.

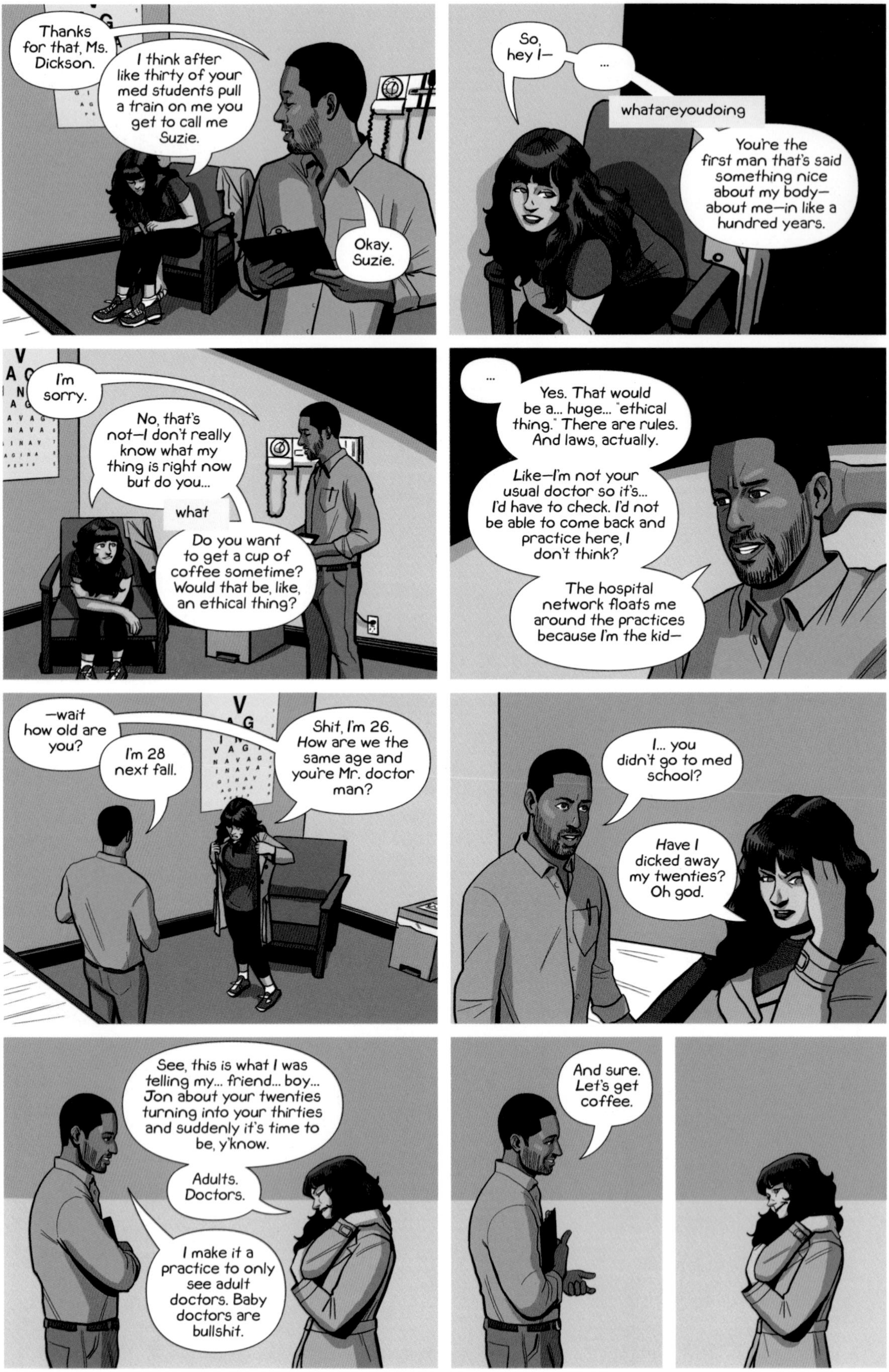
Thanks for that, Ms. Dickson.
I think after like thirty of your med students pull a train on me you get to call me Suzie.
Okay. Suzie.
So, hey I—
...
whatareyoudoing
You're the first man that's said something nice about my body—about me—in like a hundred years.
I'm sorry.
No, that's not—I don't really know what my thing is right now but do you...
what
Do you want to get a cup of coffee sometime? Would that be, like, an ethical thing?
...
Yes. That would be a... huge... "ethical thing." There are rules. And laws, actually.
Like—I'm not your usual doctor so it's... I'd have to check. I'd not be able to come back and practice here, I don't think?
The hospital network floats me around the practices because I'm the kid—
—wait how old are you?
I'm 28 next fall.
Shit, I'm 26. How are we the same age and you're Mr. doctor man?
I... you didn't go to med school?
Have I dicked away my twenties? Oh god.
See, this is what I was telling my... friend... boy... Jon about your twenties turning into your thirties and suddenly it's time to be, y'know.
Adults. Doctors.
I make it a practice to only see adult doctors. Baby doctors are bullshit.
And sure. Let's get coffee.

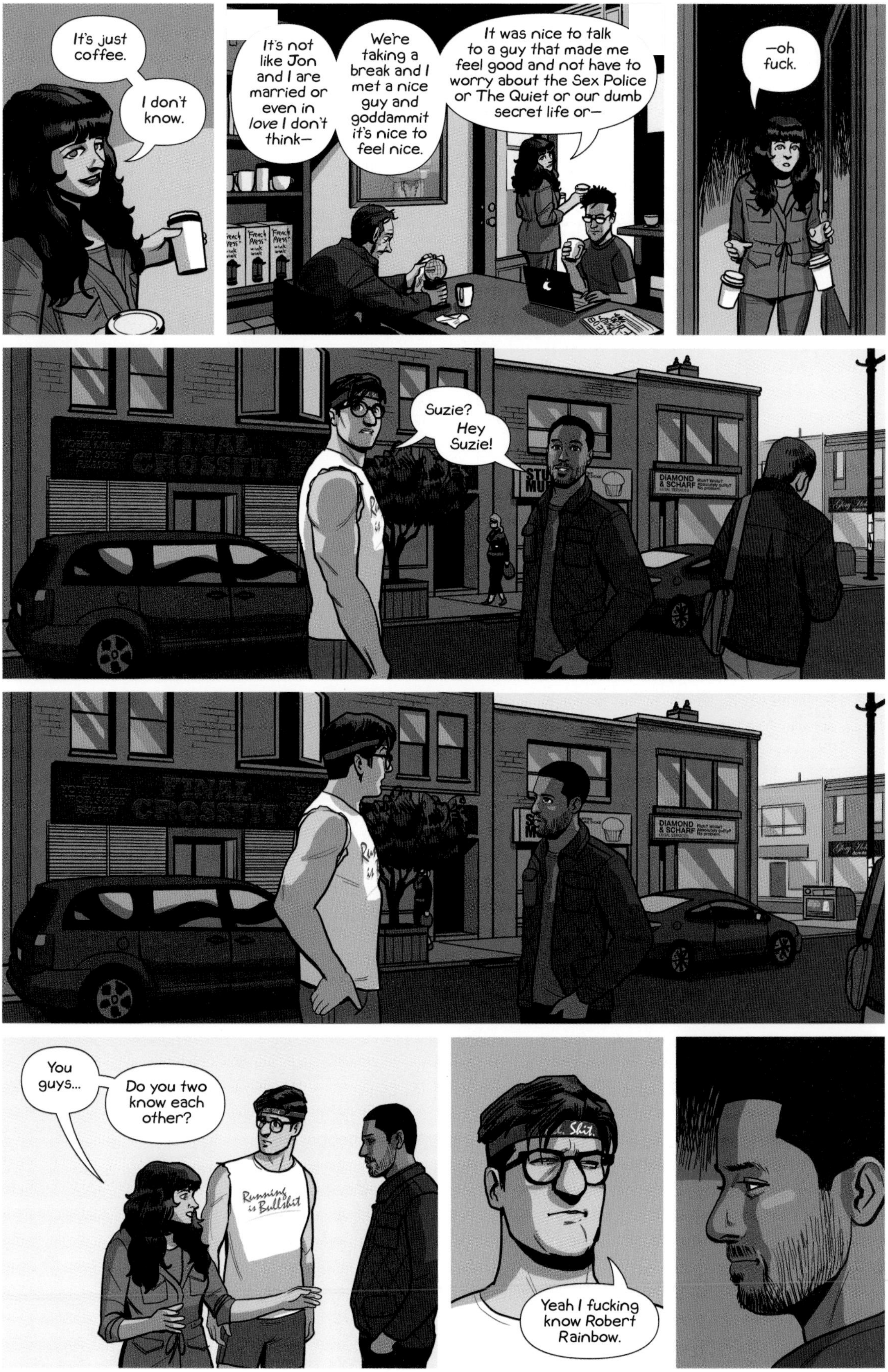
It's just coffee.
I don't know.
It's not like Jon and I are married or even in love I don't think—
We're taking a break and I met a nice guy and goddammit it's nice to feel nice.
It was nice to talk to a guy that made me feel good and not have to worry about the Sex Police or The Quiet or our dumb secret life or—
—oh fuck.
Suzie? Hey Suzie!
DIAMOND & SCHARF
You guys...
Do you two know each other?
Running is Bullshit
Yeah I fucking know Robert Rainbow.

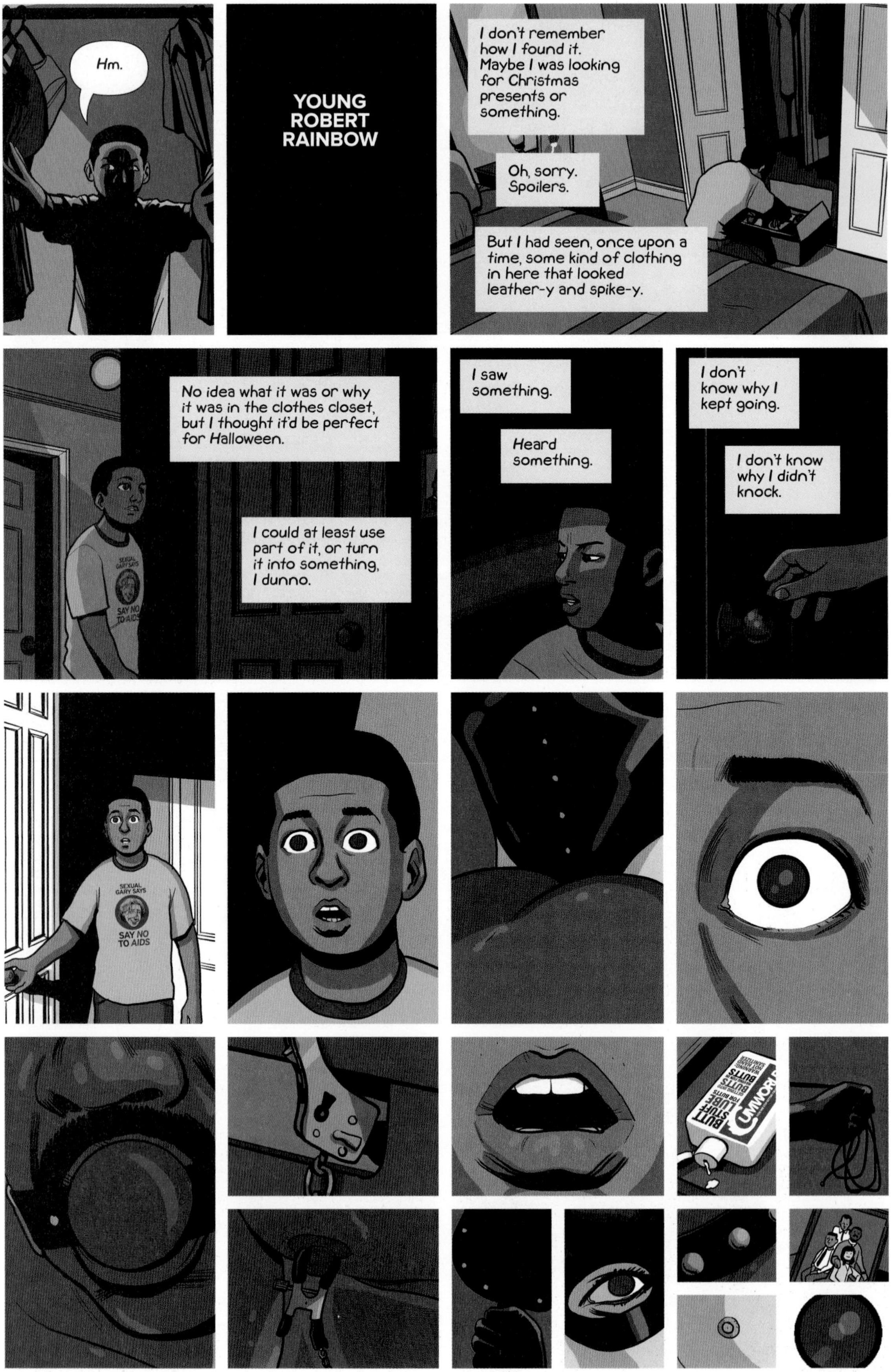

Hm.
YOUNG ROBERT RAINBOW
I don't remember how I found it. Maybe I was looking for Christmas presents or something.
Oh, sorry. Spoilers.
But I had seen, once upon a time, some kind of clothing in here that looked leather-y and spike-y.
No idea what it was or why it was in the clothes closet, but I thought it'd be perfect for Halloween.
I could at least use part of it, or turn it into something, I dunno.
I saw something.
Heard something.
I don't know why I kept going.
I don't know why I didn't knock.
SEXUAL GARY SAYS
SAY NO TO AIDS

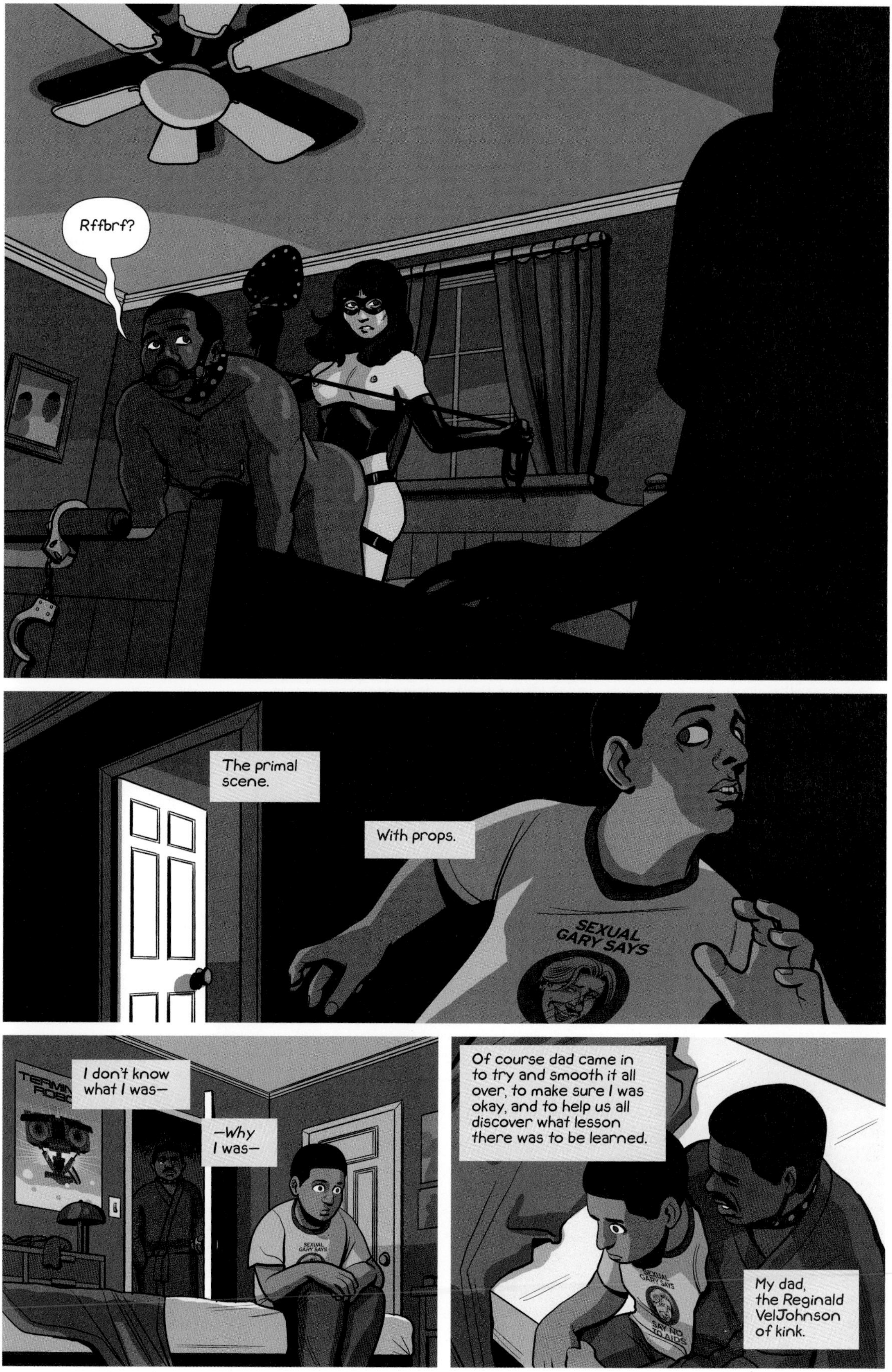
Rffbrf?
The primal scene.
With props.
SEXUAL GARY SAYS
I don't know what I was—
—Why I was—
Of course dad came in to try and smooth it all over, to make sure I was okay, and to help us all discover what lesson there was to be learned.
My dad, the Reginald VelJohnson of kink.

He and mom love each other very much.

What I'd seen was consensual and planned and, while maybe not common, is a thing they enjoy very much.

He kept apologizing.

All I could think was, *why the fuck did I open that door?*

Why the fuck didn't I realize what I'd found when I found it?

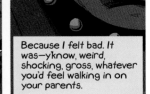

Because I felt bad. It was—yknow, weird, shocking, gross, whatever you'd feel walking in on your parents.

But I felt bad I'd embarrassed them.

And I couldn't stop looking at the dog collar.

Dad, look—

I'm sorry. I don't know what I was doing. I should've knocked.

You and mom don't have anything to apologize for.

What followed was the most mature thing I'd ever said to date.

You and mom are, like, the only parents out of all of my friends that are still together. Literally.

If you're happy? Stay happy.

I don't know if I believed it, but it was true.

Mostly I just wanted to get this over with and get on to my goddamn Halloween plans, right?

I think Dad was happy to be let off the hook.

Christ knows I was.

So I wouldn't have any cool shit to wear. Fine.

The *face* was all that mattered anyway.

It was meditative, putting it on.

I worked on compartmentalizing my Freudian horror as I became Cat Man.

Pfft.

You are *such* an embarrassment to the scene.

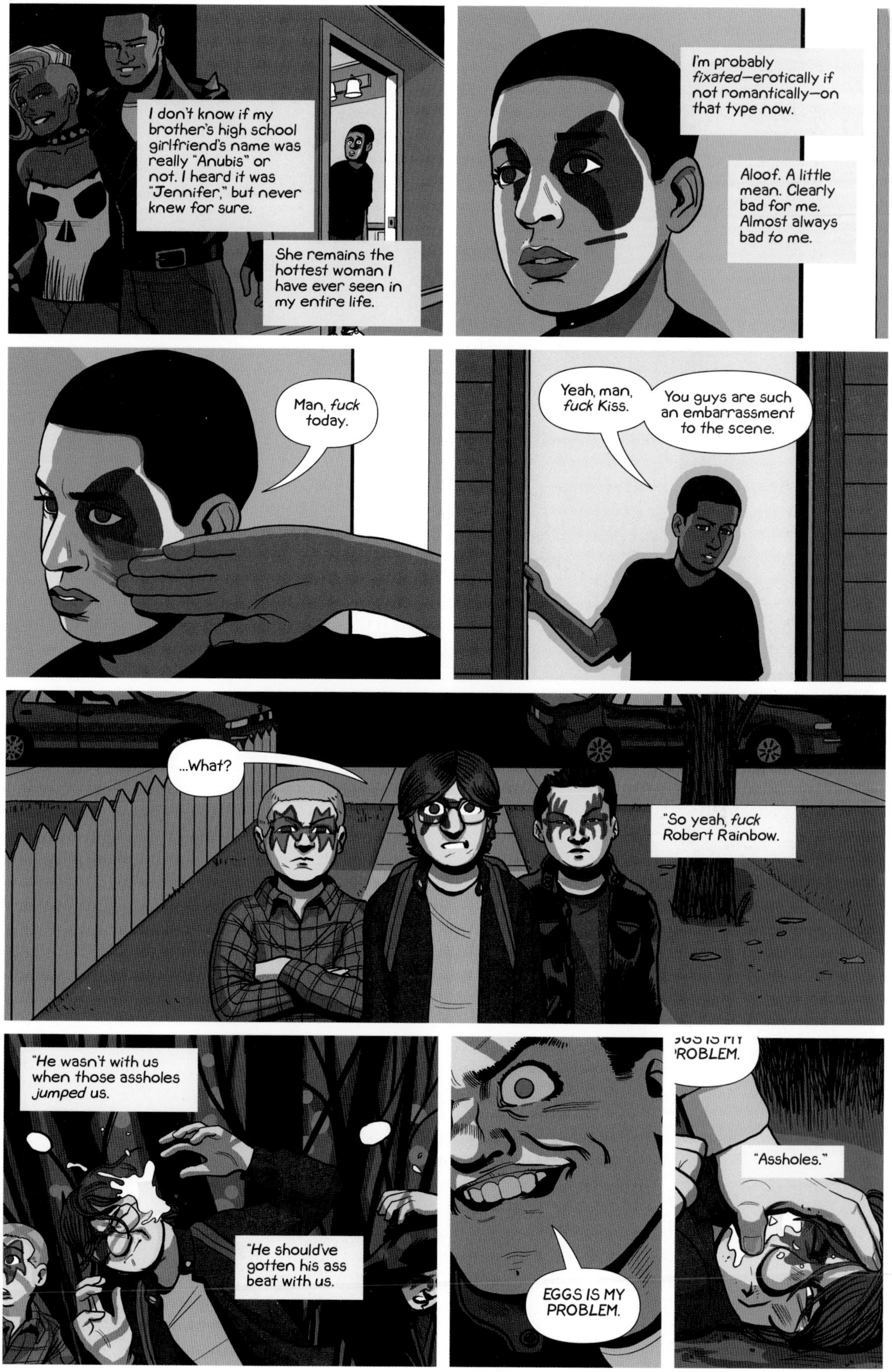
I don't know if my brother's high school girlfriend's name was really "Anubis" or not. I heard it was "Jennifer," but never knew for sure.
She remains the hottest woman I have ever seen in my entire life.
I'm probably *fixated*—erotically if not romantically—on that type now.
Aloof. A little mean. Clearly bad for me. Almost always bad *to* me.
Man, *fuck* today.
Yeah, man, *fuck* Kiss.
You guys are such an embarrassment to the scene.
...What?
"So yeah, *fuck* Robert Rainbow.
"He wasn't with us when those assholes *jumped* us.
"He should've gotten his ass beat with us.
EGGS IS MY PROBLEM.
"Assholes."

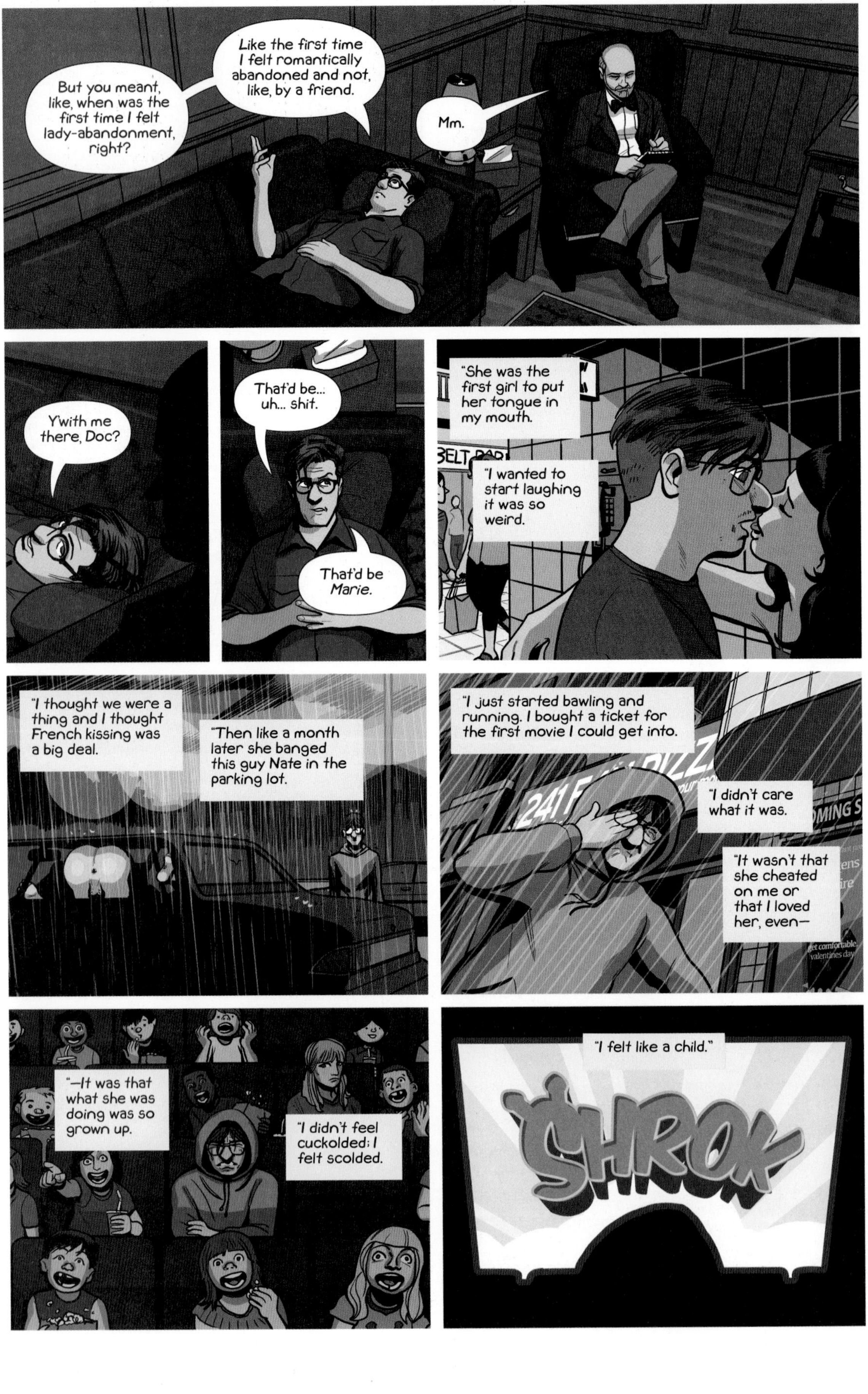
But you meant, like, when was the first time I felt lady-abandonment, right?
Like the first time I felt romantically abandoned and not, like, by a friend.
Mm.
Y'with me there, Doc?
That'd be... uh... shit.
That'd be Marie.
"She was the first girl to put her tongue in my mouth.
"I wanted to start laughing it was so weird.
"I thought we were a thing and I thought French kissing was a big deal.
"Then like a month later she banged this guy Nate in the parking lot.
"I just started bawling and running. I bought a ticket for the first movie I could get into.
241 F
"I didn't care what it was.
"It wasn't that she cheated on me or that I loved her, even—
get comfortable
valentines day
"—It was that what she was doing was so grown up.
"I didn't feel cuckolded; I felt scolded.
"I felt like a child."
SHROK

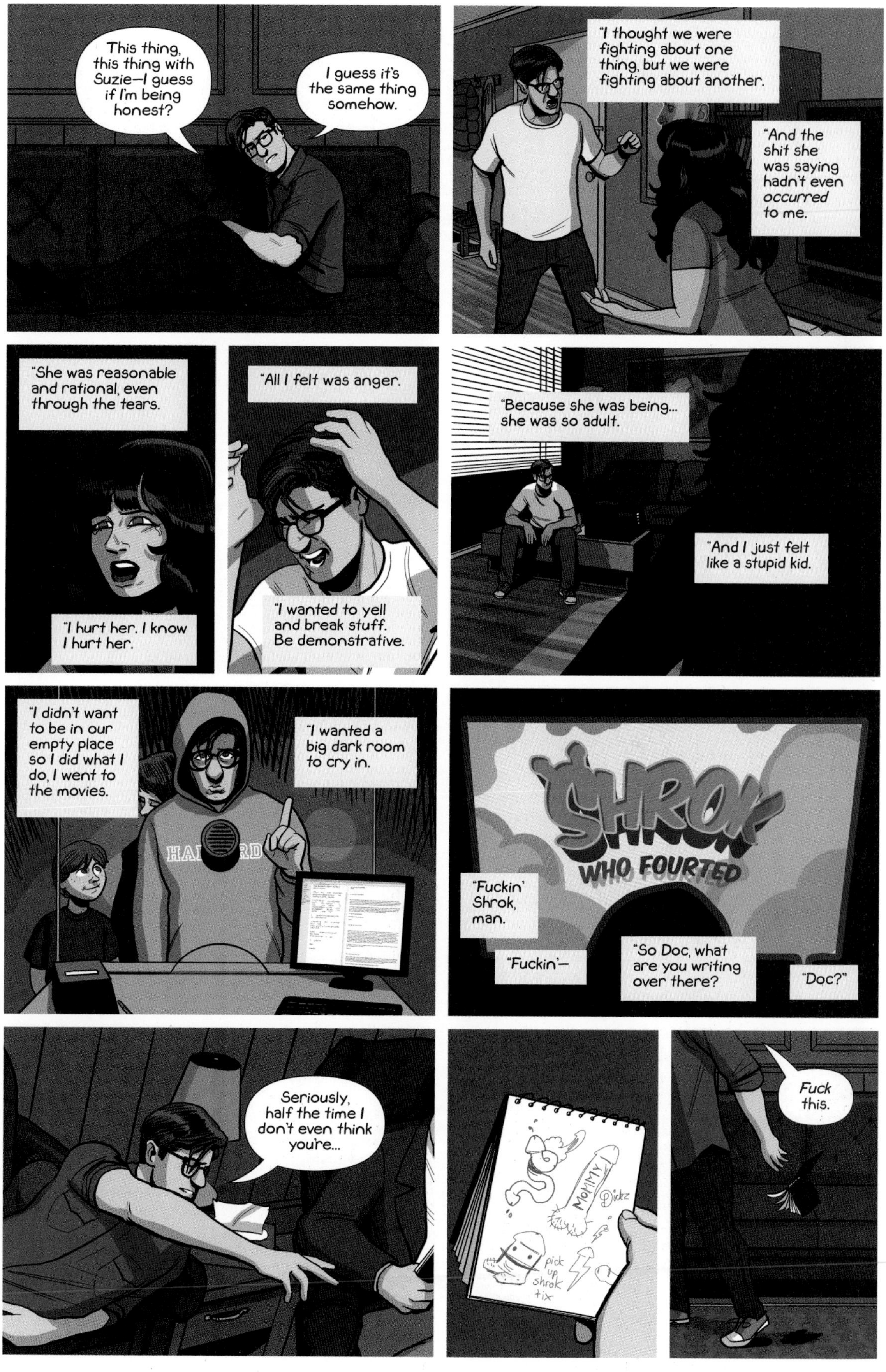
This thing, this thing with Suzie—I guess if I'm being honest?
I guess it's the same thing somehow.
"I thought we were fighting about one thing, but we were fighting about another.
"And the shit she was saying hadn't even *occurred* to me.
"She was reasonable and rational, even through the tears.
"I hurt her. I know I hurt her.
"All I felt was anger.
"I wanted to yell and break stuff. Be demonstrative.
"Because she was being... she was so adult.
"And I just felt like a stupid kid.
"I didn't want to be in our empty place so I did what I do, I went to the movies.
"I wanted a big dark room to cry in.
SHROK
WHO FOURTED
"Fuckin' Shrok, man.
"Fuckin'—
"So Doc, what are you writing over there?
"Doc?"
Seriously, half the time I don't even think you're...
MOMMY
Dickz
pick up shrok tix
Fuck this.

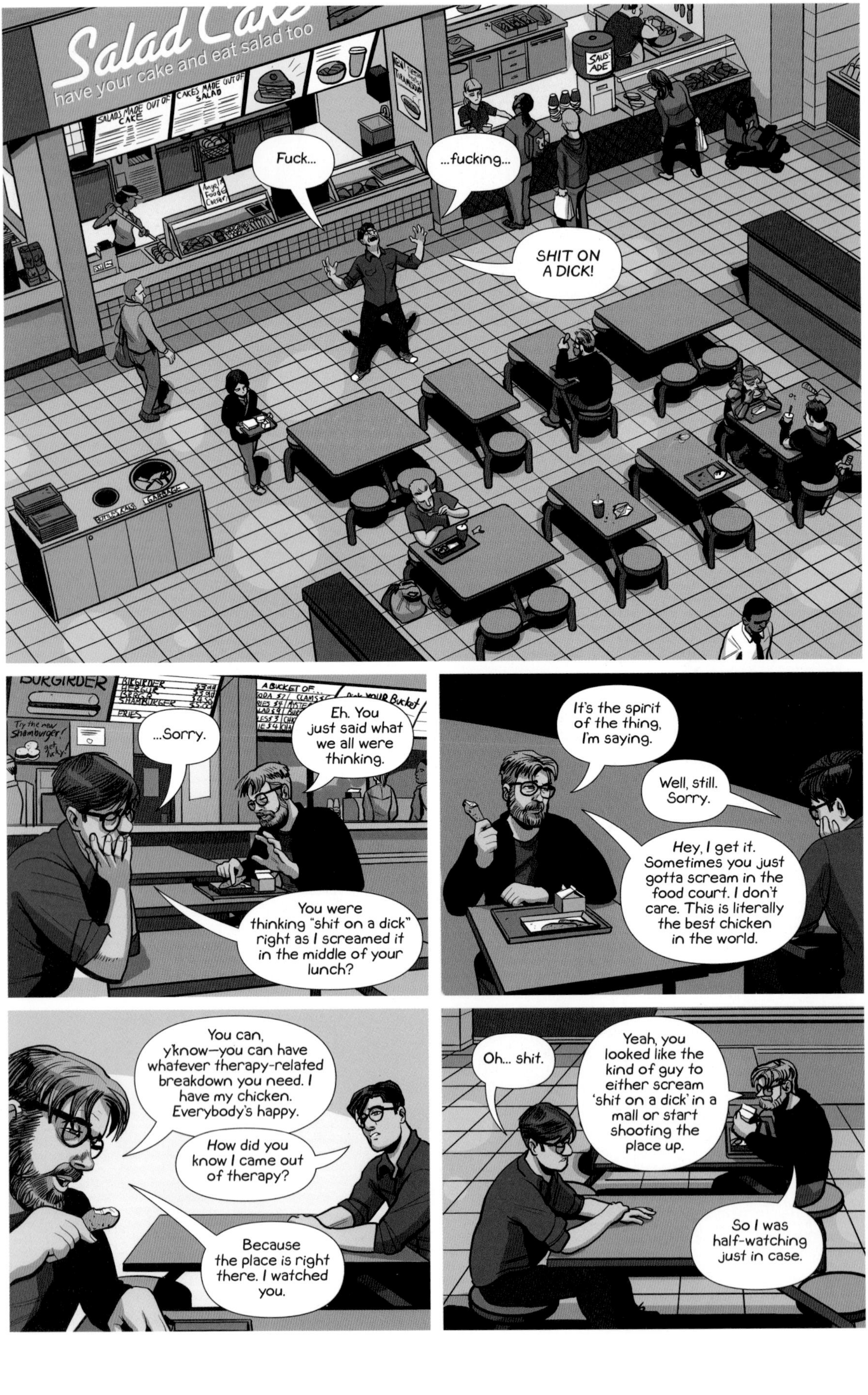
Salad Cakes
have your cake and eat salad too
SALADS MADE OUT OF CAKE
CAKES MADE OUT OF SALAD
SAUS ADE
GARBAGE
Fuck...
...fucking...
SHIT ON A DICK!
BURGIRDER
...Sorry.
Eh. You just said what we all were thinking.
You were thinking "shit on a dick" right as I screamed it in the middle of your lunch?
It's the spirit of the thing, I'm saying.
Well, still. Sorry.
Hey, I get it. Sometimes you just gotta scream in the food court. I don't care. This is literally the best chicken in the world.
You can, y'know—you can have whatever therapy-related breakdown you need. I have my chicken. Everybody's happy.
How did you know I came out of therapy?
Because the place is right there. I watched you.
Oh... shit.
Yeah, you looked like the kind of guy to either scream 'shit on a dick' in a mall or start shooting the place up.
So I was half-watching just in case.

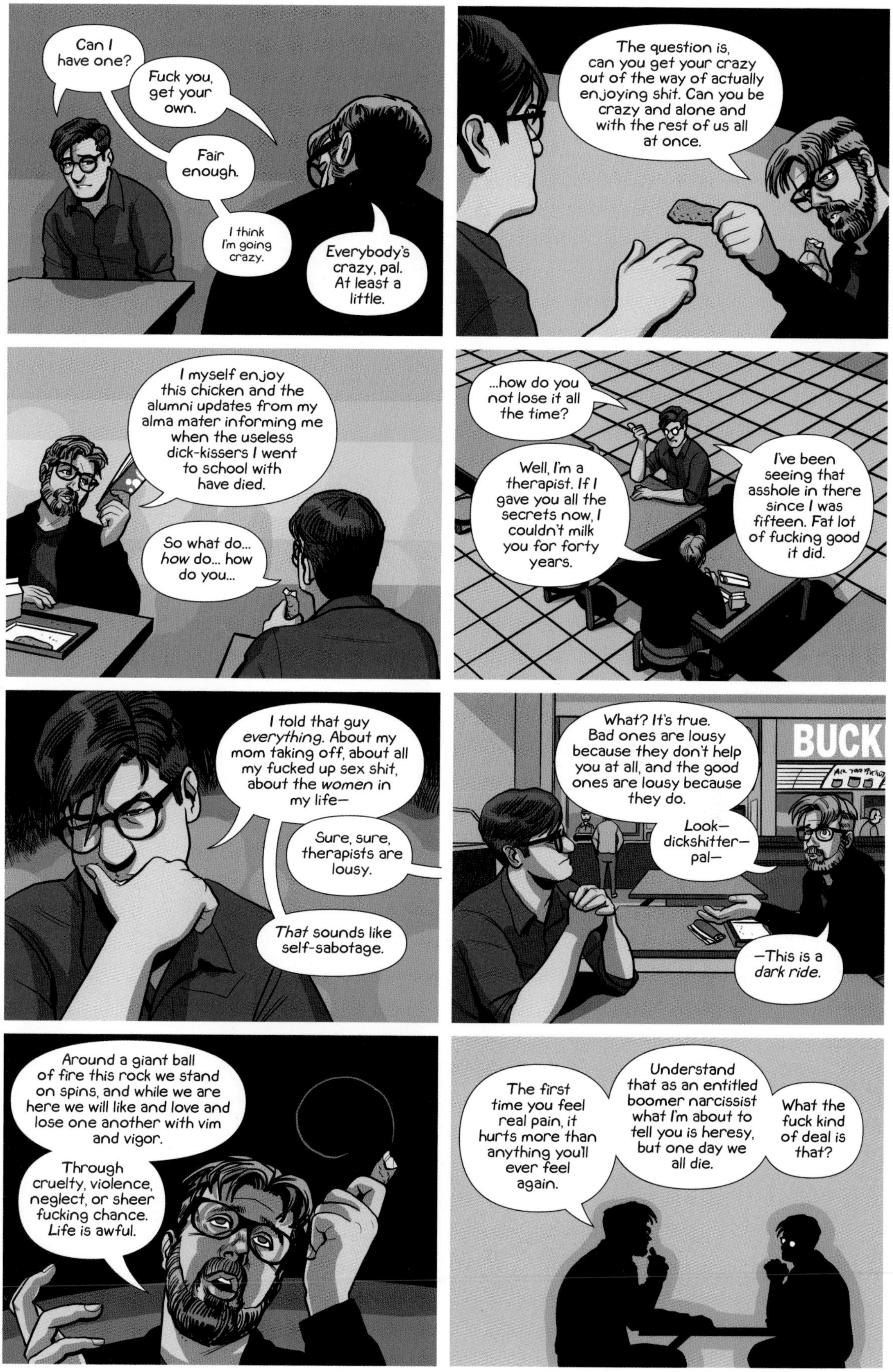
Can I have one?
Fuck you, get your own.
Fair enough.
I think I'm going crazy.
Everybody's crazy, pal. At least a little.
The question is, can you get your crazy out of the way of actually enjoying shit. Can you be crazy and alone and with the rest of us all at once.
I myself enjoy this chicken and the alumni updates from my alma mater informing me when the useless dick-kissers I went to school with have died.
So what do... *how* do... how do you...
...how do you not lose it all the time?
Well, I'm a therapist. If I gave you all the secrets now, I couldn't milk you for forty years.
I've been seeing that asshole in there since I was fifteen. Fat lot of fucking good it did.
I told that guy *everything*. About my mom taking off, about all my fucked up sex shit, about the *women* in my life—
Sure, sure, therapists are lousy.
That sounds like self-sabotage.
What? It's true. Bad ones are lousy because they don't help you at all, and the good ones are lousy because they do.
BUCK
Look—dickshitter—pal—
—This is a *dark ride*.
Around a giant ball of fire this rock we stand on spins, and while we are here we will like and love and lose one another with vim and vigor.
Through cruelty, violence, neglect, or sheer fucking chance. Life is awful.
The first time you feel real pain, it hurts more than anything you'll ever feel again.
Understand that as an entitled boomer narcissist what I'm about to tell you is heresy, but one day we all die.
What the fuck kind of deal is that?

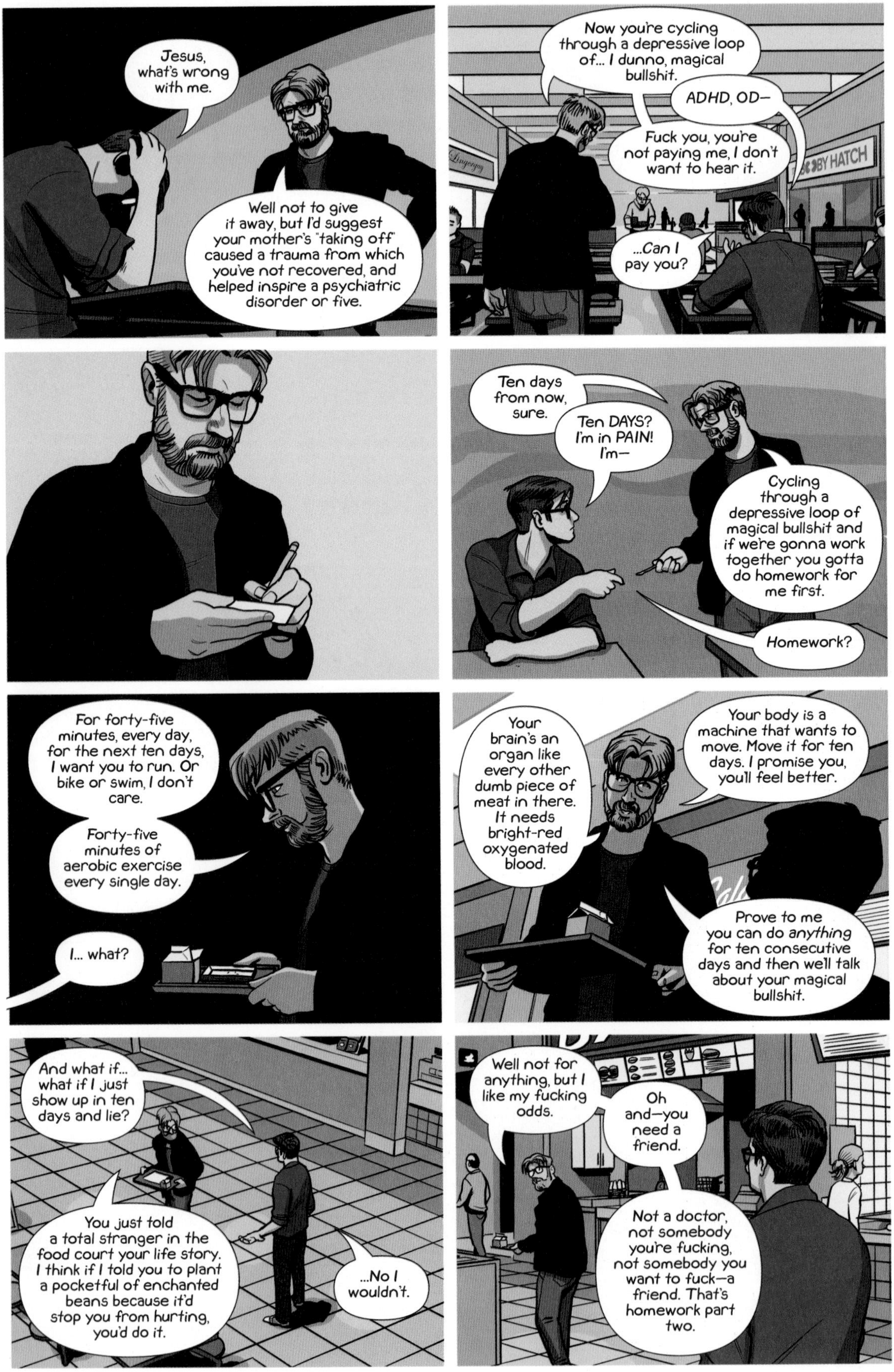
Jesus, what's wrong with me.
Well not to give it away, but I'd suggest your mother's "taking off" caused a trauma from which you've not recovered, and helped inspire a psychiatric disorder or five.
Now you're cycling through a depressive loop of... I dunno, magical bullshit.
ADHD, OD–
Fuck you, you're not paying me, I don't want to hear it.
...Can I pay you?
Ten days from now, sure.
Ten DAYS? I'm in PAIN! I'm–
Cycling through a depressive loop of magical bullshit and if we're gonna work together you gotta do homework for me first.
Homework?
For forty-five minutes, every day, for the next ten days, I want you to run. Or bike or swim, I don't care.
Forty-five minutes of aerobic exercise every single day.
I... what?
Your brain's an organ like every other dumb piece of meat in there. It needs bright-red oxygenated blood.
Your body is a machine that wants to move. Move it for ten days. I promise you, you'll feel better.
Prove to me you can do *anything* for ten consecutive days and then we'll talk about your magical bullshit.
And what if... what if I just show up in ten days and lie?
You just told a total stranger in the food court your life story. I think if I told you to plant a pocketful of enchanted beans because it'd stop you from hurting, you'd do it.
...No I wouldn't.
Well not for anything, but I like my fucking odds.
Oh and—you need a friend.
Not a doctor, not somebody you're fucking, not somebody you want to fuck—a friend. That's homework part two.

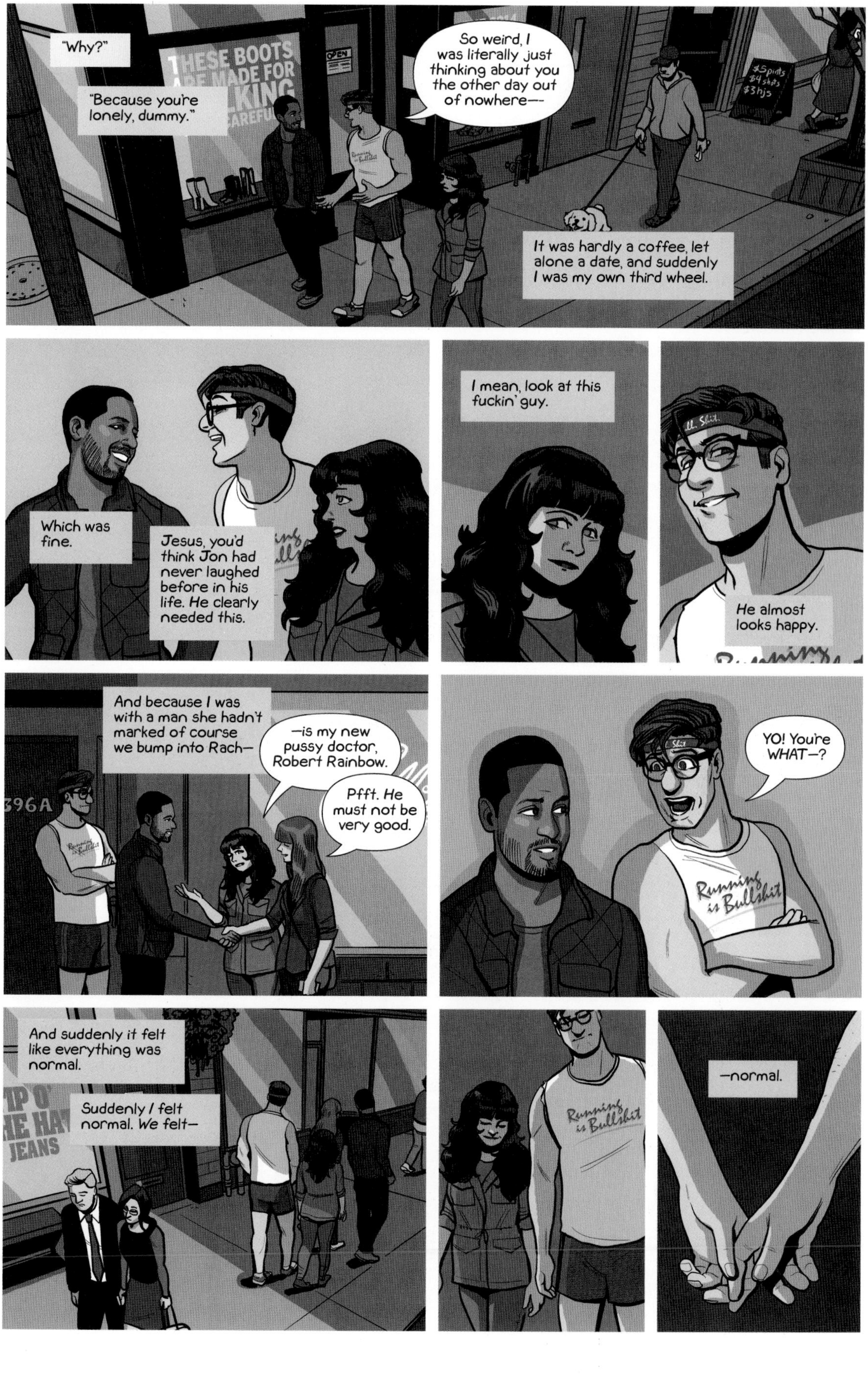

"Why?"
"Because you're lonely, dummy."
THESE BOOTS ARE MADE FOR WALKING
OPEN
So weird, I was literally just thinking about you the other day out of nowhere—
$5pints $4shots $3hjs
It was hardly a coffee, let alone a date, and suddenly I was my own third wheel.
Which was fine.
Jesus, you'd think Jon had never laughed before in his life. He clearly needed this.
I mean, look at this fuckin' guy.
He almost looks happy.
And because I was with a man she hadn't marked of course we bump into Rach—
—is my new pussy doctor, Robert Rainbow.
Pfft. He must not be very good.
396A
YO! You're WHAT—?
Running is Bullshit
And suddenly it felt like everything was normal.
Suddenly I felt normal. We felt—
JEANS
Running is Bullshit
—normal.

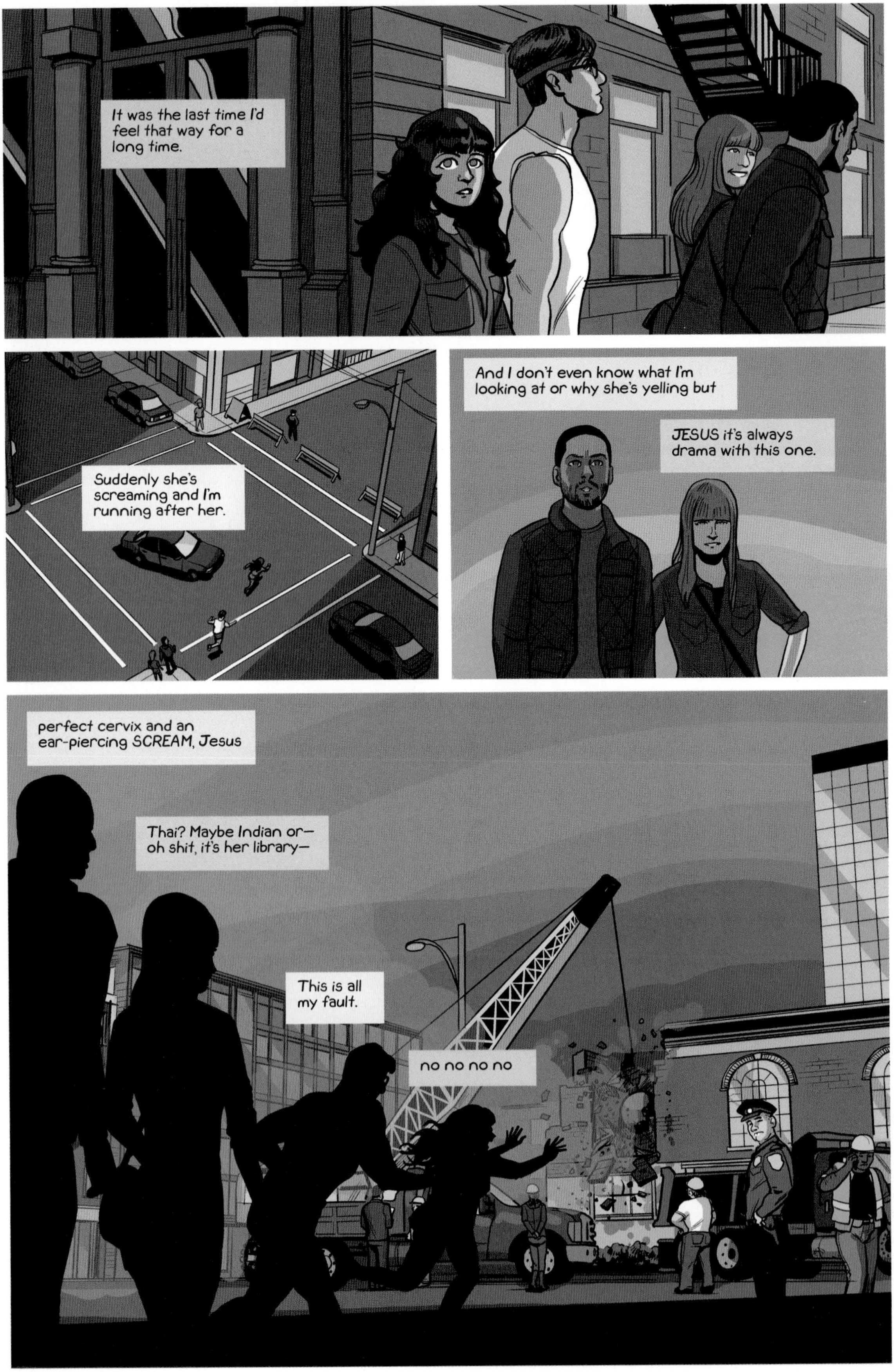
It was the last time I'd feel that way for a long time.
Suddenly she's screaming and I'm running after her.
And I don't even know what I'm looking at or why she's yelling but
JESUS it's always drama with this one.
perfect cervix and an ear-piercing SCREAM, Jesus
Thai? Maybe Indian or—oh shit, it's her library—
This is all my fault.
no no no no

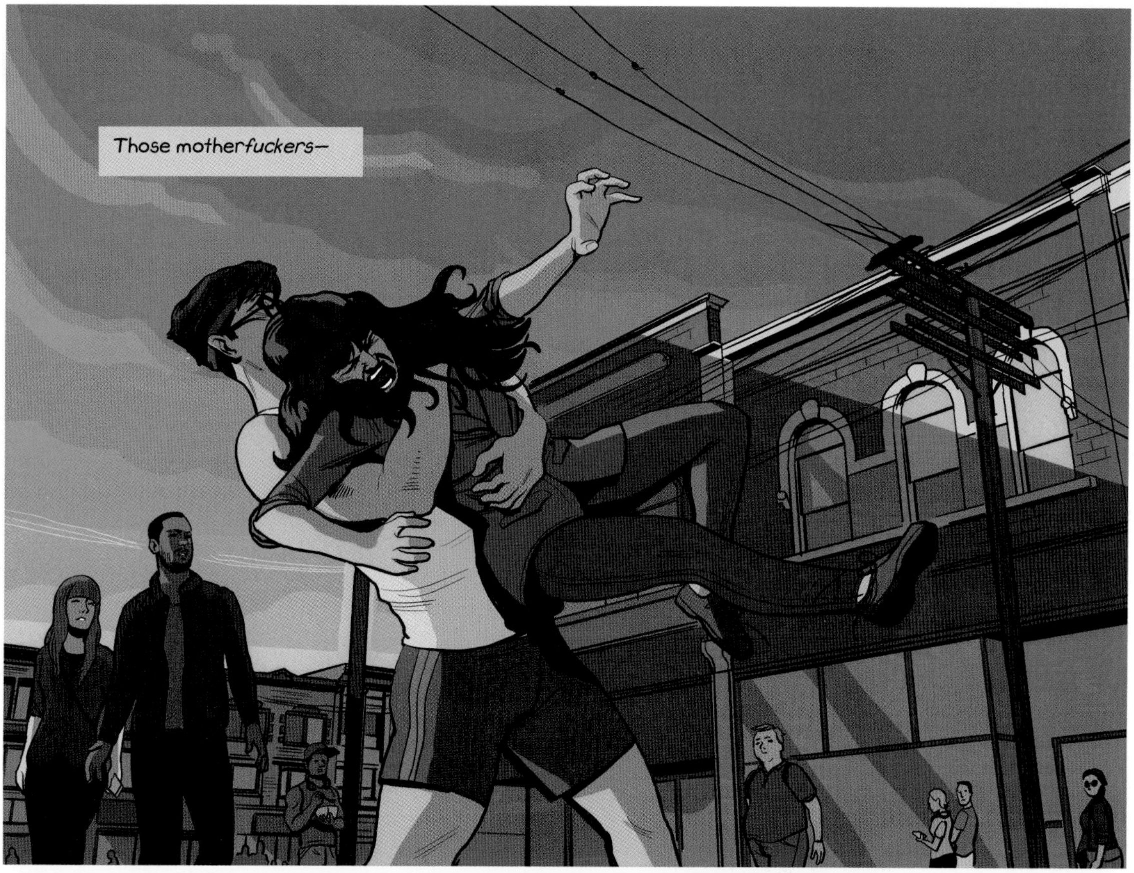
Those motherfuckers—

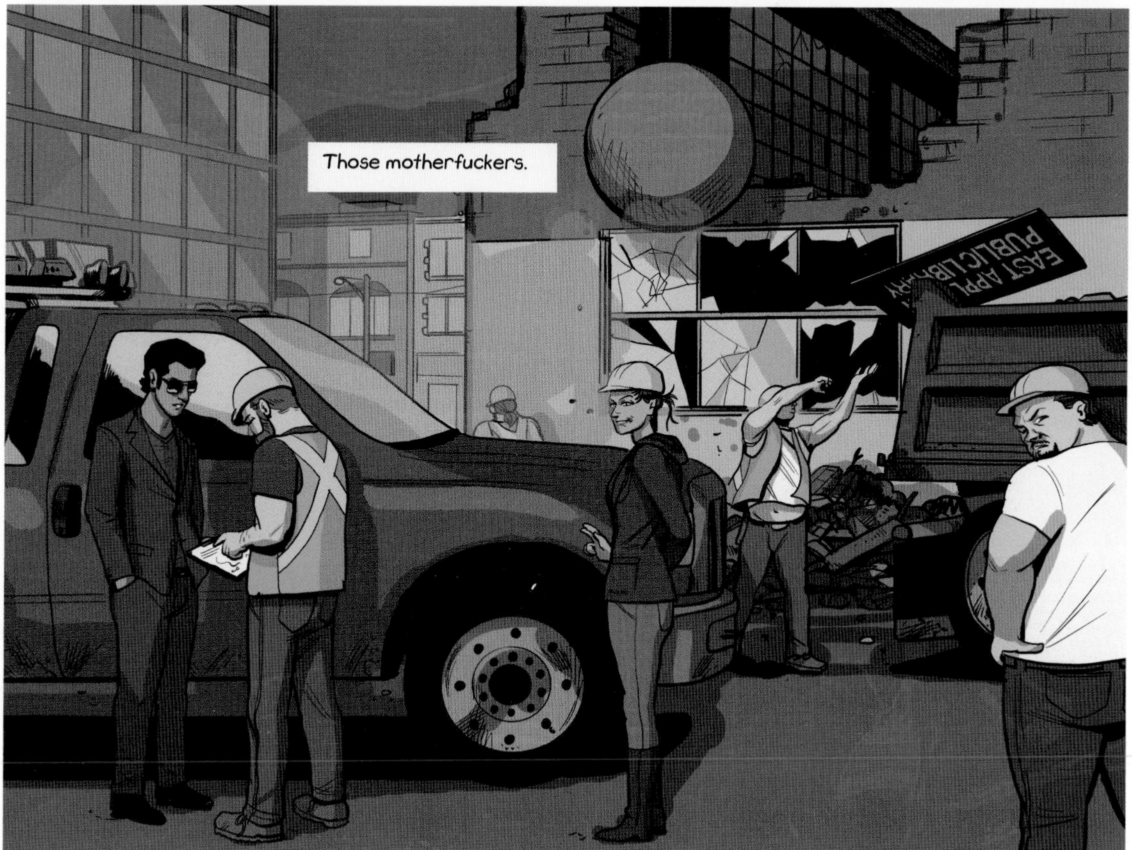
Those motherfuckers.
EAST APPL
PUBLIC LIBRARY

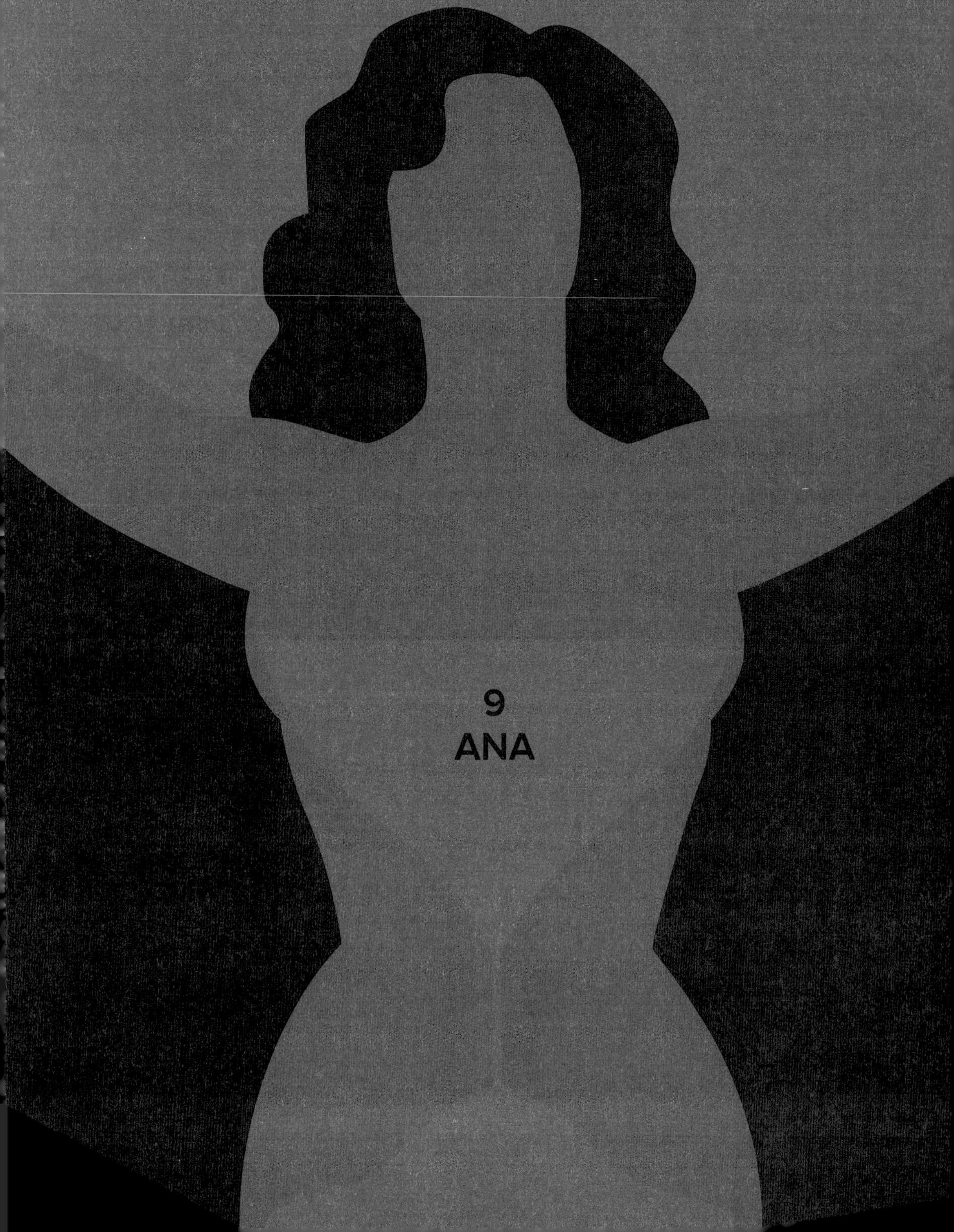

9
ANA

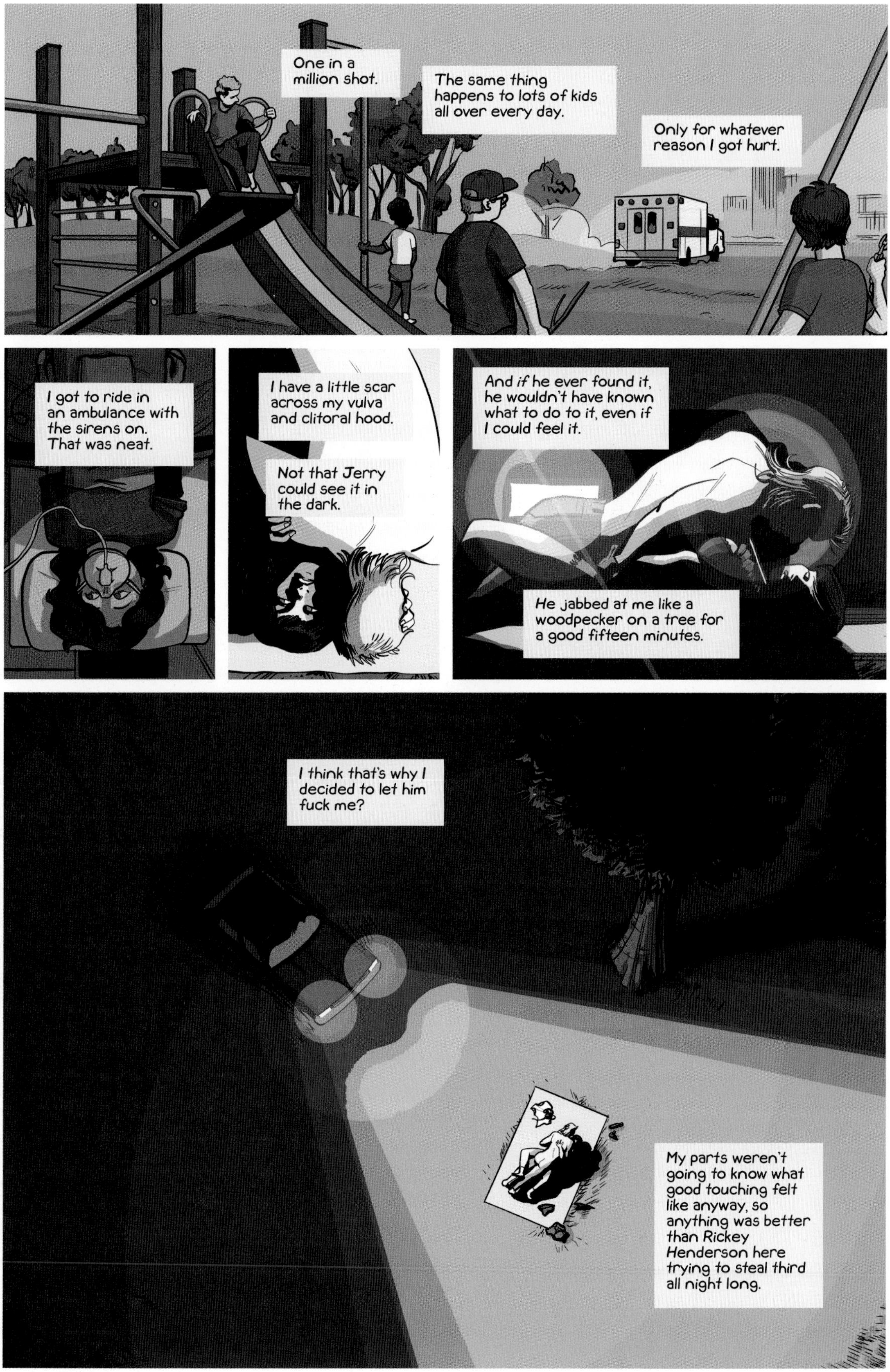

One in a million shot.
The same thing happens to lots of kids all over every day.
Only for whatever reason I got hurt.
I got to ride in an ambulance with the sirens on. That was neat.
I have a little scar across my vulva and clitoral hood.
Not that Jerry could see it in the dark.
And *if* he ever found it, he wouldn't have known what to do to it, even if I could feel it.
He jabbed at me like a woodpecker on a tree for a good fifteen minutes.
I think that's why I decided to let him fuck me?
My parts weren't going to know what good touching felt like anyway, so anything was better than Rickey Henderson here trying to steal third all night long.

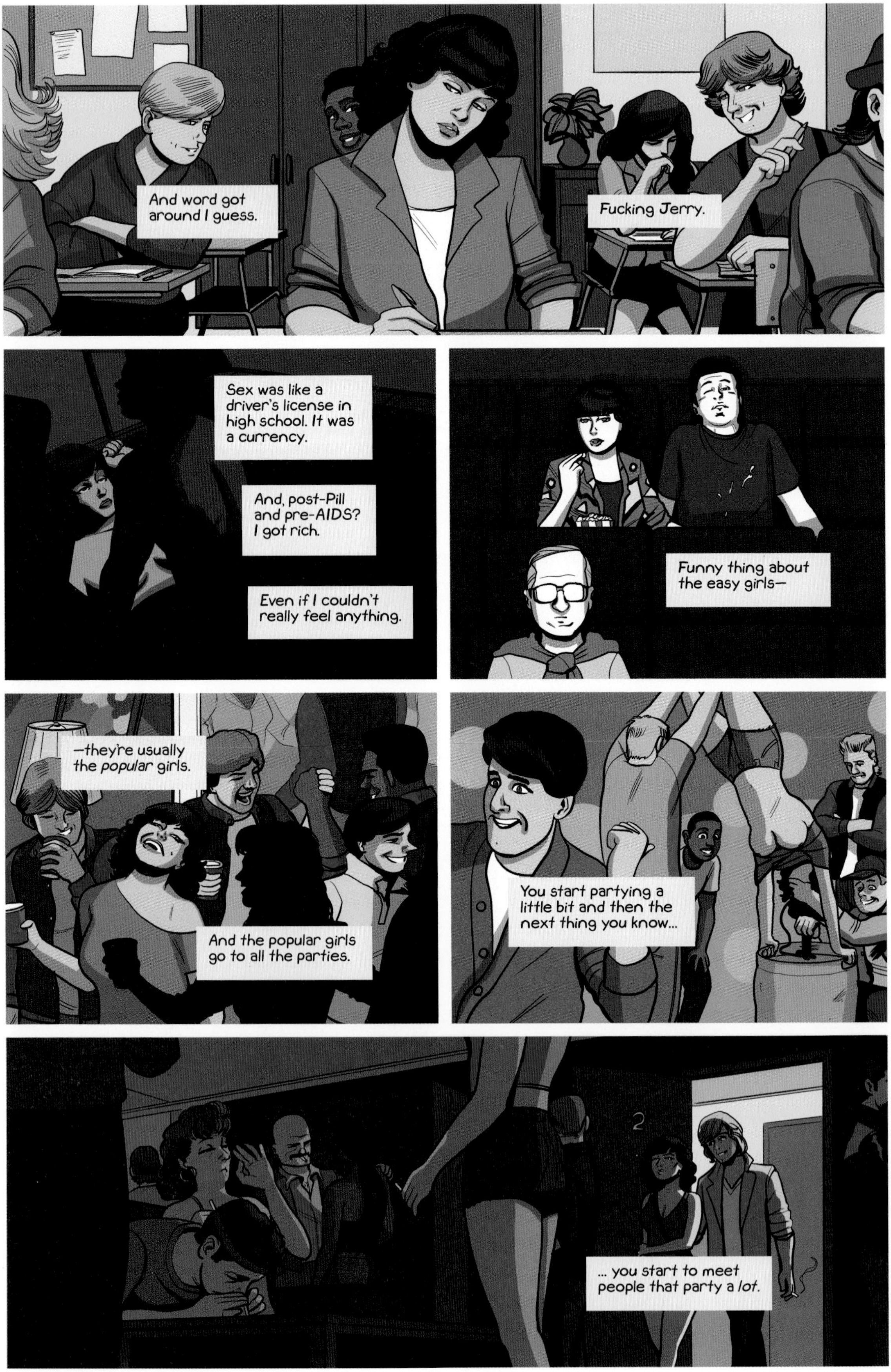
And word got around I guess.
Fucking Jerry.
Sex was like a driver's license in high school. It was a currency.
And, post-Pill and pre-AIDS? I got rich.
Even if I couldn't really feel anything.
Funny thing about the easy girls—
—they're usually the *popular* girls.
And the popular girls go to all the parties.
You start partying a little bit and then the next thing you know...
... you start to meet people that party a *lot*.

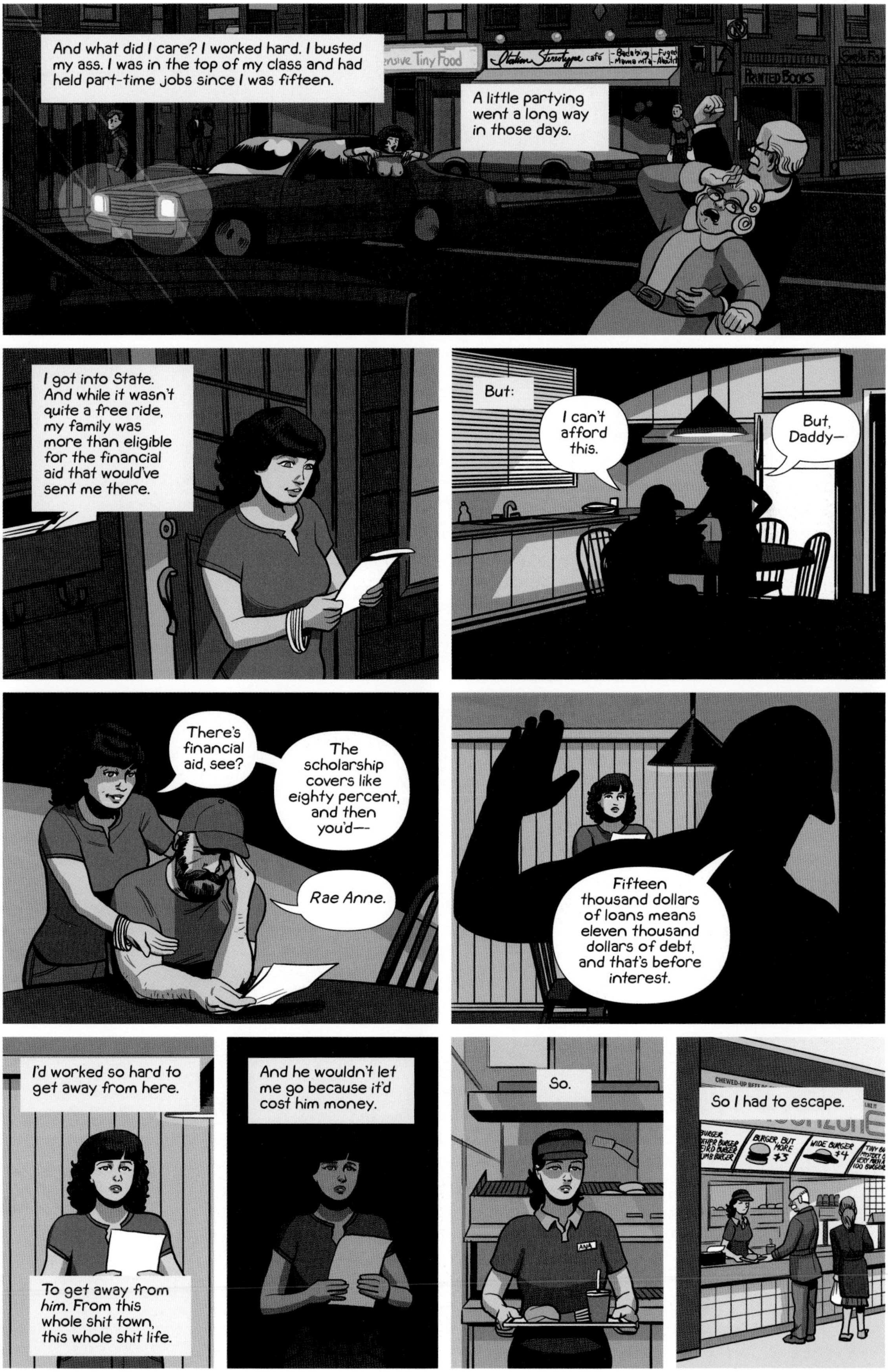

And what did I care? I worked hard. I busted my ass. I was in the top of my class and had held part-time jobs since I was fifteen.
Tiny Food
PRINTED BOOKS
A little partying went a long way in those days.
I got into State. And while it wasn't quite a free ride, my family was more than eligible for the financial aid that would've sent me there.
But:
I can't afford this.
But, Daddy—
There's financial aid, see?
The scholarship covers like eighty percent, and then you'd—
Rae Anne.
Fifteen thousand dollars of loans means eleven thousand dollars of debt, and that's before interest.
I'd worked so hard to get away from here.
To get away from *him*. From this whole shit town, this whole shit life.
And he wouldn't let me go because it'd cost him money.
So.
ANA
So I had to escape.
BURGER, BUT MORE $3
WIDE BURGER $4

Two years at a junior college wouldn't be anything. Hell, even *I* could afford *that*.

I could try again with financial aid for a free ride my last two years.

In the meantime I'd do anything to feel anything but what I was feeling.

So, if you're wondering, "how does a nice girl like me get started" doing what I did, it was just that easy.

I was hanging out with friends.

We went to a titty bar.

The end.

See, sometimes that's what party girls do, and I am nothing if not a good sport.

I was a party girl. I thought I was a smart girl. Then I learned—

—the *really* smart girls watch the fucking money.

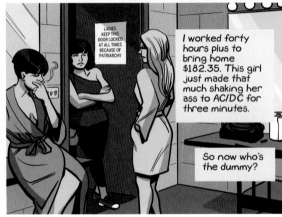

LADIES KEEP THIS DOOR LOCKED AT ALL TIMES BECAUSE OF PATRIARCHY

I worked forty hours plus to bring home $182.35. This girl just made that much shaking her ass to AC/DC for three minutes.

So now who's the dummy?

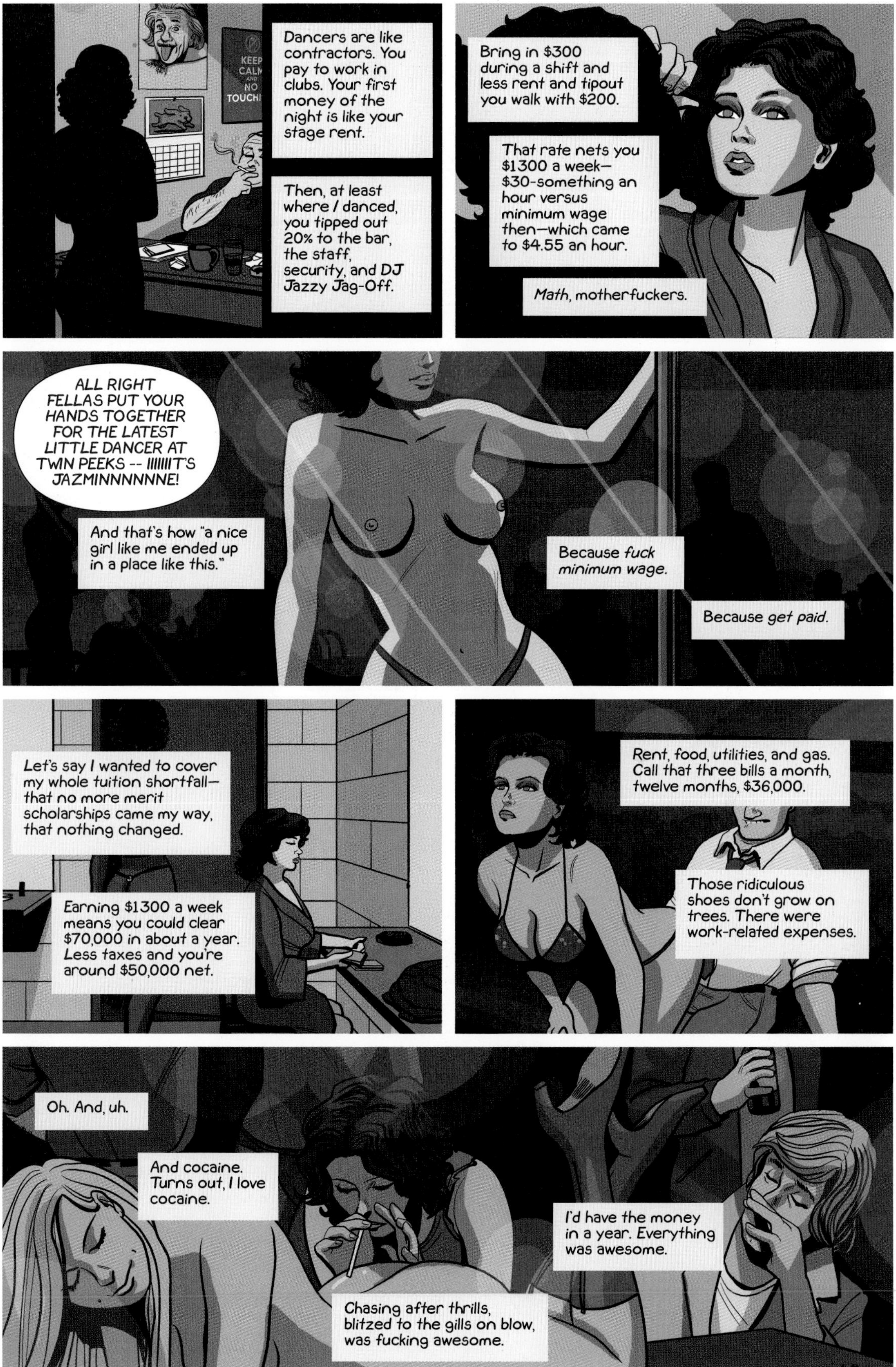
KEEP CALM AND NO TOUCHI
Dancers are like contractors. You pay to work in clubs. Your first money of the night is like your stage rent.
Then, at least where I danced, you tipped out 20% to the bar, the staff, security, and DJ Jazzy Jag-Off.
Bring in $300 during a shift and less rent and tipout you walk with $200.
That rate nets you $1300 a week—$30-something an hour versus minimum wage then—which came to $4.55 an hour.
Math, motherfuckers.
ALL RIGHT FELLAS PUT YOUR HANDS TOGETHER FOR THE LATEST LITTLE DANCER AT TWIN PEEKS -- IIIIIIIT'S JAZMINNNNNNE!
And that's how "a nice girl like me ended up in a place like this."
Because *fuck minimum wage*.
Because *get paid*.
Let's say I wanted to cover my whole tuition shortfall—that no more merit scholarships came my way, that nothing changed.
Earning $1300 a week means you could clear $70,000 in about a year. Less taxes and you're around $50,000 net.
Rent, food, utilities, and gas. Call that three bills a month, twelve months, $36,000.
Those ridiculous shoes don't grow on trees. There were work-related expenses.
Oh. And, uh.
And cocaine. Turns out, I love cocaine.
I'd have the money in a year. Everything was awesome.
Chasing after thrills, blitzed to the gills on blow, was fucking awesome.

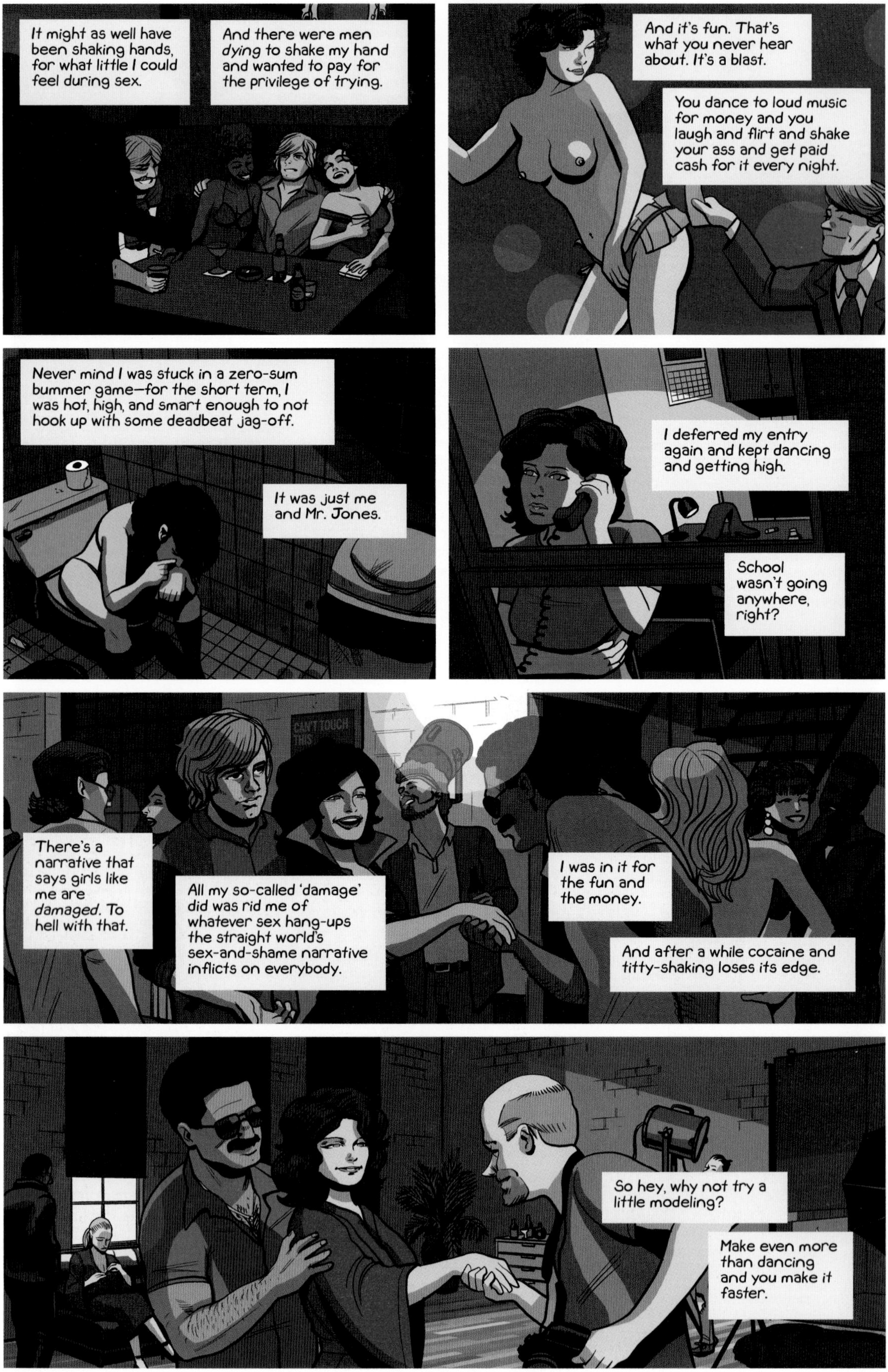
It might as well have been shaking hands, for what little I could feel during sex.
And there were men *dying* to shake my hand and wanted to pay for the privilege of trying.
And it's fun. That's what you never hear about. It's a blast.
You dance to loud music for money and you laugh and flirt and shake your ass and get paid cash for it every night.
Never mind I was stuck in a zero-sum bummer game—for the short term, I was hot, high, and smart enough to not hook up with some deadbeat jag-off.
It was just me and Mr. Jones.
I deferred my entry again and kept dancing and getting high.
School wasn't going anywhere, right?
There's a narrative that says girls like me are *damaged*. To hell with that.
All my so-called 'damage' did was rid me of whatever sex hang-ups the straight world's sex-and-shame narrative inflicts on everybody.
I was in it for the fun and the money.
And after a while cocaine and titty-shaking loses its edge.
So hey, why not try a little modeling?
Make even more than dancing and you make it faster.

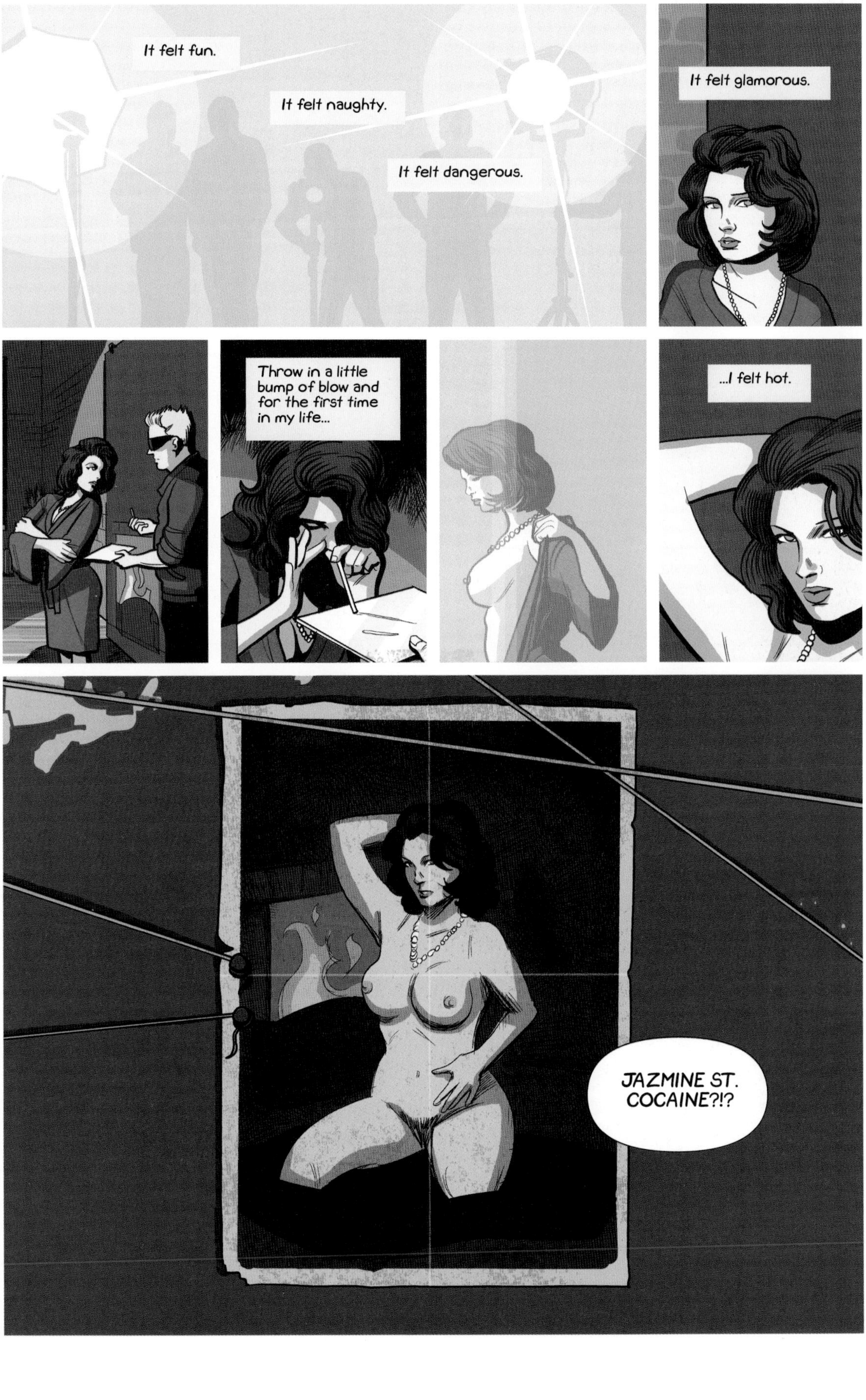
It felt fun.
It felt naughty.
It felt dangerous.
It felt glamorous.
Throw in a little bump of blow and for the first time in my life...
...I felt hot.
JAZMINE ST. COCAINE?!?

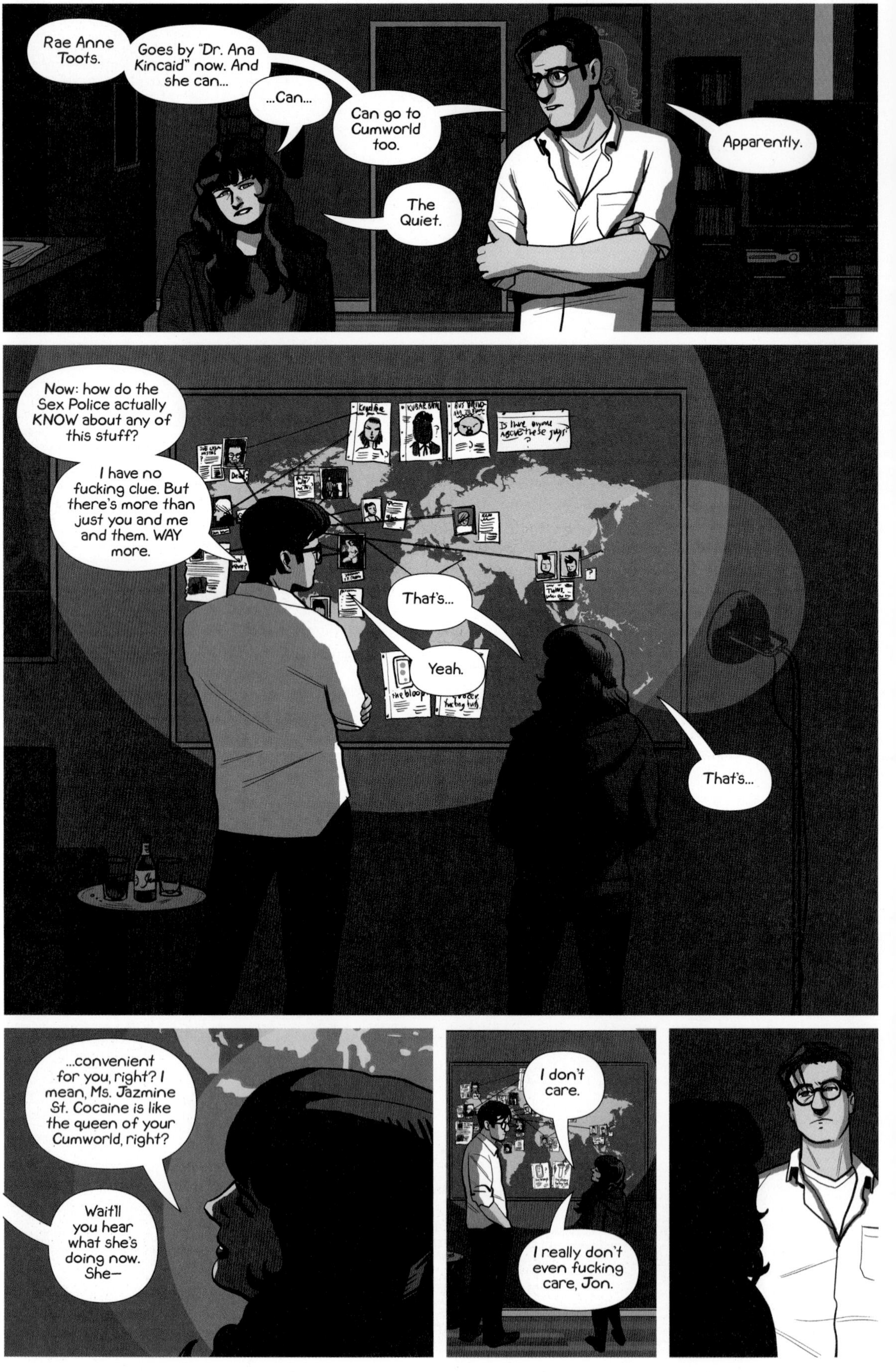

Rae Anne Toots.
Goes by "Dr. Ana Kincaid" now. And she can...
...Can...
Can go to Cumworld too.
The Quiet.
Apparently.
Now: how do the Sex Police actually KNOW about any of this stuff?
I have no fucking clue. But there's more than just you and me and them. WAY more.
That's...
Yeah.
That's...
...convenient for you, right? I mean, Ms. Jazmine St. Cocaine is like the queen of your Cumworld, right?
Wait'll you hear what she's doing now. She—
I don't care.
I really don't even fucking care, Jon.

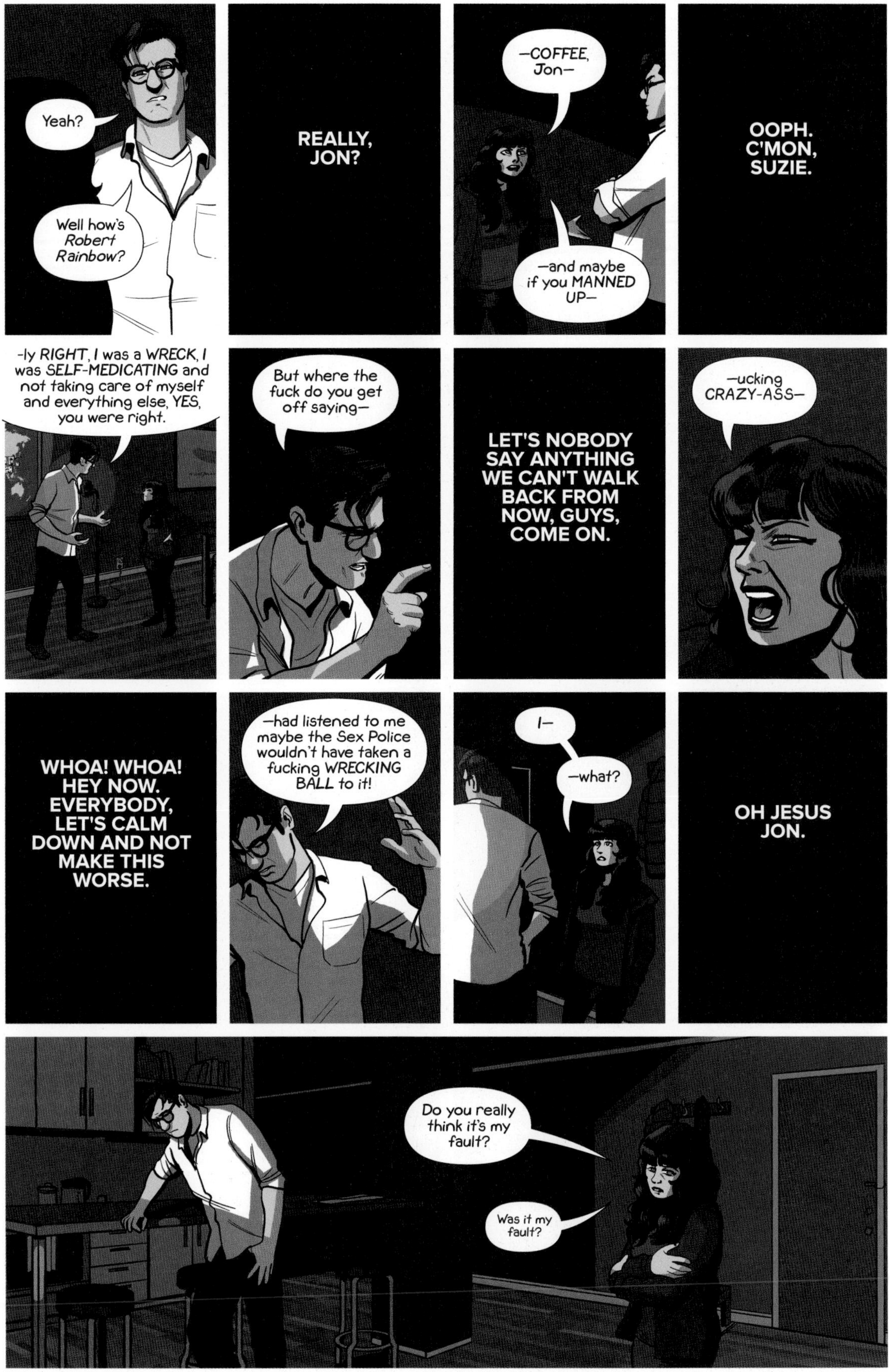
Yeah?
Well how's *Robert Rainbow?*
REALLY, JON?
—COFFEE, Jon—
—and maybe if you MANNED UP—
OOPH. C'MON, SUZIE.
-ly *RIGHT*, I was a *WRECK*, I was *SELF-MEDICATING* and not taking care of myself and everything else, *YES*, you were right.
But where the fuck do you get off saying—
LET'S NOBODY SAY ANYTHING WE CAN'T WALK BACK FROM NOW, GUYS, COME ON.
—ucking CRAZY-ASS—
WHOA! WHOA! HEY NOW. EVERYBODY, LET'S CALM DOWN AND NOT MAKE THIS WORSE.
—had listened to me maybe the Sex Police wouldn't have taken a fucking *WRECKING BALL* to it!
I—
—what?
OH JESUS JON.
Do you really think it's my fault?
Was it my fault?

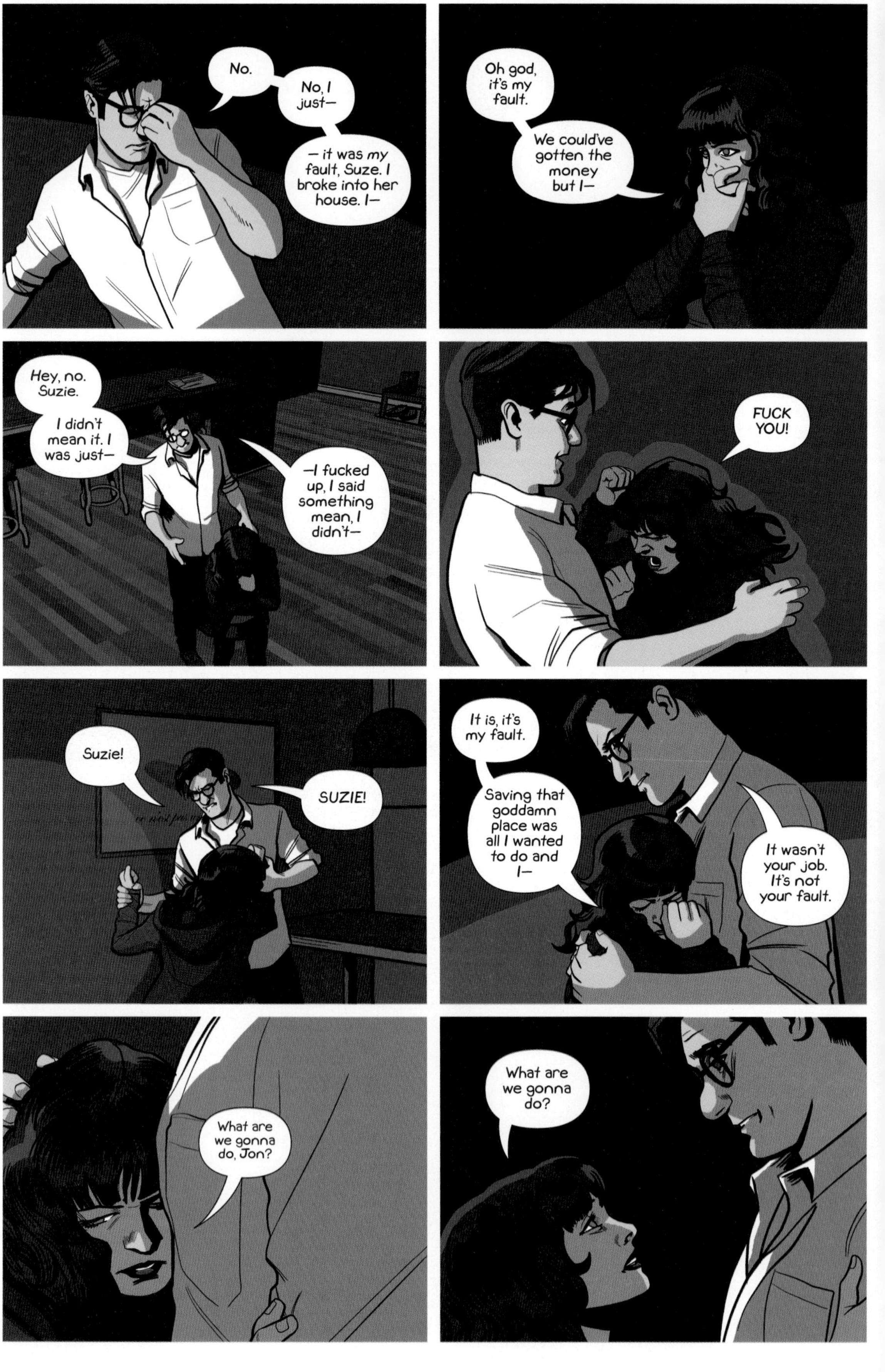
No.
No, I just—
— it was my fault, Suze. I broke into her house. I—
Oh god, it's my fault.
We could've gotten the money but I—
Hey, no. Suzie.
I didn't mean it. I was just—
—I fucked up, I said something mean, I didn't—
FUCK YOU!
Suzie!
SUZIE!
It is, it's my fault.
Saving that goddamn place was all I wanted to do and I—
It wasn't your job. It's not your fault.
What are we gonna do, Jon?
What are we gonna do?

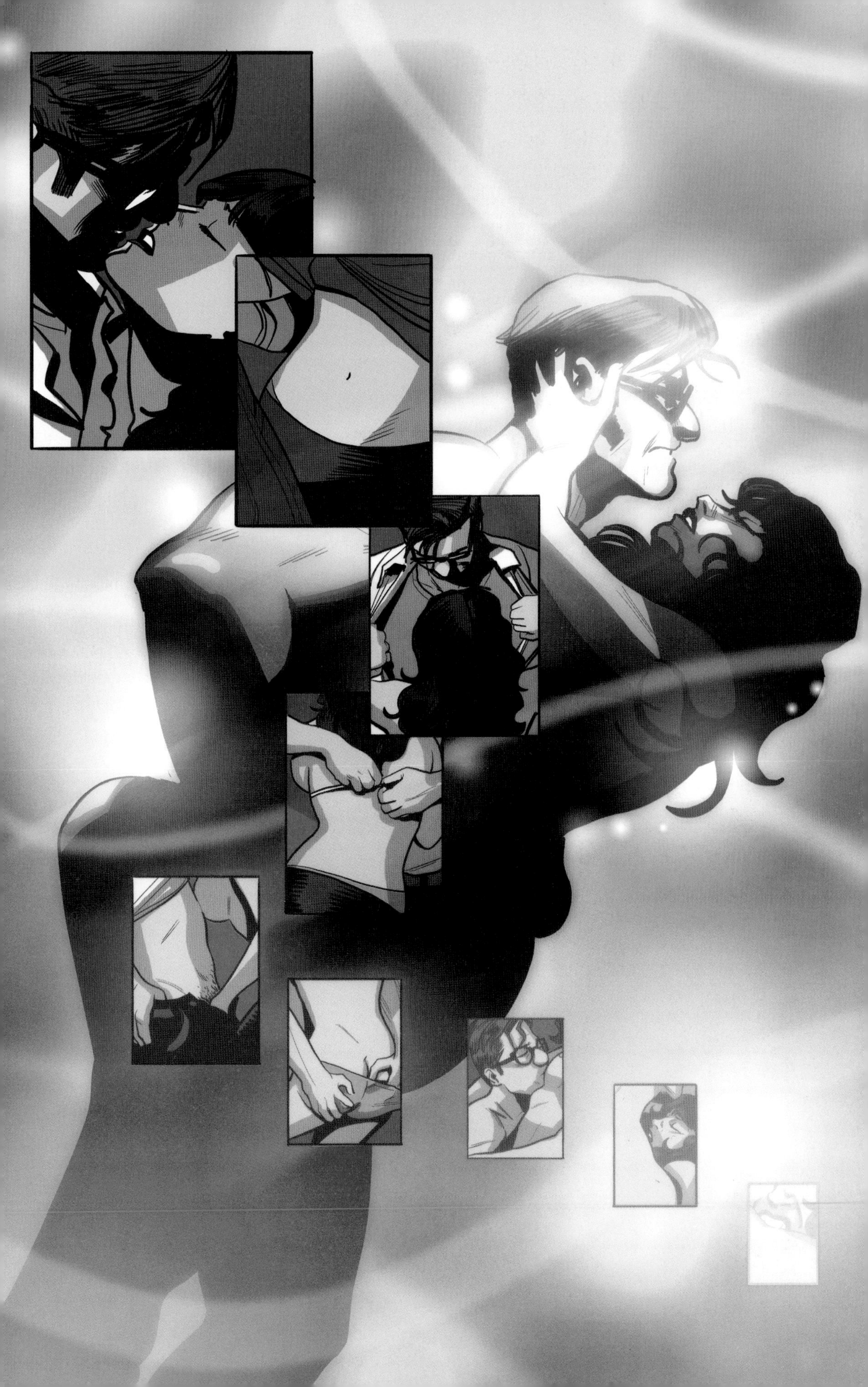

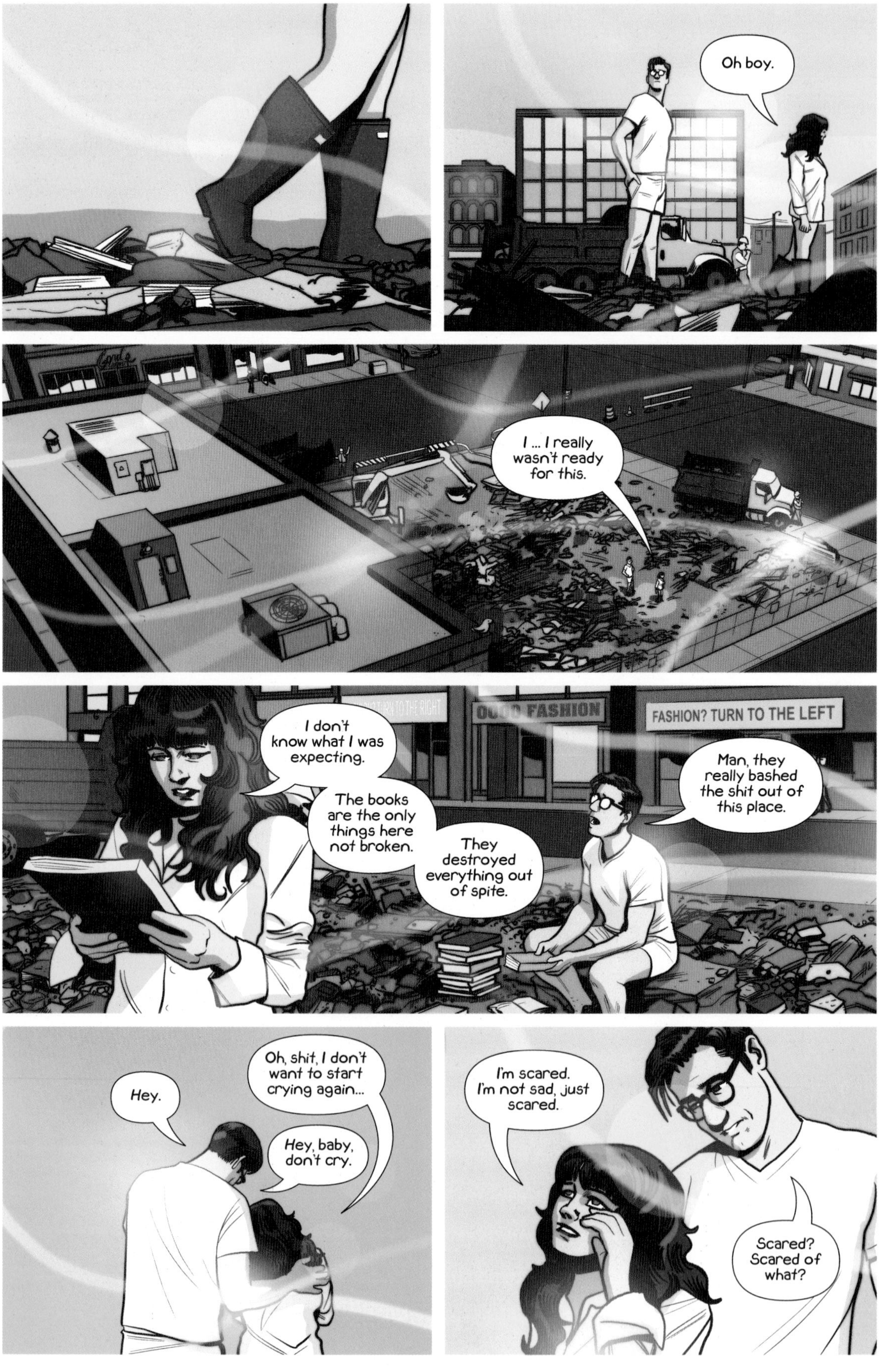
Oh boy.
I ... I really wasn't ready for this.
FASHION? TURN TO THE LEFT
I don't know what I was expecting.
Man, they really bashed the shit out of this place.
The books are the only things here not broken.
They destroyed everything out of spite.
Hey.
Oh, shit, I don't want to start crying again...
Hey, baby, don't cry.
I'm scared. I'm not sad, just scared.
Scared? Scared of what?

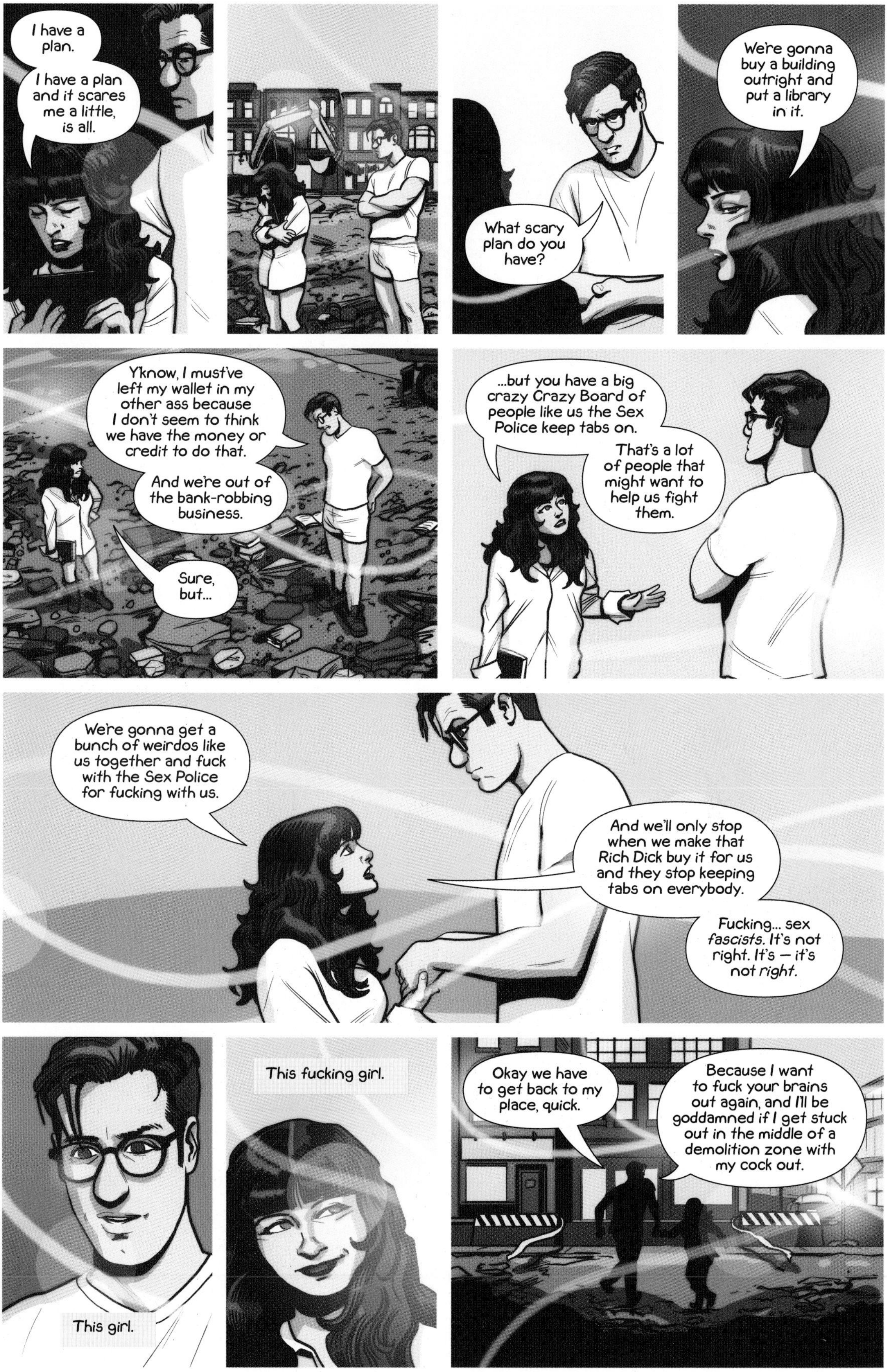
I have a plan.
I have a plan and it scares me a little, is all.
What scary plan do you have?
We're gonna buy a building outright and put a library in it.
Y'know, I must've left my wallet in my other ass because I don't seem to think we have the money or credit to do that.
And we're out of the bank-robbing business.
Sure, but...
...but you have a big crazy Crazy Board of people like us the Sex Police keep tabs on.
That's a lot of people that might want to help us fight them.
We're gonna get a bunch of weirdos like us together and fuck with the Sex Police for fucking with us.
And we'll only stop when we make that Rich Dick buy it for us and they stop keeping tabs on everybody.
Fucking... sex *fascists*. It's not right. It's — it's not *right*.
This girl.
This fucking girl.
Okay we have to get back to my place, quick.
Because I want to fuck your brains out again, and I'll be goddamned if I get stuck out in the middle of a demolition zone with my cock out.

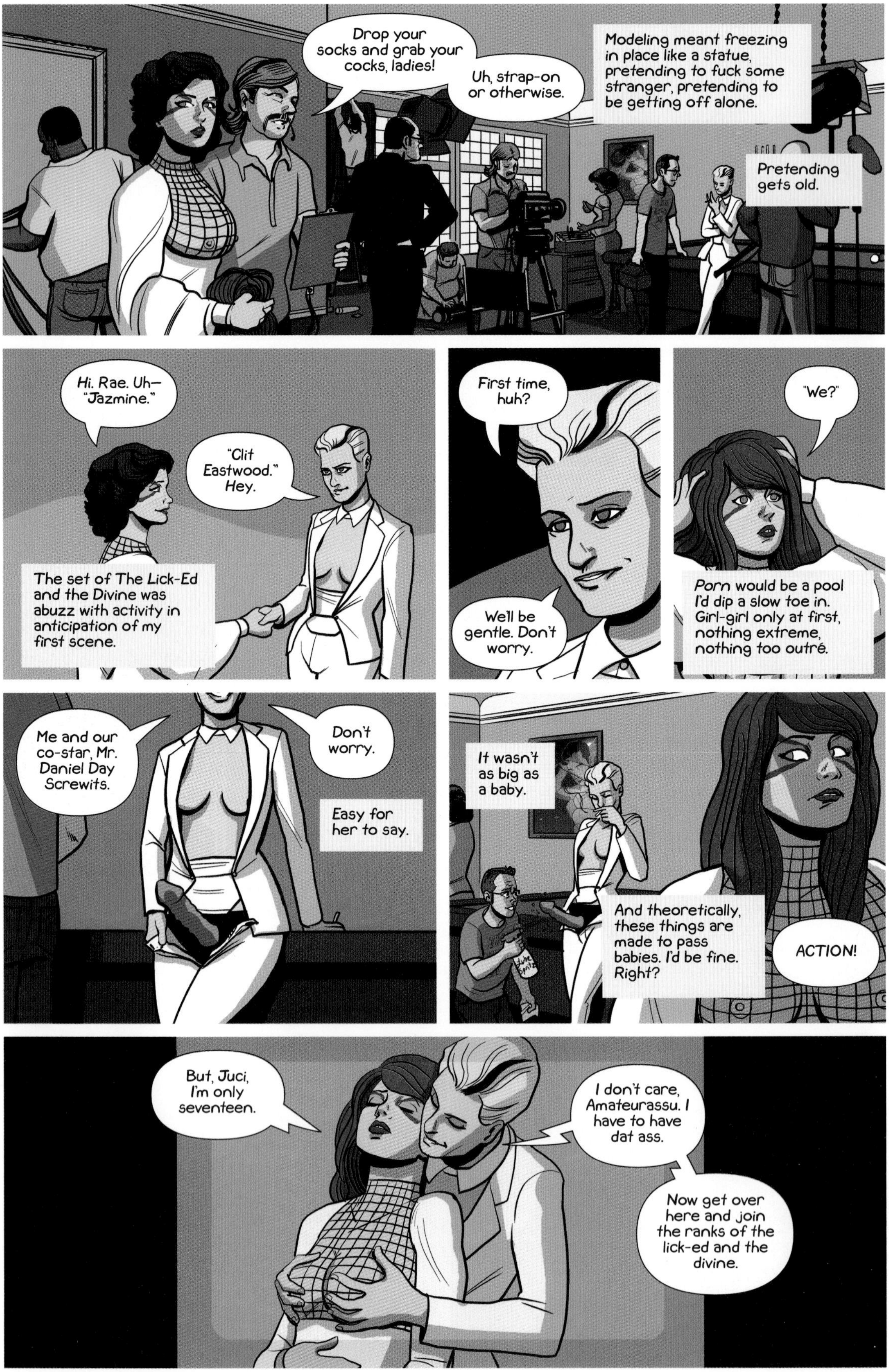
Drop your socks and grab your cocks, ladies!
Uh, strap-on or otherwise.
Modeling meant freezing in place like a statue, pretending to fuck some stranger, pretending to be getting off alone.
Pretending gets old.
Hi. Rae. Uh— "Jazmine."
"Clit Eastwood." Hey.
The set of The Lick-Ed and the Divine was abuzz with activity in anticipation of my first scene.
First time, huh?
We'll be gentle. Don't worry.
"We?"
Porn would be a pool I'd dip a slow toe in. Girl-girl only at first, nothing extreme, nothing too outré.
Me and our co-star, Mr. Daniel Day Screwits.
Don't worry.
Easy for her to say.
It wasn't as big as a baby.
And theoretically, these things are made to pass babies. I'd be fine. Right?
ACTION!
But, Juci, I'm only seventeen.
I don't care, Amateurassu. I have to have dat ass.
Now get over here and join the ranks of the lick-ed and the divine.

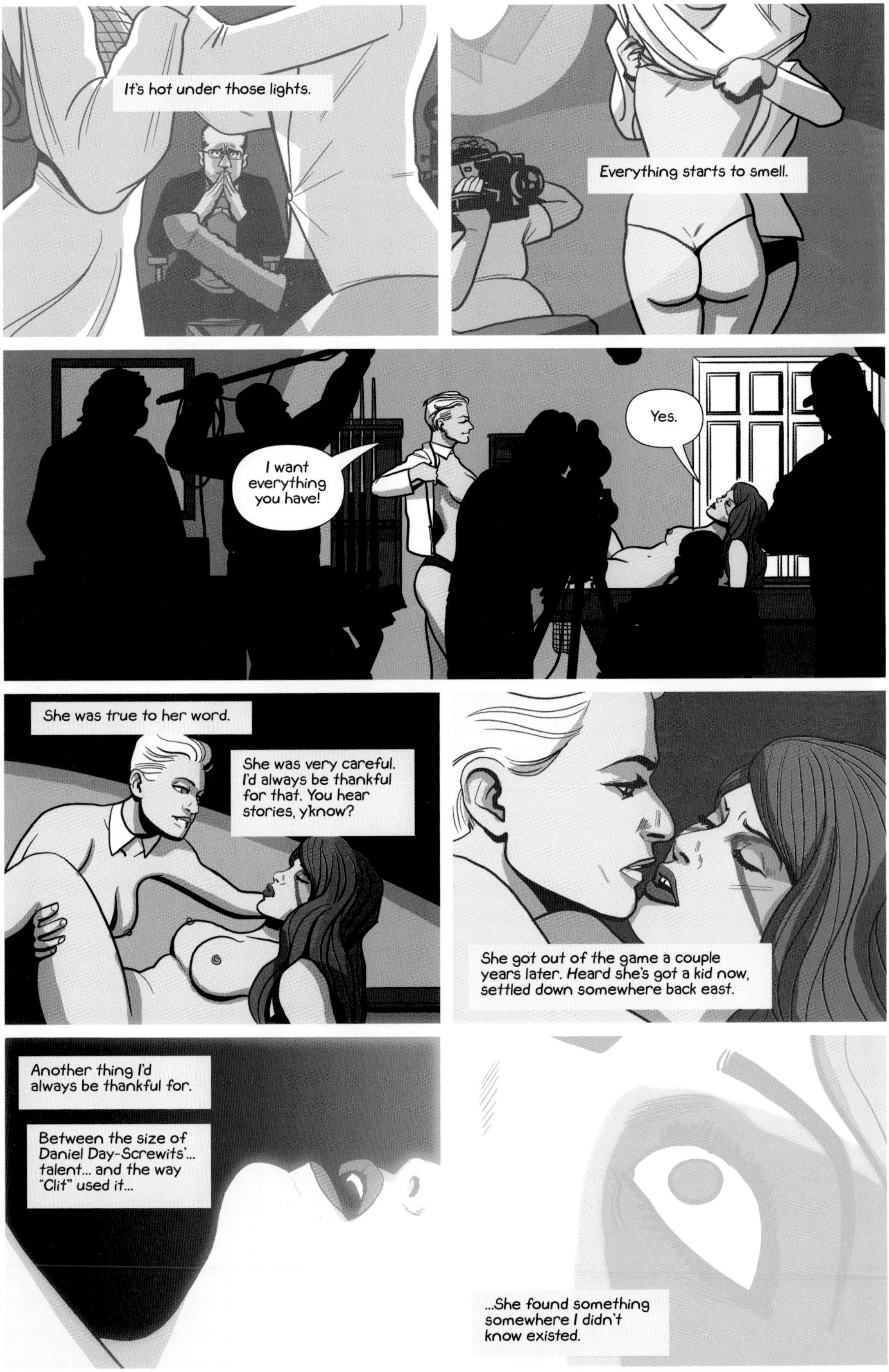
It's hot under those lights.
Everything starts to smell.
I want everything you have!
Yes.
She was true to her word.
She was very careful. I'd always be thankful for that. You hear stories, yknow?
She got out of the game a couple years later. Heard she's got a kid now, settled down somewhere back east.
Another thing I'd always be thankful for.
Between the size of Daniel Day-Screwits'... talent... and the way "Clit" used it...
...She found something somewhere I didn't know existed.

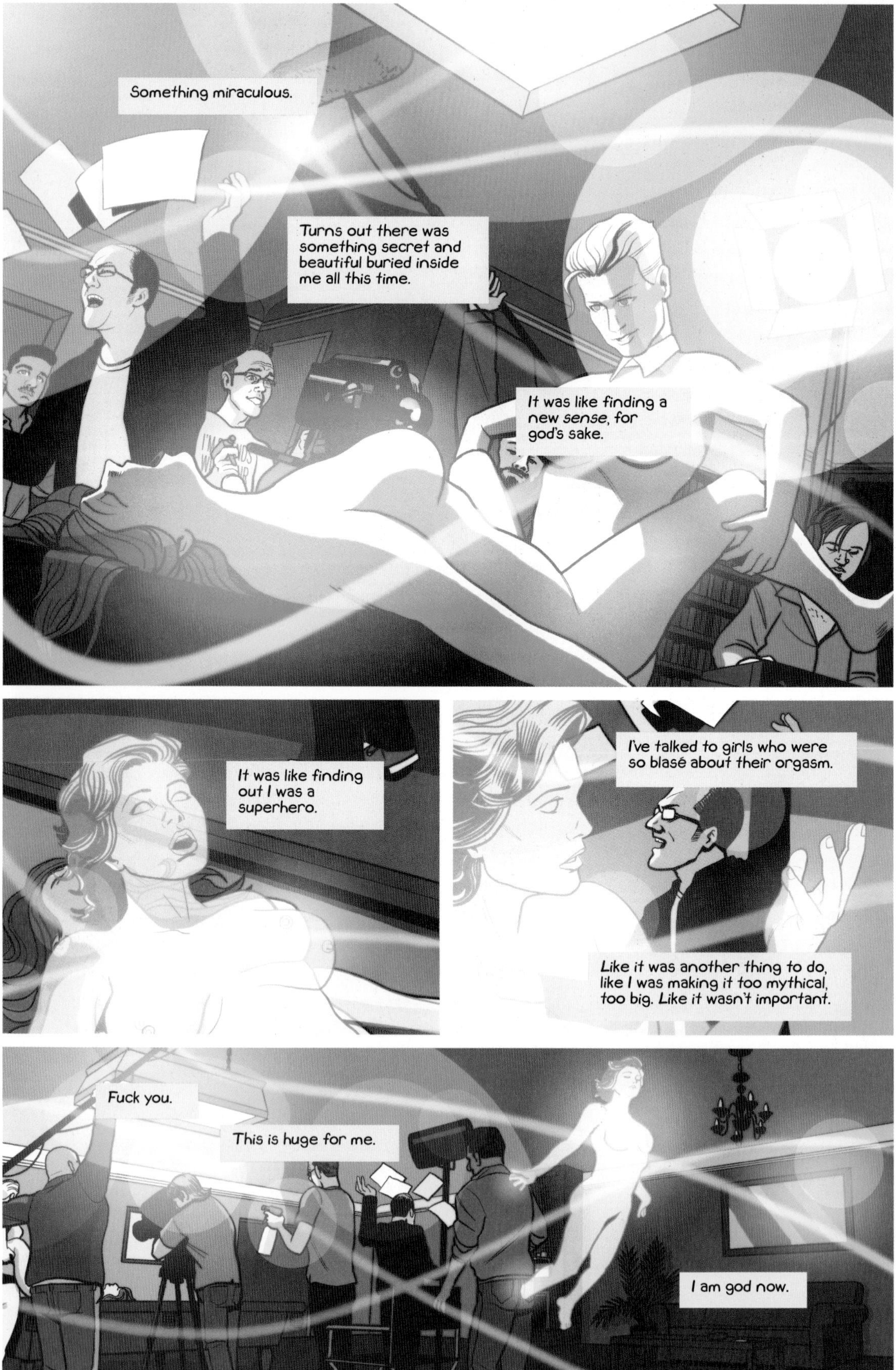
Something miraculous.
Turns out there was something secret and beautiful buried inside me all this time.
It was like finding a new *sense*, for god's sake.
It was like finding out I was a superhero.
I've talked to girls who were so blasé about their orgasm.
Like it was another thing to do, like I was making it too mythical, too big. Like it wasn't important.
Fuck you.
This is huge for me.
I am god now.

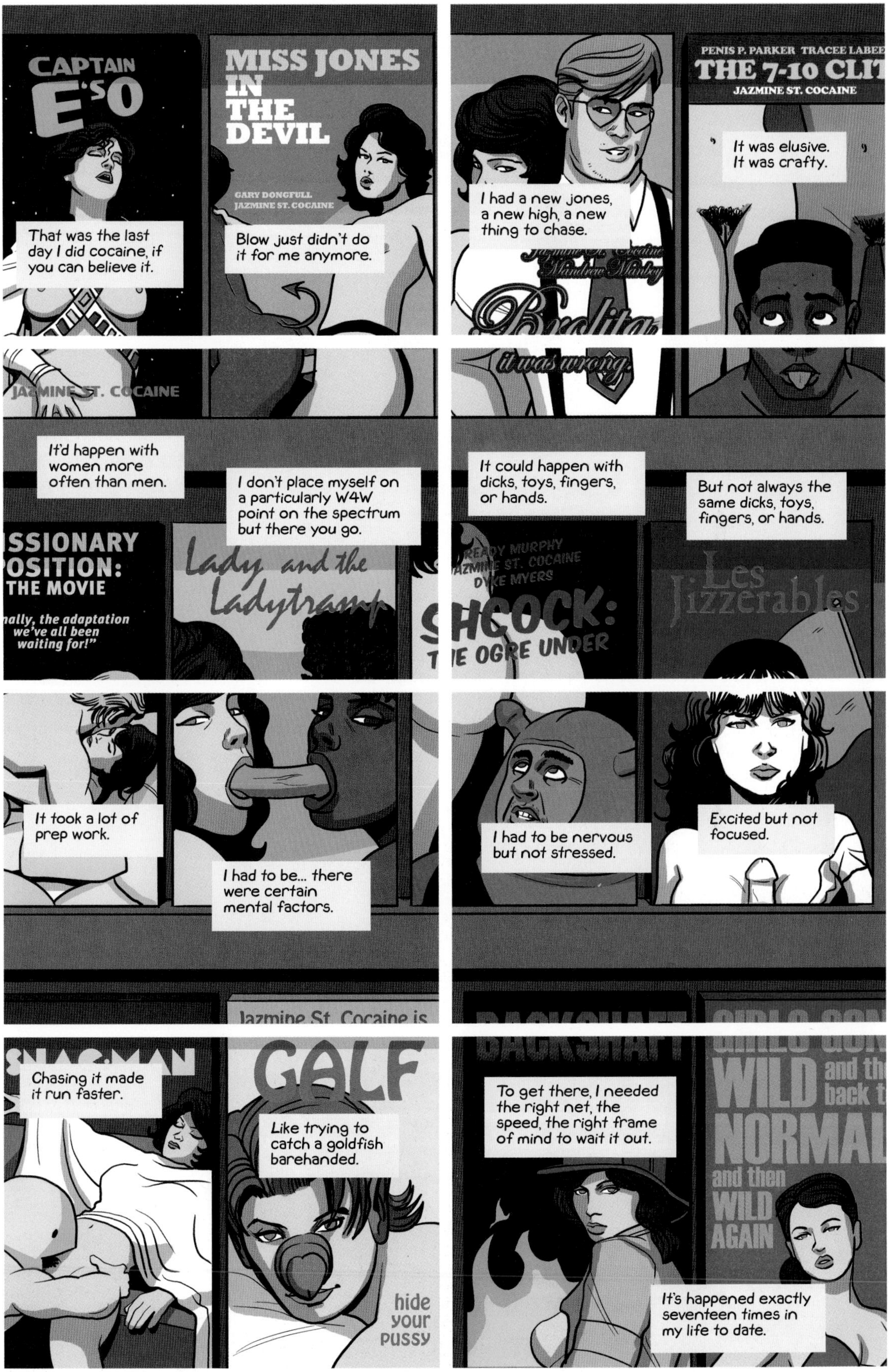
CAPTAIN E'SO
MISS JONES IN THE DEVIL
GARY DONGFULL
JAZMINE ST. COCAINE
That was the last day I did cocaine, if you can believe it.
Blow just didn't do it for me anymore.
JAZMINE ST. COCAINE
PENIS P. PARKER TRACEE LABEE
THE 7-10 CLIT
JAZMINE ST. COCAINE
I had a new jones, a new high, a new thing to chase.
It was elusive. It was crafty.
it was wrong.
It'd happen with women more often than men.
I don't place myself on a particularly W4W point on the spectrum but there you go.
SSIONARY POSITION: THE MOVIE
nally, the adaptation we've all been waiting for!"
Lady and the Ladytramp
It could happen with dicks, toys, fingers, or hands.
But not always the same dicks, toys, fingers, or hands.
DYKE MYERS
THE OGRE UNDER
Les Jizzerables
It took a lot of prep work.
I had to be... there were certain mental factors.
I had to be nervous but not stressed.
Excited but not focused.
Jazmine St. Cocaine is
GALF
Chasing it made it run faster.
Like trying to catch a goldfish barehanded.
hide your pussy
WILD and th back t NORMAL and then WILD AGAIN
To get there, I needed the right net, the speed, the right frame of mind to wait it out.
It's happened exactly seventeen times in my life to date.

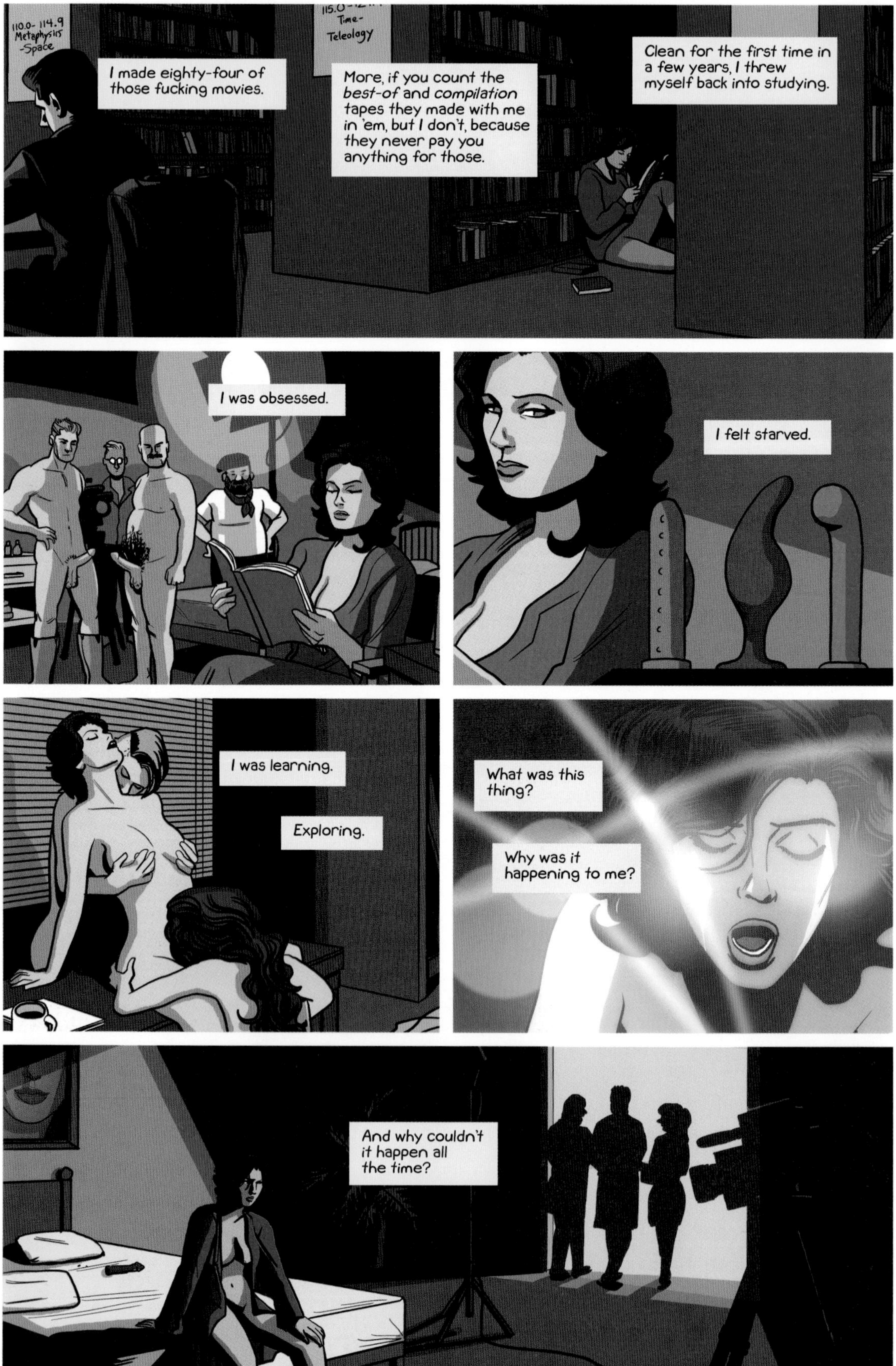
110.0- 114.9 Metaphysics -Space
I made eighty-four of those fucking movies.
Time- Teleology
More, if you count the *best-of* and *compilation* tapes they made with me in 'em, but I don't, because they never pay you anything for those.
Clean for the first time in a few years, I threw myself back into studying.
I was obsessed.
I felt starved.
I was learning.
Exploring.
What was this thing?
Why was it happening to me?
And why couldn't it happen all the time?

I went to seven colleges in all.

PRINCETOWN UNIVERSITY
EST. 1892
"Together, we are a school"

Someone would *recognize* me.

I didn't care, but sooner or later it became a distraction and I'd transfer.

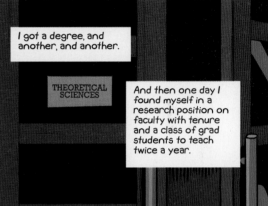

I got a degree, and another, and another.

THEORETICAL SCIENCES

And then one day I found myself in a research position on faculty with tenure and a class of grad students to teach twice a year.

As I'm not in the literature department, I can't say if it's irony or parody that I teach *horology*.

See, even before I froze it, I was obsessed with the study of *time*.

Now it's my job to pick it apart.

Sex and time. Time and sex.

Dr. Ana Kincaid
HOROLOGY

NO more office hours this semester. FUCK. OFF.

My magnetic north and so–

Um, Dr. Kincaid?

Goddammit...

Can't you read? If you didn't already schedule office hours, then I can't–

–you're not my students. Who are you?

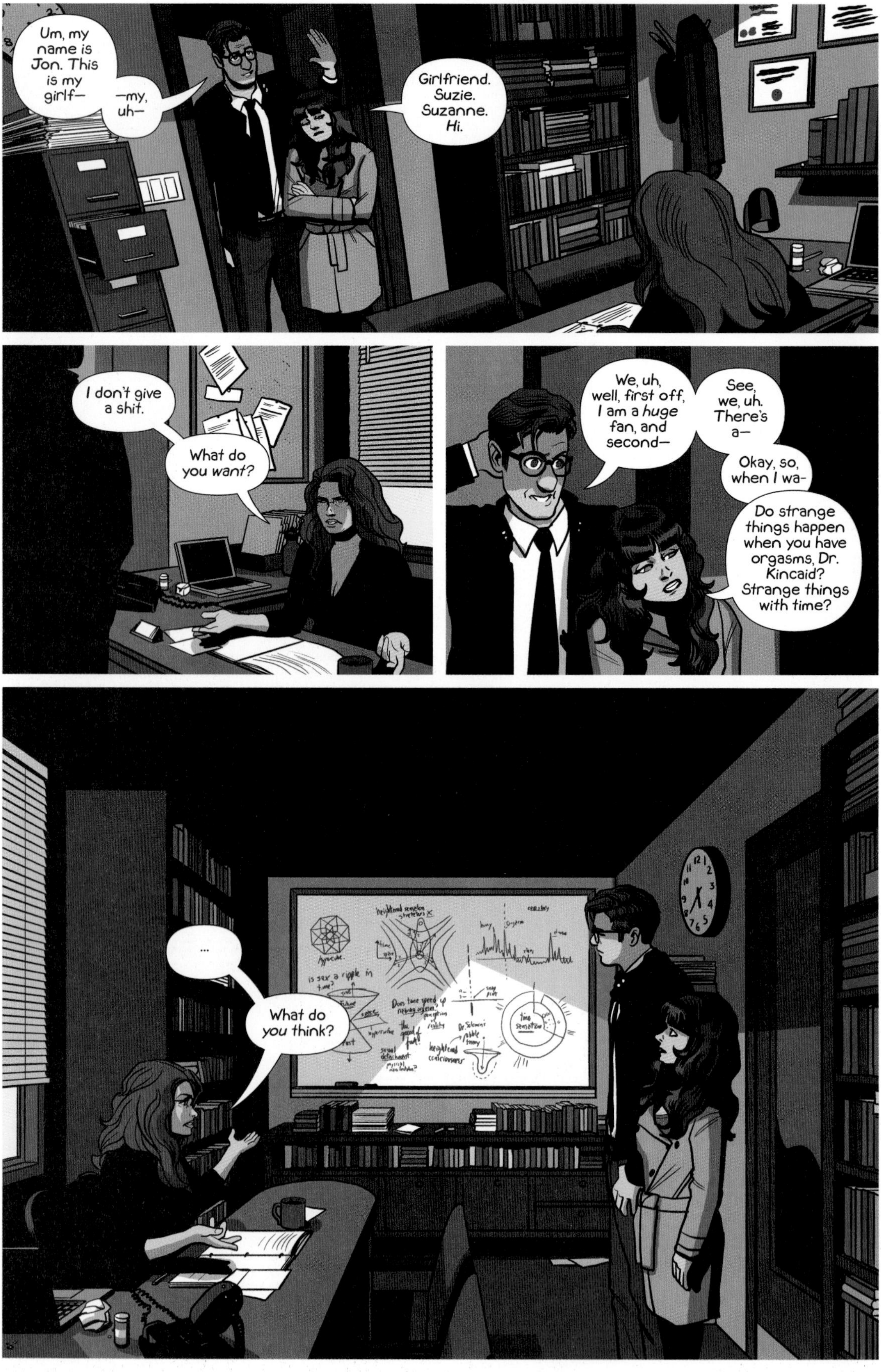

Um, my name is Jon. This is my girlf—
—my, uh—
Girlfriend. Suzie. Suzanne. Hi.
I don't give a shit.
What do you want?
We, uh, well, first off, I am a *huge* fan, and second—
See, we, uh. There's a—
Okay, so, when I wa-
Do strange things happen when you have orgasms, Dr. Kincaid? Strange things with time?
...
What do you think?

10
ALONE TOGETHER

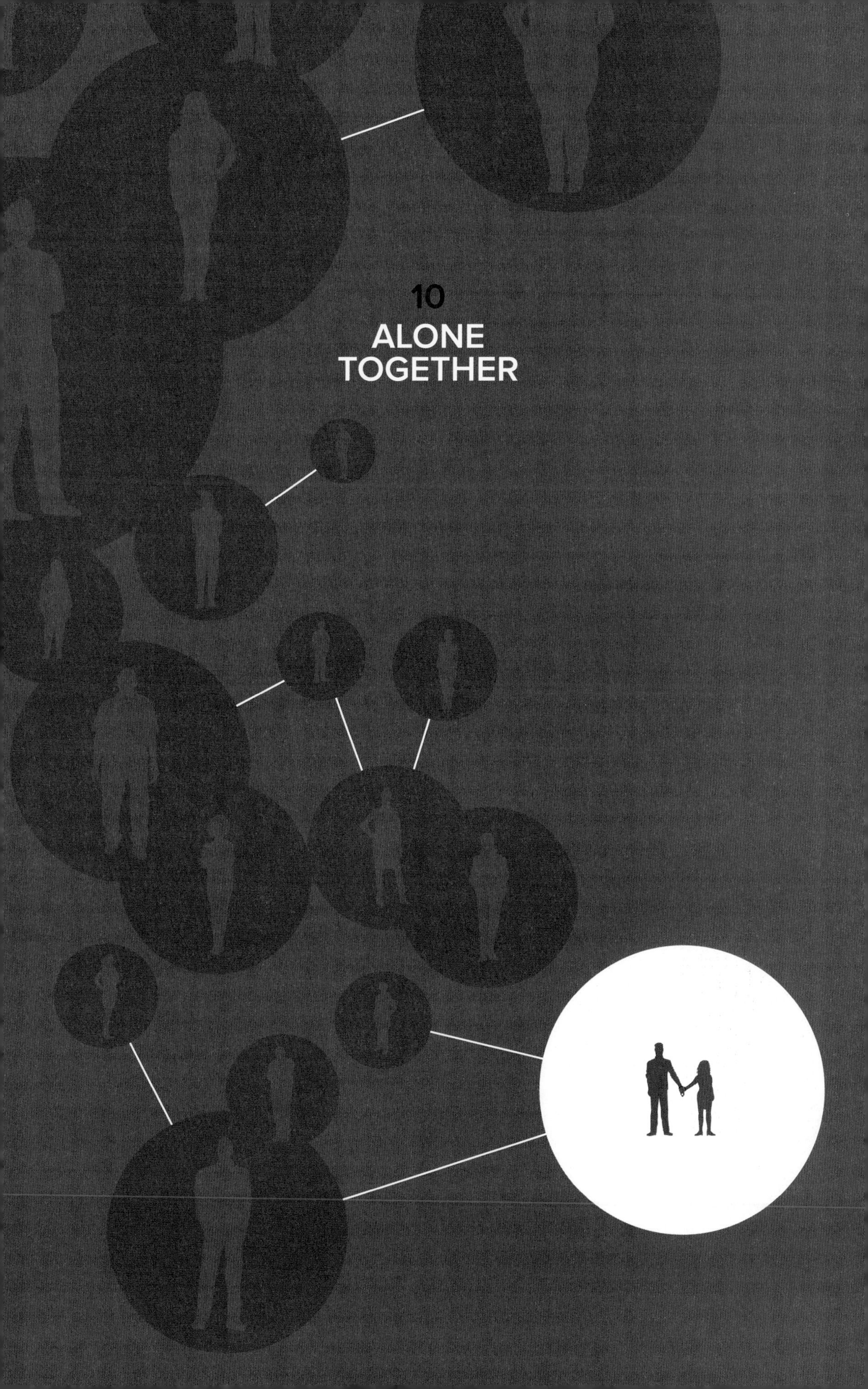

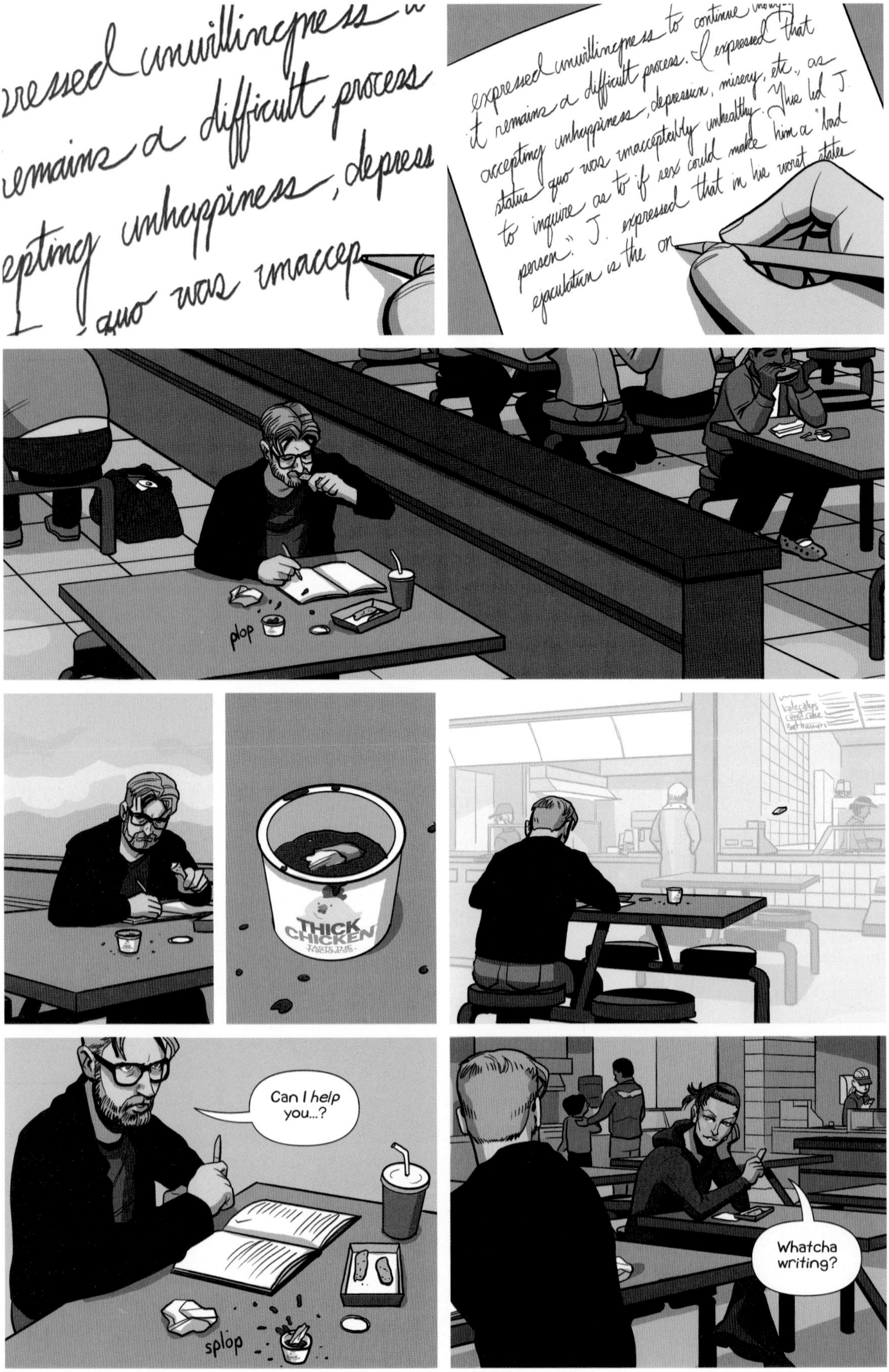
ressed unwillingness
remains a difficult process
epting unhappiness, depress
quo was unaccep
expressed unwillingness to continue
it remains a difficult process. I expressed that
accepting unhappiness, depression, misery, etc., as
status quo was unacceptably unhealthy. This led J.
to inquire as to if sex could make him a "bad
person." J. expressed that in his worst states
ejaculation is the on
plop
THICK CHICKEN
TASTE THE THICKNESS
Can I help you...?
splop
Whatcha writing?

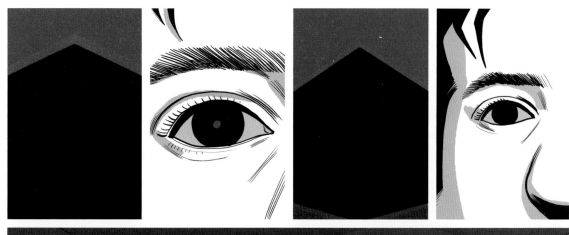

"It's okay."

"...Not being okay."

Yknow, Jon?

It's okay.

...Yeah.

Yeah.

What's *not* okay is to be okay with that.

Suffering, sickness. Sure. Acceptance. No.

It's like a parasite, Jon.

After a while, it'll kill you.

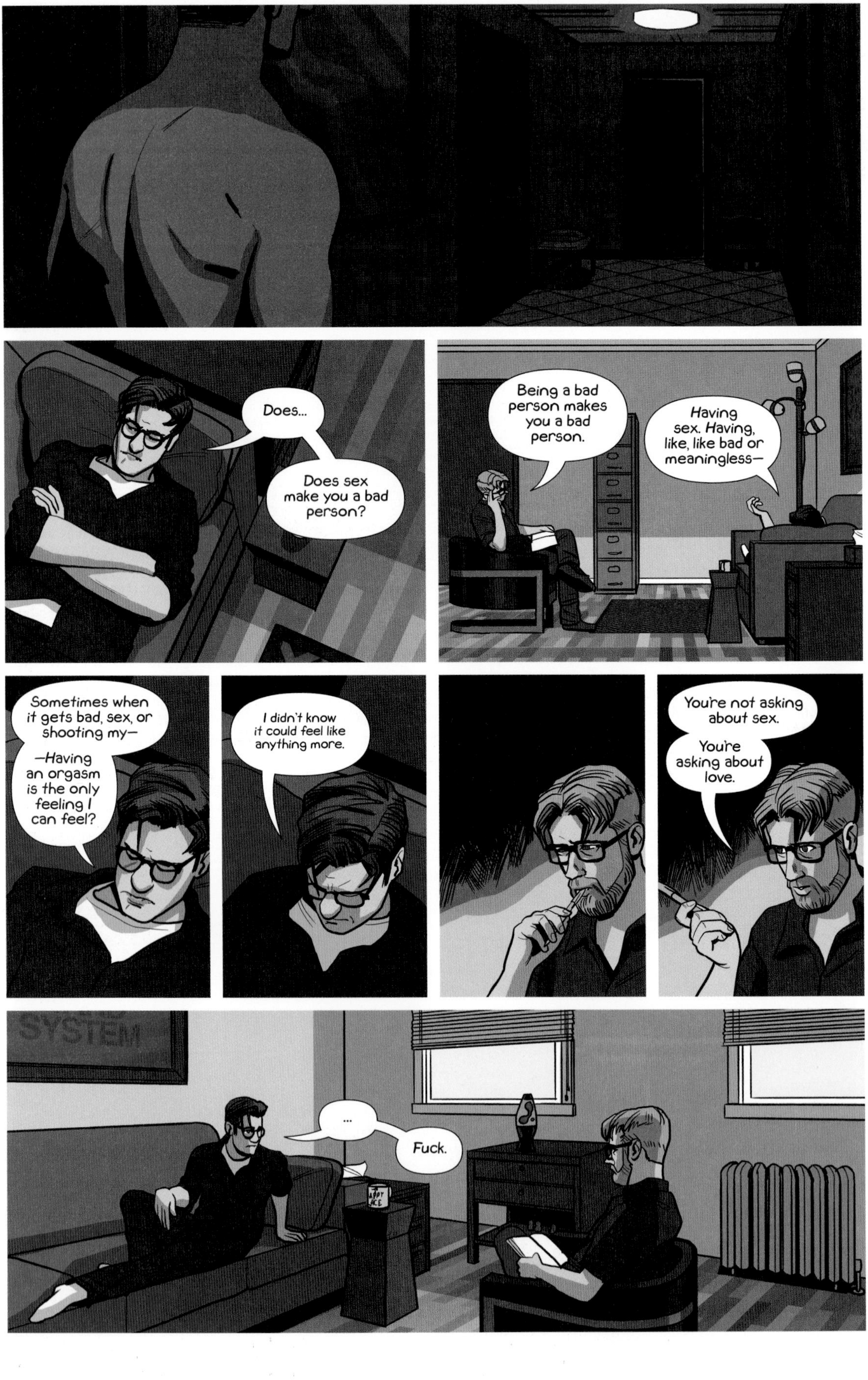

Does...
Does sex make you a bad person?
Being a bad person makes you a bad person.
Having sex. Having, like, like bad or meaningless—
Sometimes when it gets bad, sex, or shooting my—
—Having an orgasm is the only feeling I can feel?
I didn't know it could feel like anything more.
You're not asking about sex.
You're asking about love.
...
Fuck.

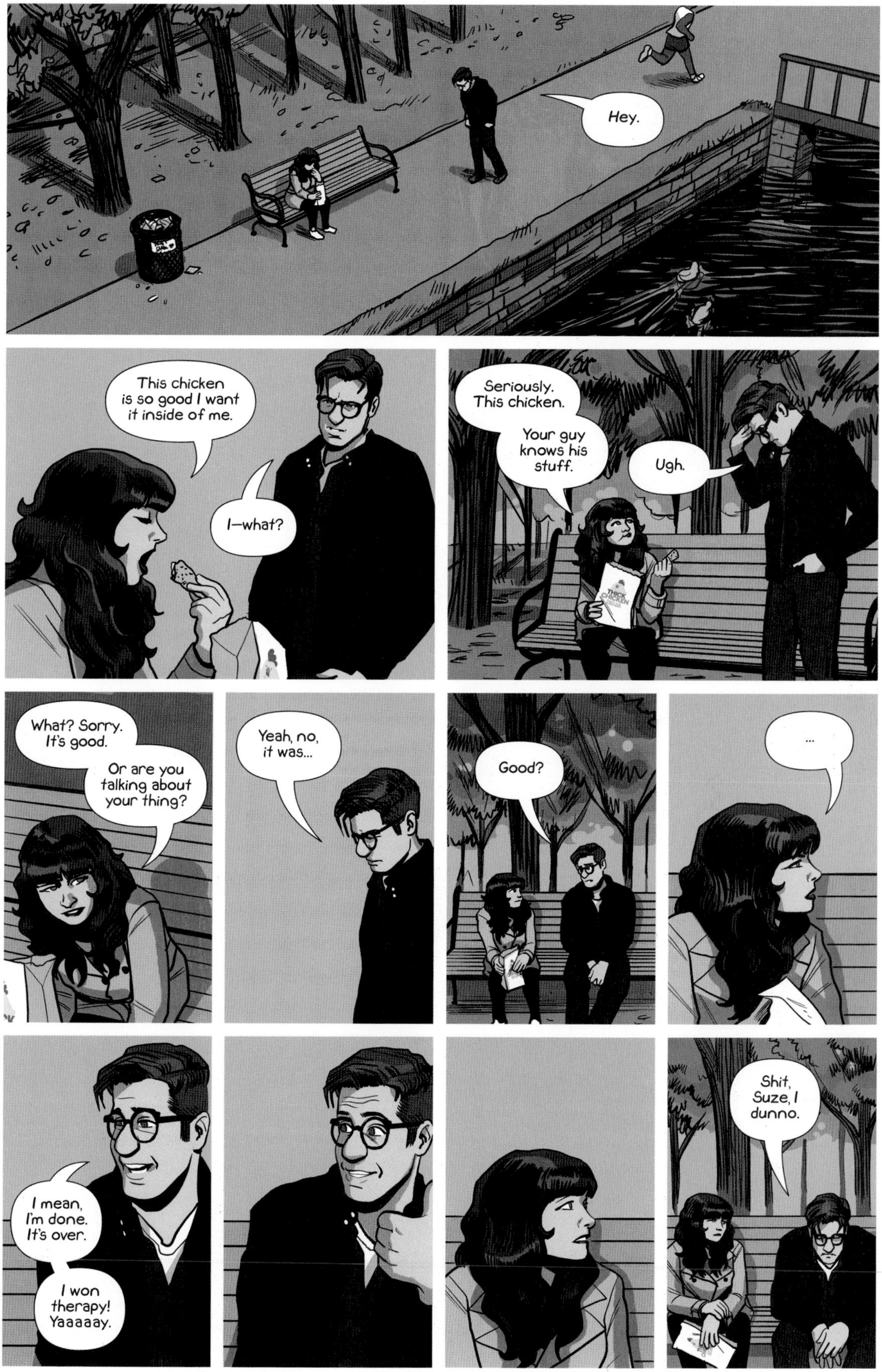
Hey.
This chicken is so good I want it inside of me.
I—what?
Seriously. This chicken.
Your guy knows his stuff.
Ugh.
THICK CHICKEN
What? Sorry. It's good.
Or are you talking about your thing?
Yeah, no, it was...
Good?
...
I mean, I'm done. It's over.
I won therapy! Yaaaaay.
Shit, Suze, I dunno.

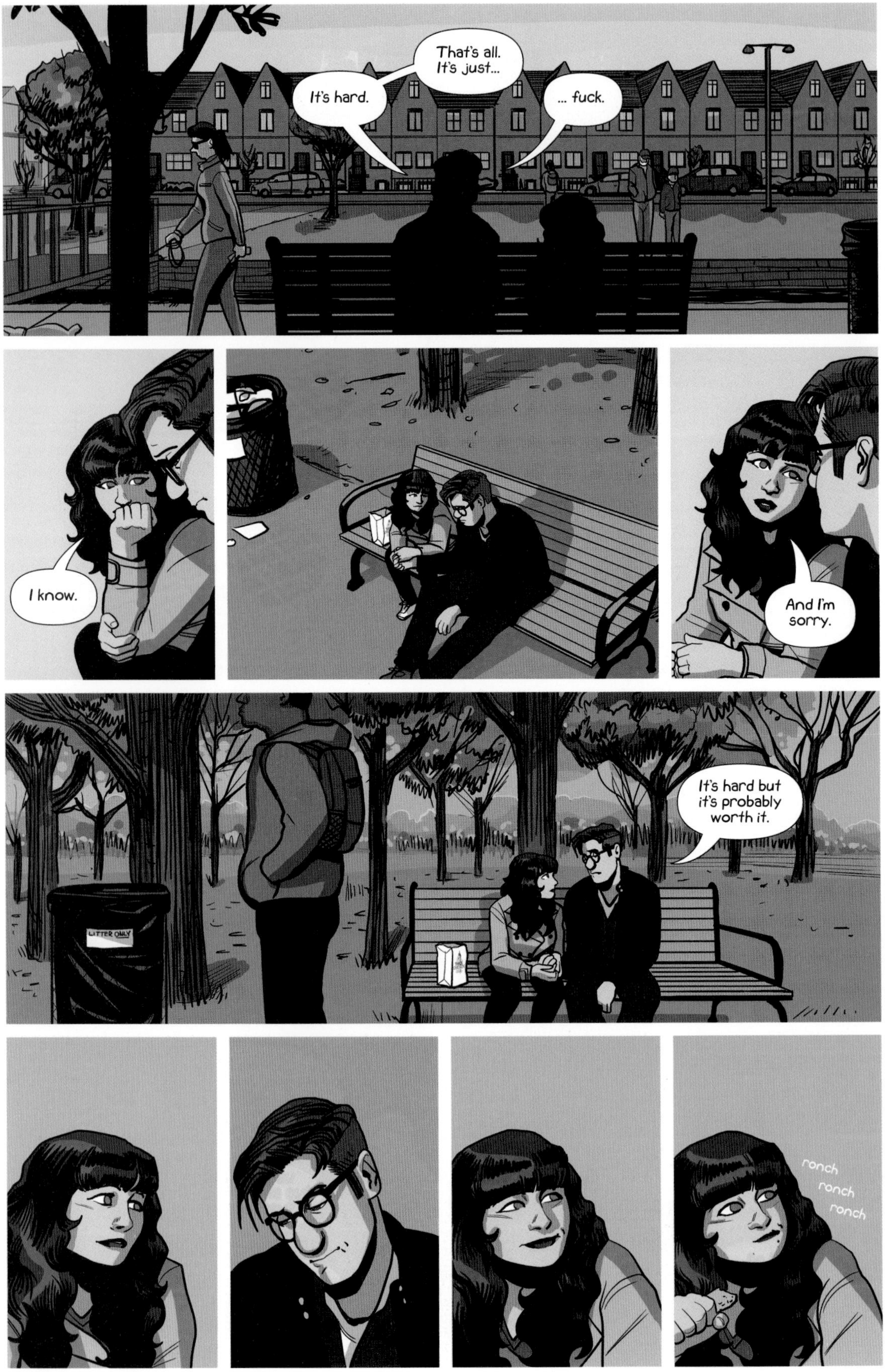
It's hard.
That's all.
It's just...
... fuck.
I know.
And I'm sorry.
It's hard but it's probably worth it.
LITTER ONLY
ronch
ronch
ronch

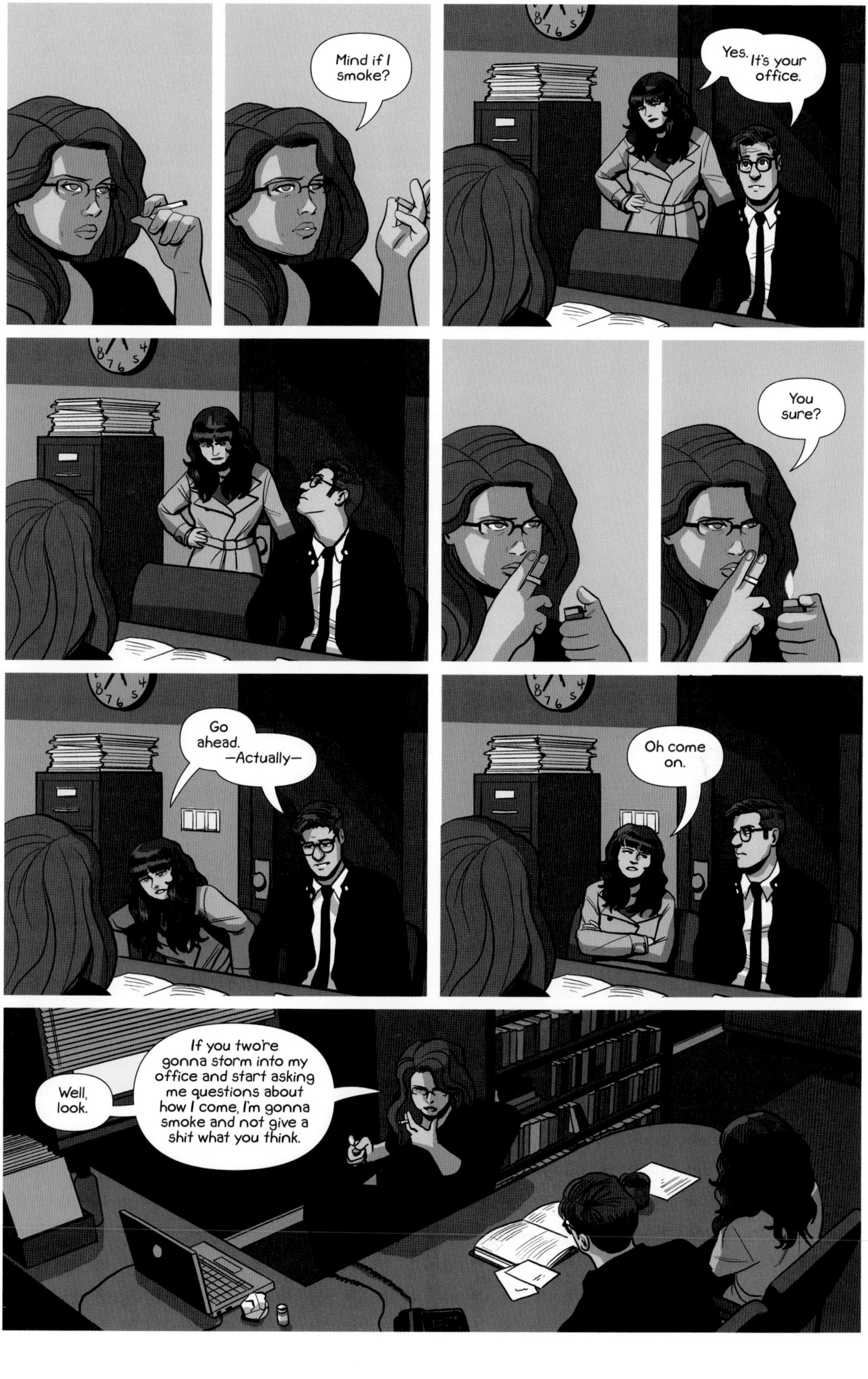
Mind if I smoke?
Yes. It's your office.
You sure?
Go ahead. —Actually—
Oh come on.
Well, look.
If you two're gonna storm into my office and start asking me questions about how I come, I'm gonna smoke and not give a shit what you think.

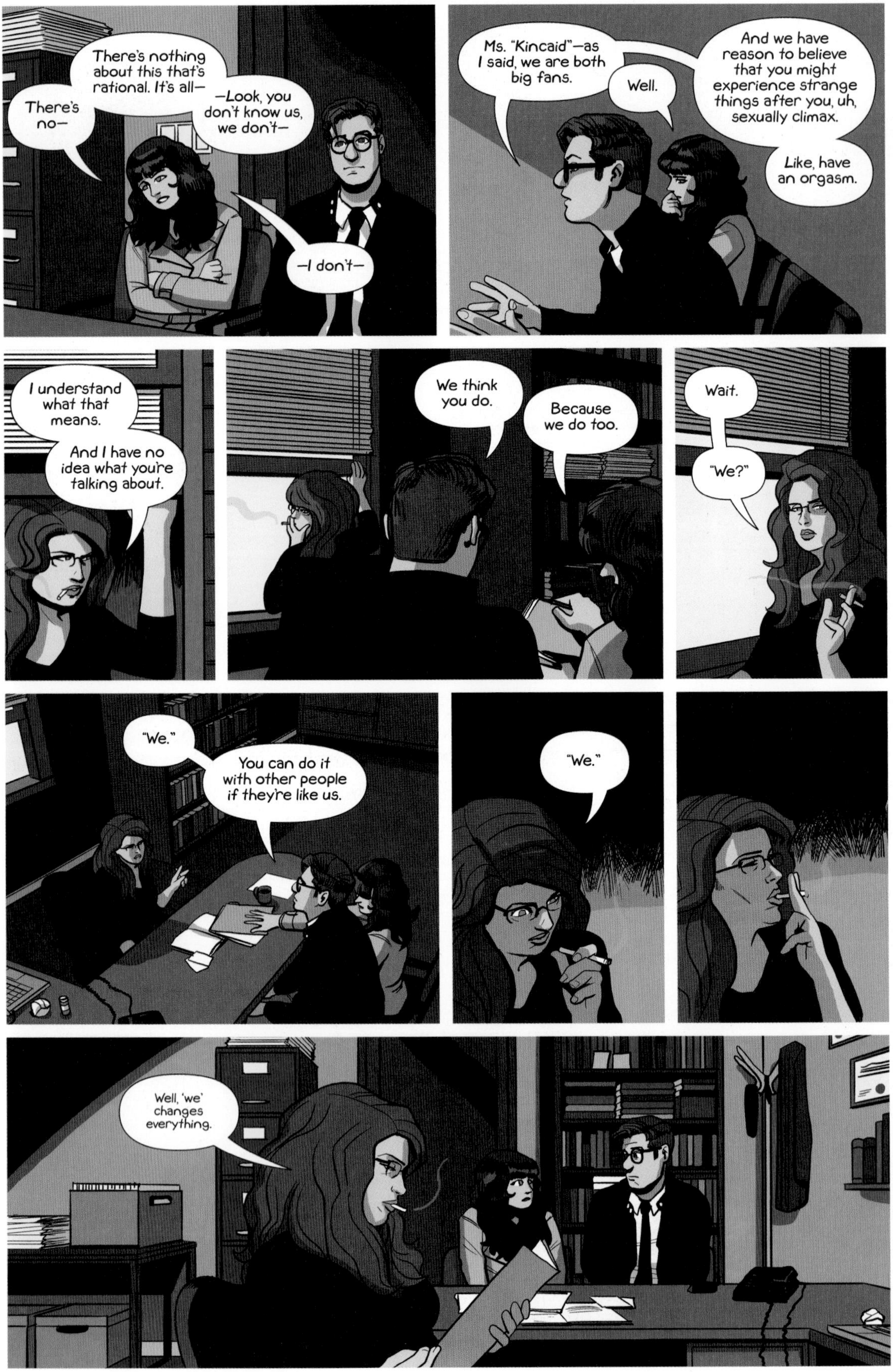
There's no—
There's nothing about this that's rational. It's all—
—Look, you don't know us, we don't—
—I don't—
Ms. "Kincaid"—as I said, we are both big fans.
Well.
And we have reason to believe that you might experience strange things after you, uh, sexually climax.
Like, have an orgasm.
I understand what that means.
And I have no idea what you're talking about.
We think you do.
Because we do too.
Wait.
"We?"
"We."
You can do it with other people if they're like us.
"We."
Well, 'we' changes everything.

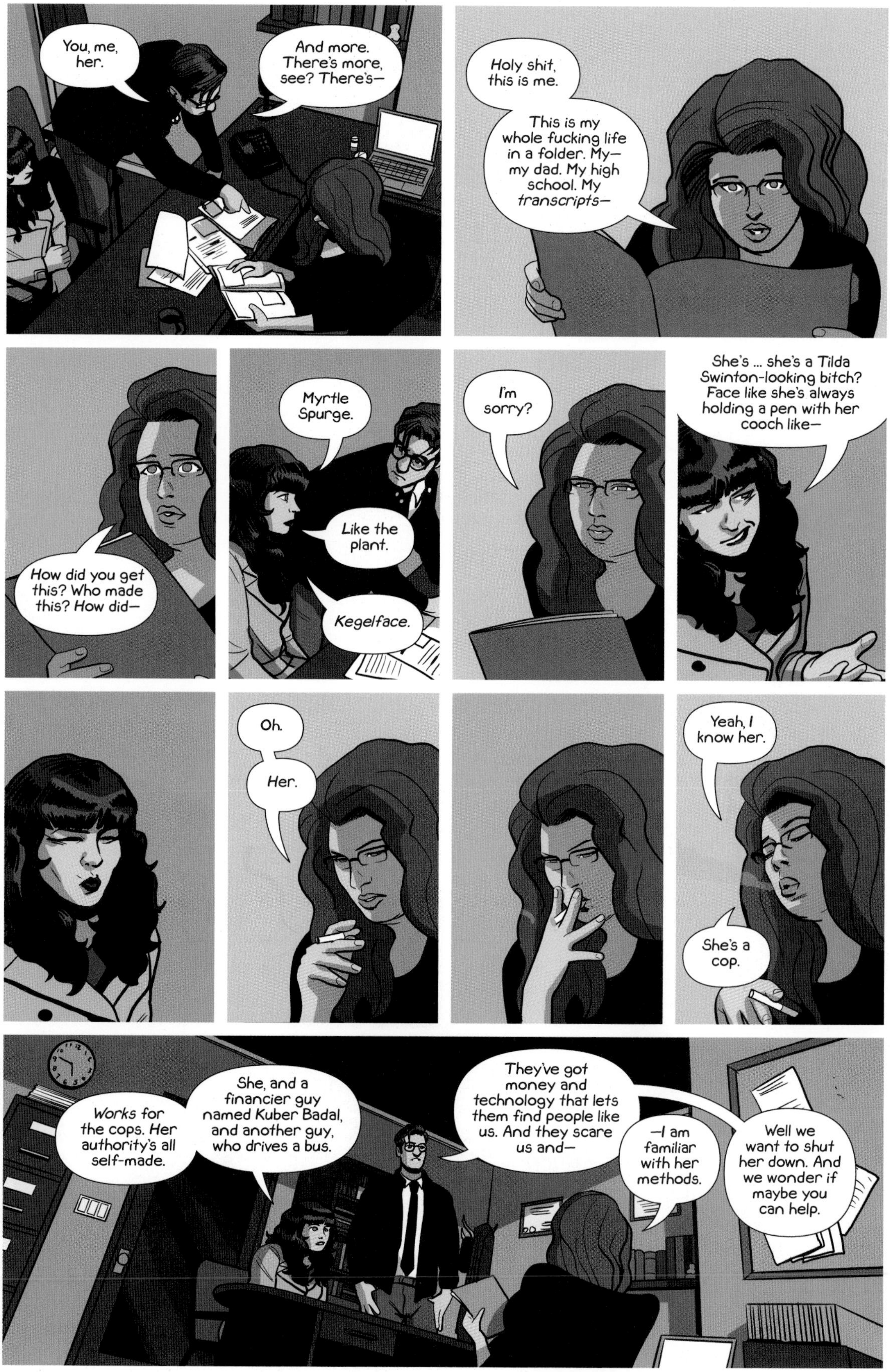
You, me, her.
And more. There's more, see? There's—
Holy shit, this is me.
This is my whole fucking life in a folder. My— my dad. My high school. My *transcripts*—
How did you get this? Who made this? How did—
Myrtle Spurge.
Like the plant.
Kegelface.
I'm sorry?
She's ... she's a Tilda Swinton-looking bitch? Face like she's always holding a pen with her cooch like—
Oh.
Her.
Yeah, *I* know her.
She's a cop.
Works for the cops. Her authority's all self-made.
She, and a financier guy named Kuber Badal, and another guy, who drives a bus.
They've got money and technology that lets them find people like us. And they scare us and—
—I am familiar with her methods.
Well we want to shut her down. And we wonder if maybe you can help.

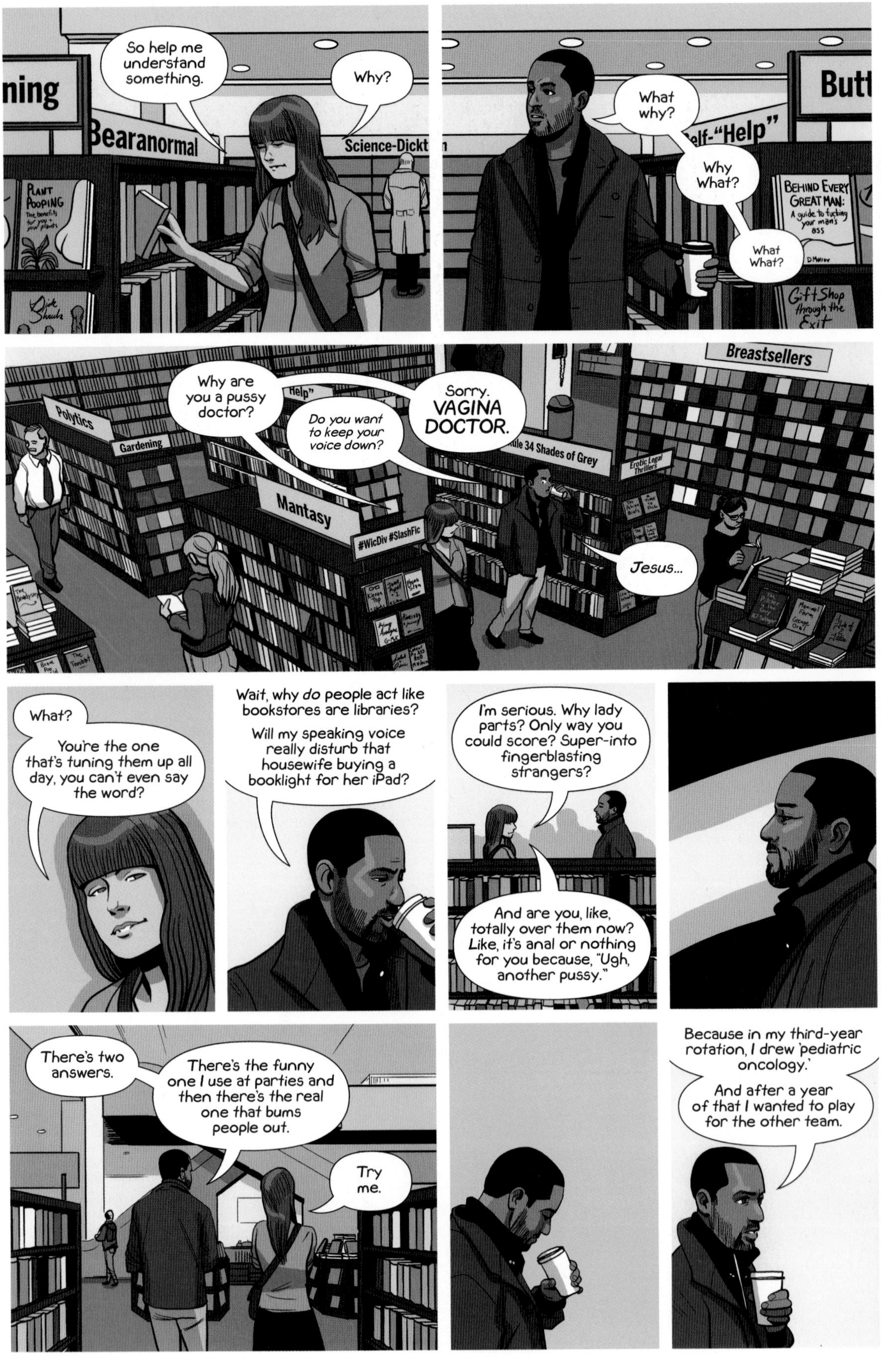

Bearanormal
Science-Dickt
So help me understand something.
Why?
What why?
Why What?
What What?
Self-"Help"
BEHIND EVERY GREAT MAN: A guide to fucking your man's ass
Gift Shop through the Exit
Breastsellers
Polytics
Gardening
Mantasy
#WicDiv #SlashFic
Erotic Legal Thrillers
Why are you a pussy doctor?
Do you want to keep your voice down?
Sorry. VAGINA DOCTOR.
Jesus...
What?
You're the one that's tuning them up all day, you can't even say the word?
Wait, why *do* people act like bookstores are libraries?
Will my speaking voice really disturb that housewife buying a booklight for her iPad?
I'm serious. Why lady parts? Only way you could score? Super-into fingerblasting strangers?
And are you, like, totally over them now? Like, it's anal or nothing for you because, "Ugh, another pussy."
There's two answers.
There's the funny one I use at parties and then there's the real one that bums people out.
Try me.
Because in my third-year rotation, I drew 'pediatric oncology.'
And after a year of that I wanted to play for the other team.

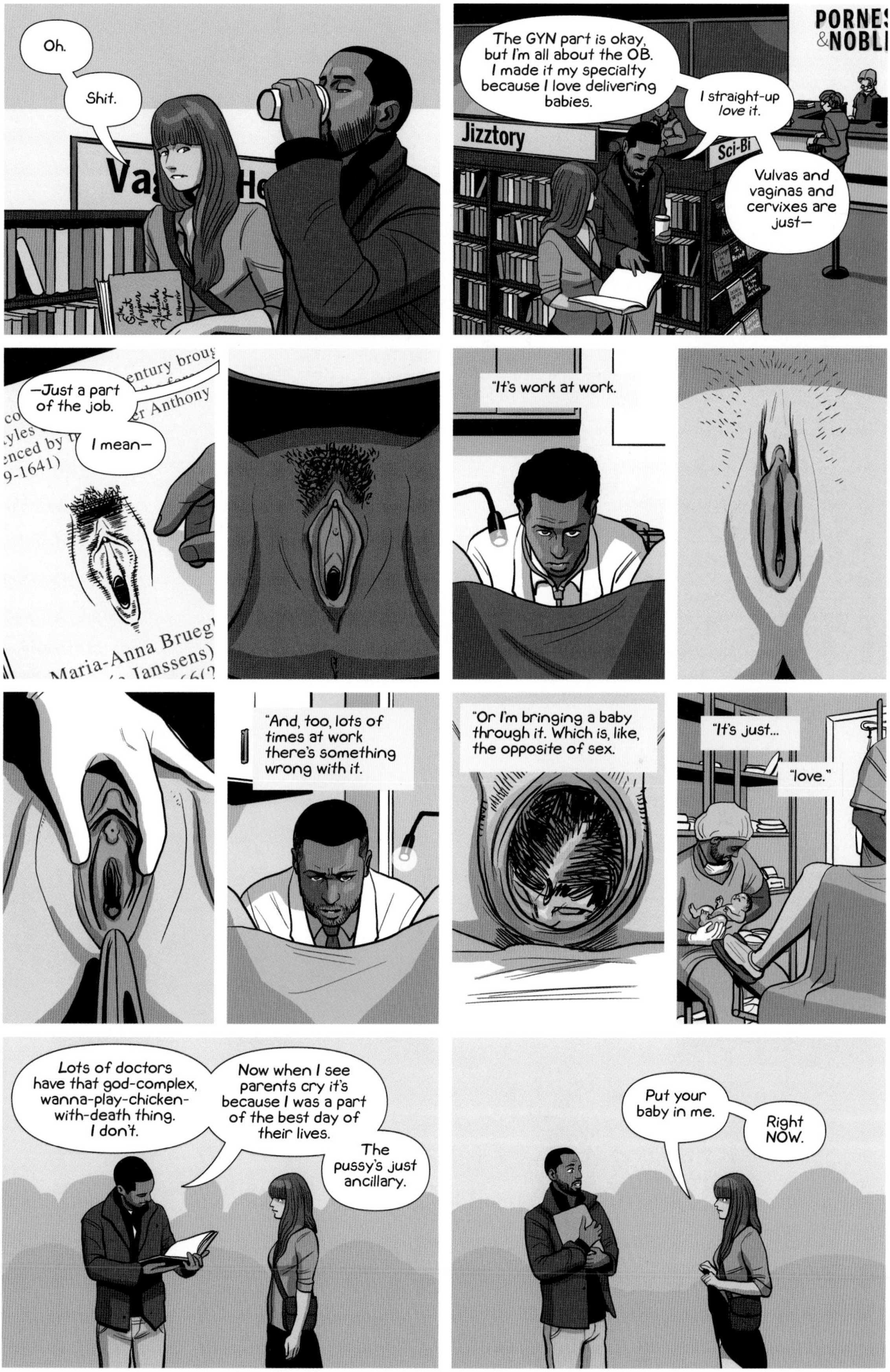
Oh.
Shit.
The GYN part is okay, but I'm all about the OB. I made it my specialty because I love delivering babies.
I straight-up love it.
Jizztory
Sci-Bi
Vulvas and vaginas and cervixes are just—
—Just a part of the job.
I mean—
"It's work at work.
"And, too, lots of times at work there's something wrong with it.
"Or I'm bringing a baby through it. Which is, like, the opposite of sex.
"It's just...
"love."
Lots of doctors have that god-complex, wanna-play-chicken-with-death thing. I don't.
Now when I see parents cry it's because I was a part of the best day of their lives.
The pussy's just ancillary.
Put your baby in me.
Right NOW.

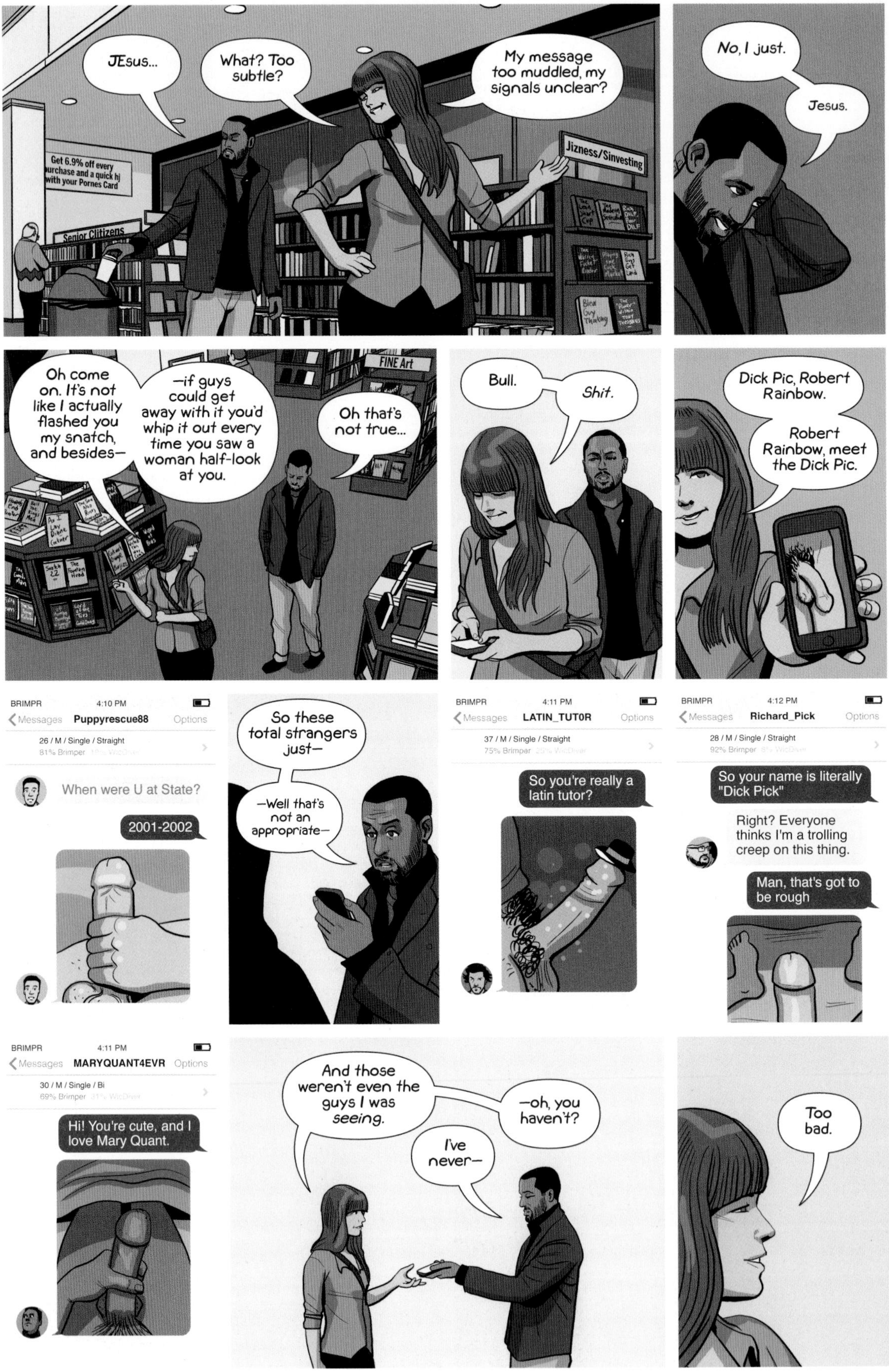
JEsus...
What? Too subtle?
My message too muddled, my signals unclear?
Get 6.9% off every purchase and a quick hj with your Pornes Card
Senior Citizens
Jizness/Sinvesting
No, I just.
Jesus.
Oh come on. It's not like I actually flashed you my snatch, and besides—
—if guys could get away with it you'd whip it out every time you saw a woman half-look at you.
FINE Art
Oh that's not true...
Bull.
Shit.
Dick Pic, Robert Rainbow.
Robert Rainbow, meet the Dick Pic.
BRIMPR 4:10 PM
Messages Puppyrescue88 Options
26 / M / Single / Straight
81% Brimper
When were U at State?
2001-2002
So these total strangers just—
—Well that's not an appropriate—
BRIMPR 4:11 PM
Messages LATIN_TUTOR Options
37 / M / Single / Straight
75% Brimper
So you're really a latin tutor?
BRIMPR 4:12 PM
Messages Richard_Pick Options
28 / M / Single / Straight
92% Brimper
So your name is literally "Dick Pick"
Right? Everyone thinks I'm a trolling creep on this thing.
Man, that's got to be rough
BRIMPR 4:11 PM
Messages MARYQUANT4EVR Options
30 / M / Single / Bi
69% Brimper
Hi! You're cute, and I love Mary Quant.
And those weren't even the guys I was seeing.
I've never—
—oh, you haven't?
Too bad.

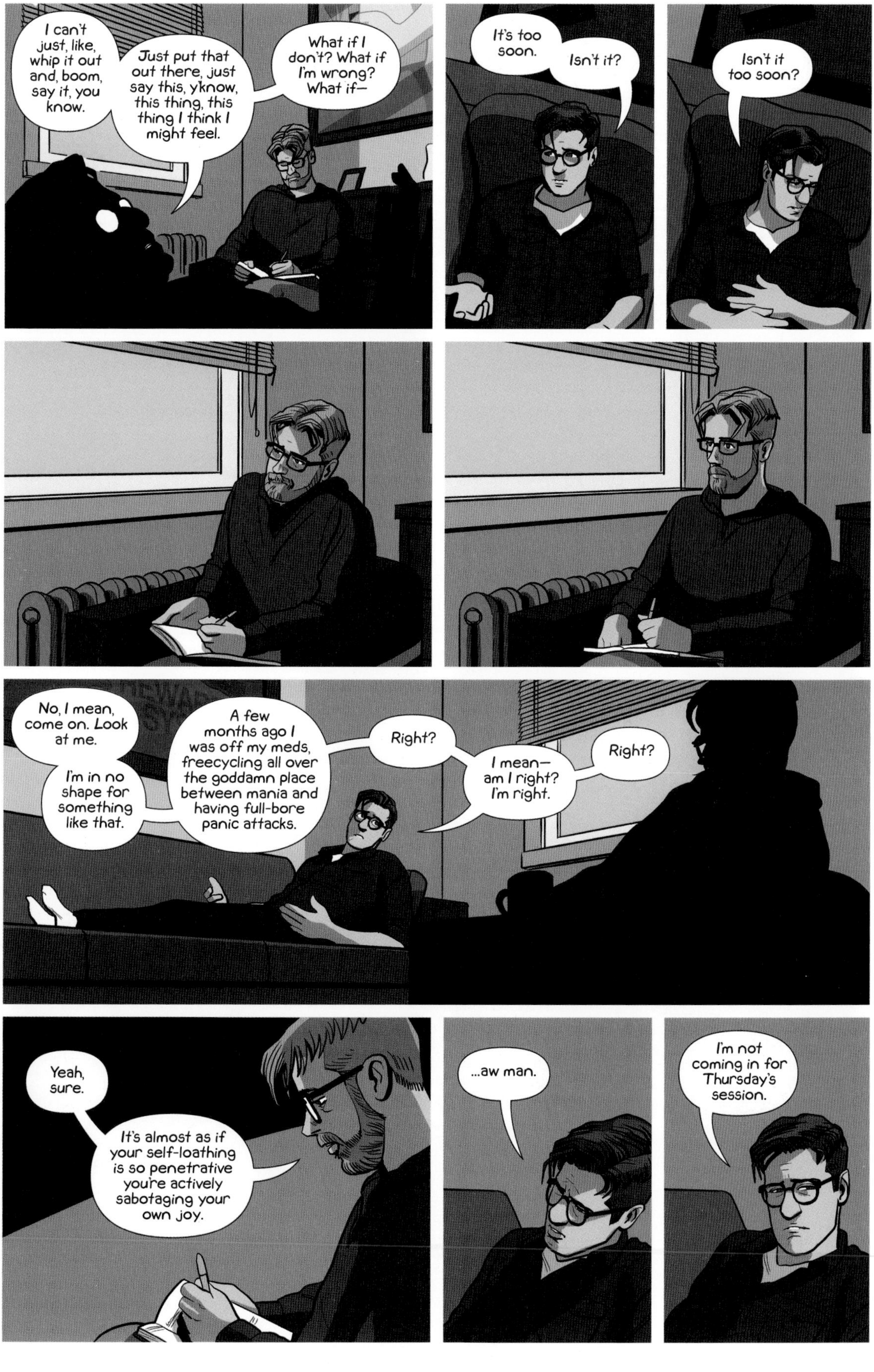
I can't just, like, whip it out and, boom, say it, you know.
Just put that out there, just say this, y'know, this thing, this thing I think I might feel.
What if I don't? What if I'm wrong? What if—
It's too soon.
Isn't it?
Isn't it too soon?
No, I mean, come on. Look at me.
I'm in no shape for something like that.
A few months ago I was off my meds, freecycling all over the goddamn place between mania and having full-bore panic attacks.
Right?
I mean— am I right? I'm right.
Right?
Yeah, sure.
It's almost as if your self-loathing is so penetrative you're actively sabotaging your own joy.
...aw man.
I'm not coming in for Thursday's session.

Aw, fuck you.

Leave my care if you want, I'm abrasive, I understand, but let me refer you to someone—

—no, no, nothing like that, Doc. I'm gonna be out of town, 'sall.

Yeah? Where are you going?

We, uh. Suzie and I.

And a couple of friends, her old roommate Rachelle and Robert, my pal, you remember—

"We're going on a road trip.

"This some kind of library sciences thing?"

"There's this, uh. There's a project Suzie's working on and we're gonna go up to State."

"Yeah.

"Something like that.

"There's a professor up there she—

Dr. Ana Kincaid, Ph.D. Horology.

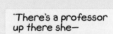

"—we—

"Want to meet.

"Yeah.

"Should be a pip."

Bloop.

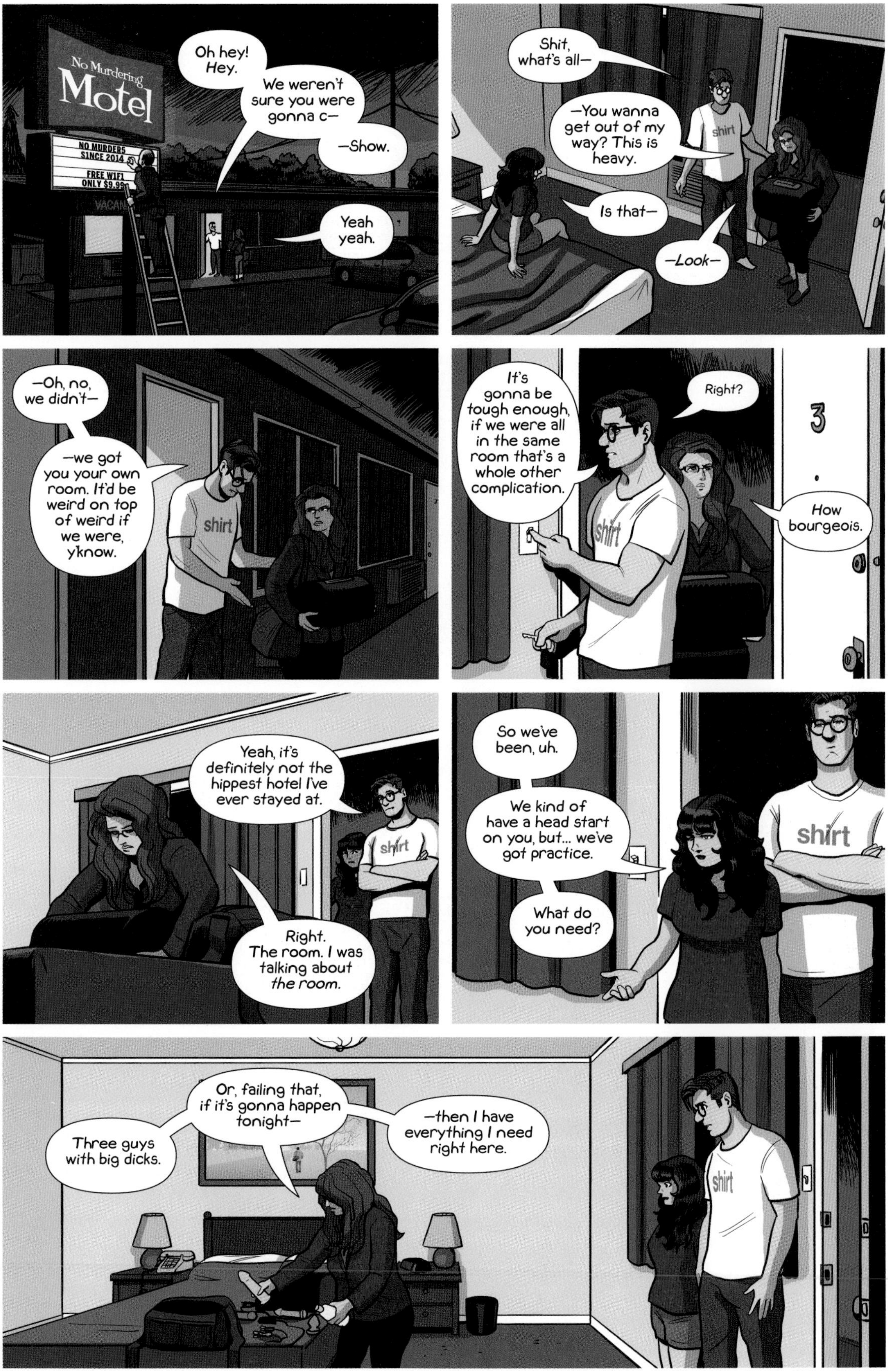

No Murdering Motel
NO MURDERS SINCE 2014
FREE WIFI ONLY $9.99
Oh hey! Hey.
We weren't sure you were gonna c—
—Show.
Yeah yeah.
Shit, what's all—
—You wanna get out of my way? This is heavy.
shirt
Is that—
—*Look*—
—Oh, no, we didn't—
—we got you your own room. It'd be weird on top of weird if we were, yknow.
shirt
It's gonna be tough enough, if we were all in the same room that's a whole other complication.
Right?
3
How bourgeois.
shirt
Yeah, it's definitely not the hippest hotel I've ever stayed at.
Right. The room. I was talking about *the room.*
So we've been, uh.
We kind of have a head start on you, but... we've got practice.
What do you need?
shirt
Three guys with big dicks.
Or, failing that, if it's gonna happen tonight—
—then I have everything I need right here.
shirt

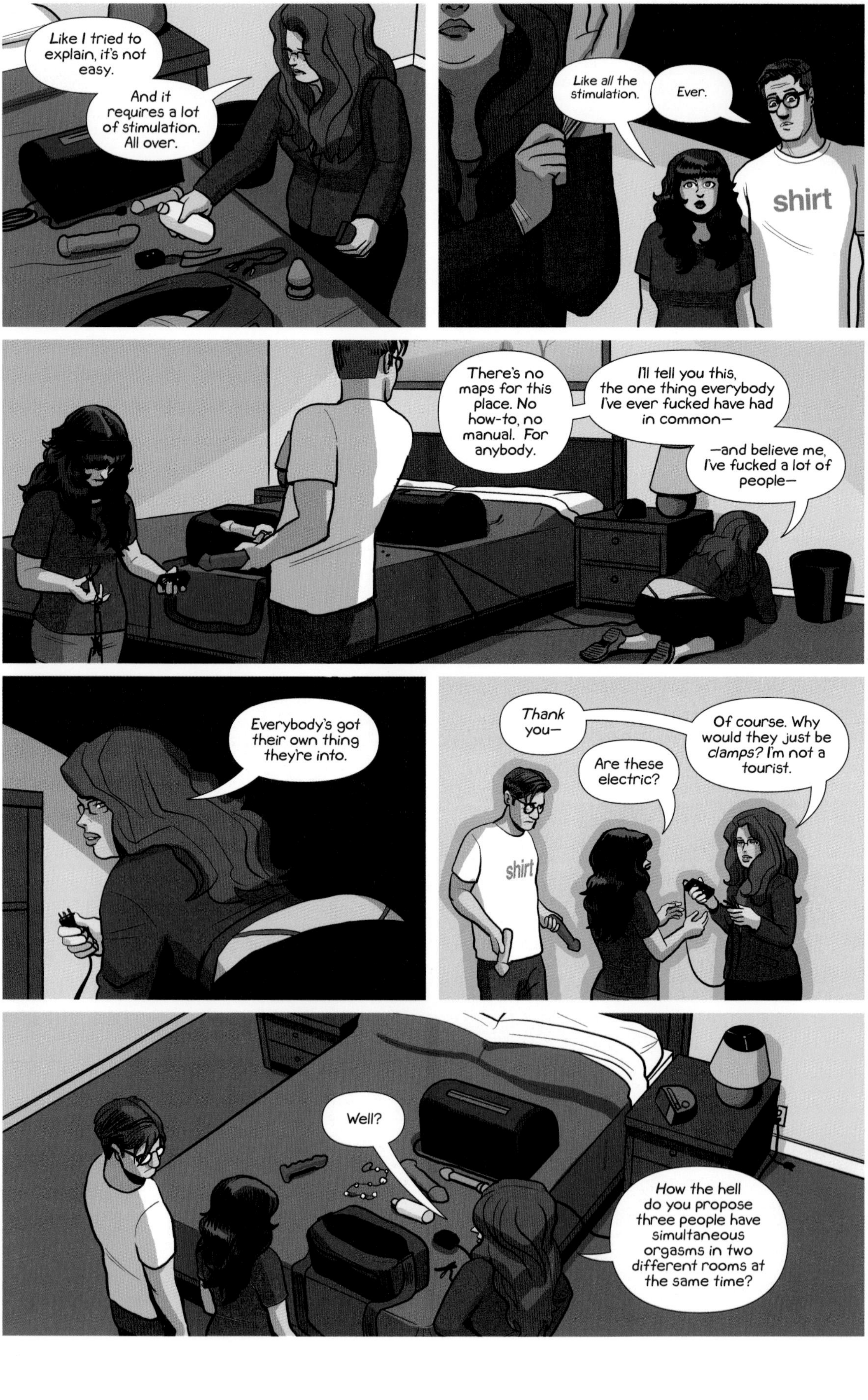

Like I tried to explain, it's not easy.
And it requires a lot of stimulation. All over.
Like *all* the stimulation.
Ever.
shirt
There's no maps for this place. No how-to, no manual. For anybody.
I'll tell you this, the one thing everybody I've ever fucked have had in common—
—and believe me, I've fucked a lot of people—
Everybody's got their own thing they're into.
Thank you—
Are these electric?
Of course. Why would they just be *clamps?* I'm not a tourist.
shirt
Well?
How the hell do you propose three people have simultaneous orgasms in two different rooms at the same time?

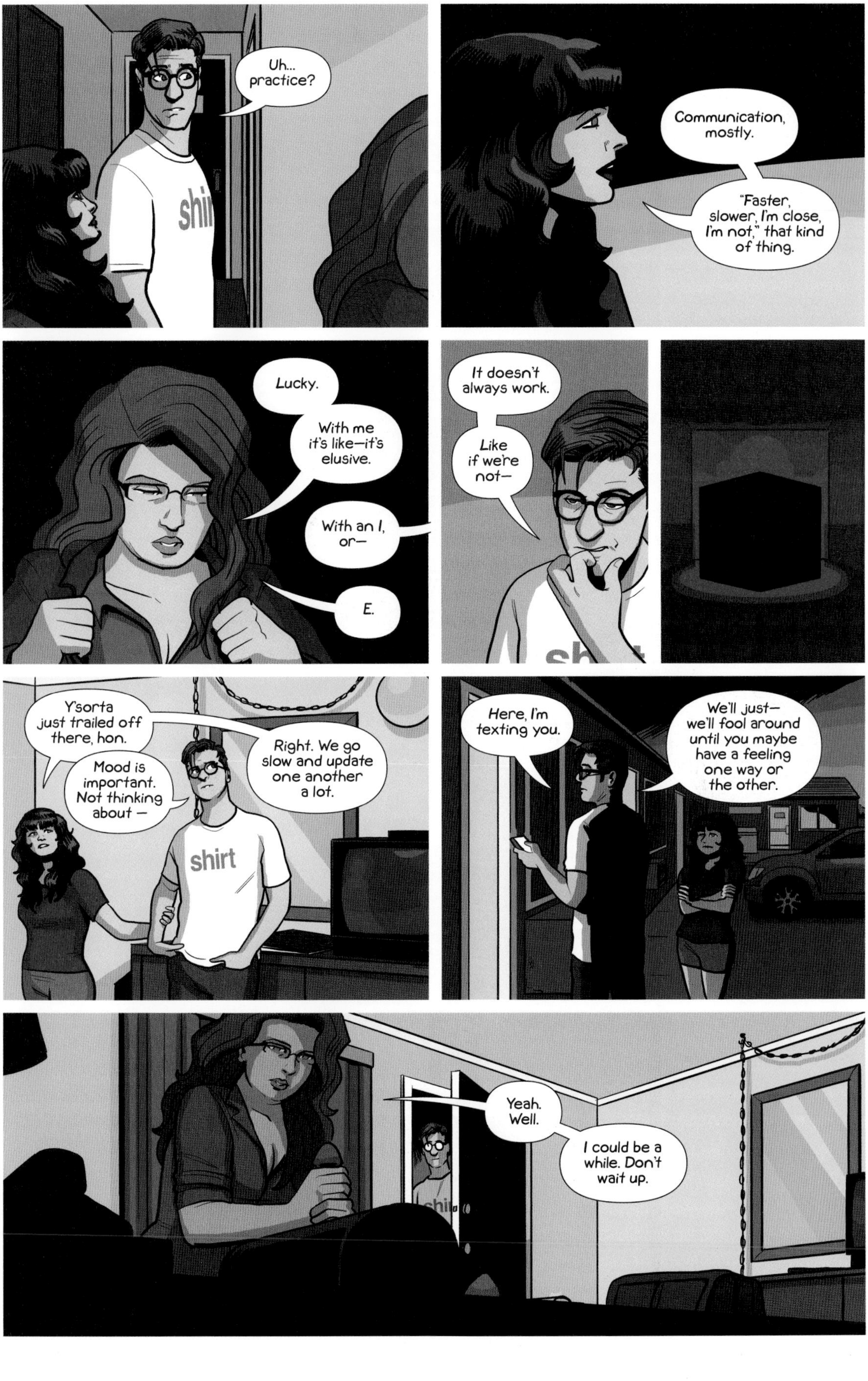
Uh... practice?
Communication, mostly.
"Faster, slower, I'm close, I'm not," that kind of thing.
Lucky.
With me it's like—it's elusive.
With an I, or—
E.
It doesn't always work.
Like if we're not—
Y'sorta just trailed off there, hon.
Mood is important. Not thinking about –
Right. We go slow and update one another a lot.
Here, I'm texting you.
We'll just—we'll fool around until you maybe have a feeling one way or the other.
Yeah. Well.
I could be a while. Don't wait up.

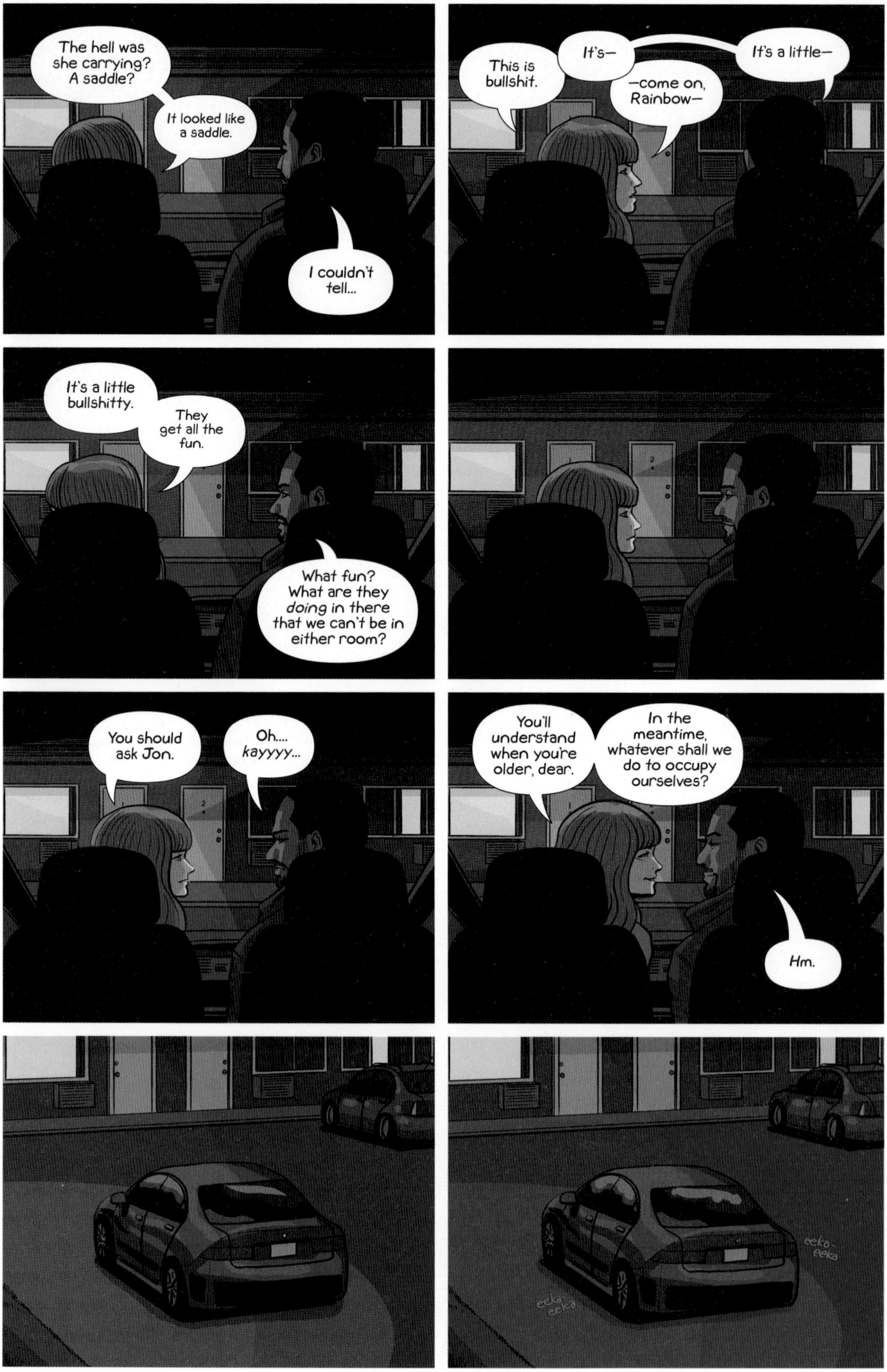

The hell was she carrying? A saddle?
It looked like a saddle.
I couldn't tell...
This is bullshit.
It's—
—come on, Rainbow—
It's a little—
It's a little bullshitty.
They get all the fun.
What fun? What are they *doing* in there that we can't be in either room?
You should ask Jon.
Oh.... *kayyyy*...
You'll understand when you're older, dear.
In the meantime, whatever shall we do to occupy ourselves?
Hm.
eeka eeka
eeka eeka

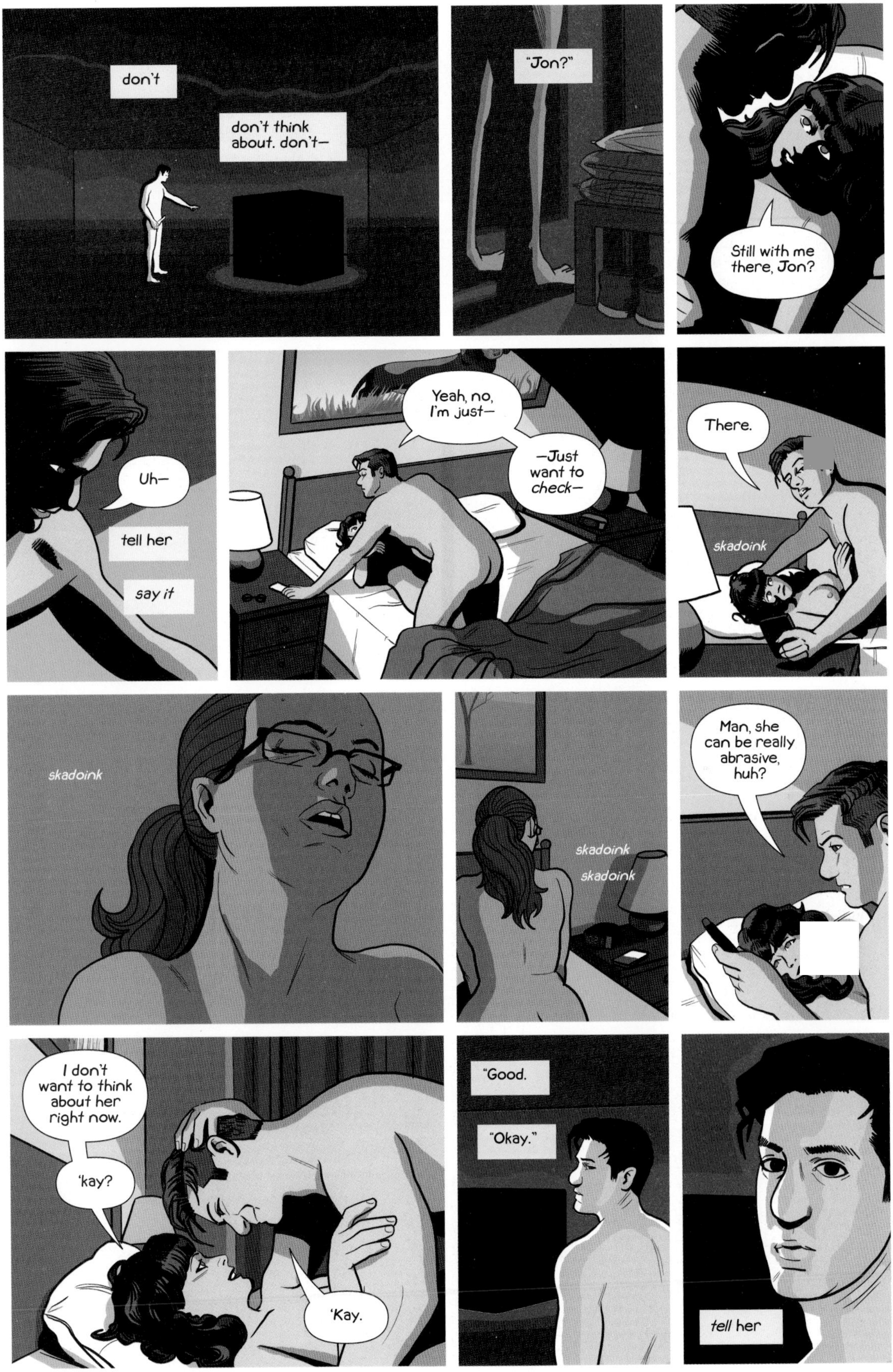

don't
don't think about. don't—
"Jon?"
Still with me there, Jon?
Uh—
tell her
say it
Yeah, no, I'm just—
—Just want to check—
There.
skadoink
skadoink
skadoink
skadoink
Man, she can be really abrasive, huh?
I don't want to think about her right now.
'kay?
'Kay.
"Good.
"Okay."
tell her

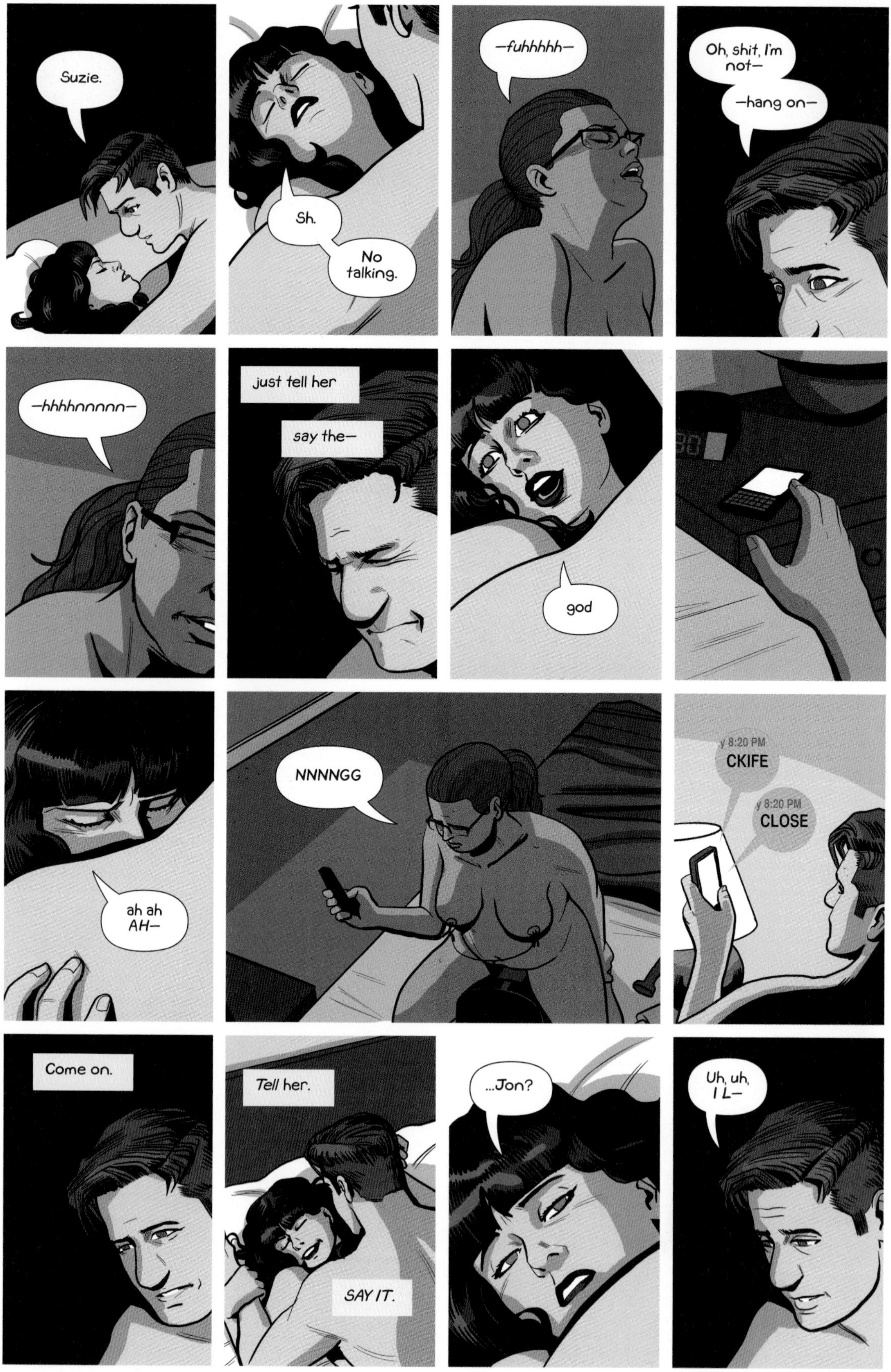
Suzie.
Sh.
No talking.
—fuhhhhh—
Oh, shit, I'm not—
—hang on—
—hhhhnnnnn—
just tell her
say the—
god
ah ah AH—
NNNNGG
8:20 PM
CKIFE
8:20 PM
CLOSE
Come on.
Tell her.
SAY IT.
...Jon?
Uh, uh, I L—

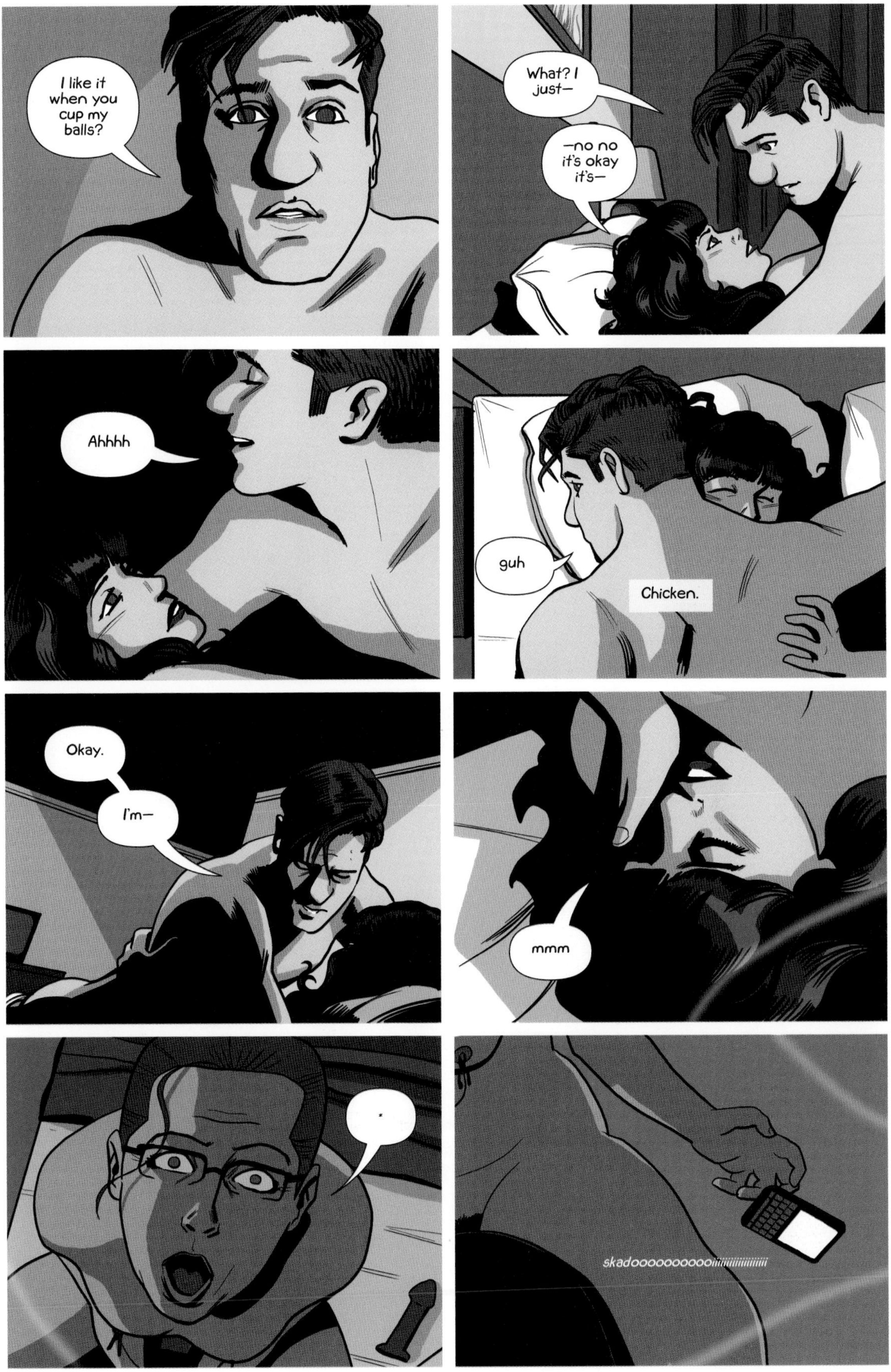
I like it when you cup my balls?
What? I just—
—no no it's okay it's—
Ahhhh
guh
Chicken.
Okay.
I'm—
mmm
*
skadooooooooooiiiiiiiiiiiiiiiiiiiii

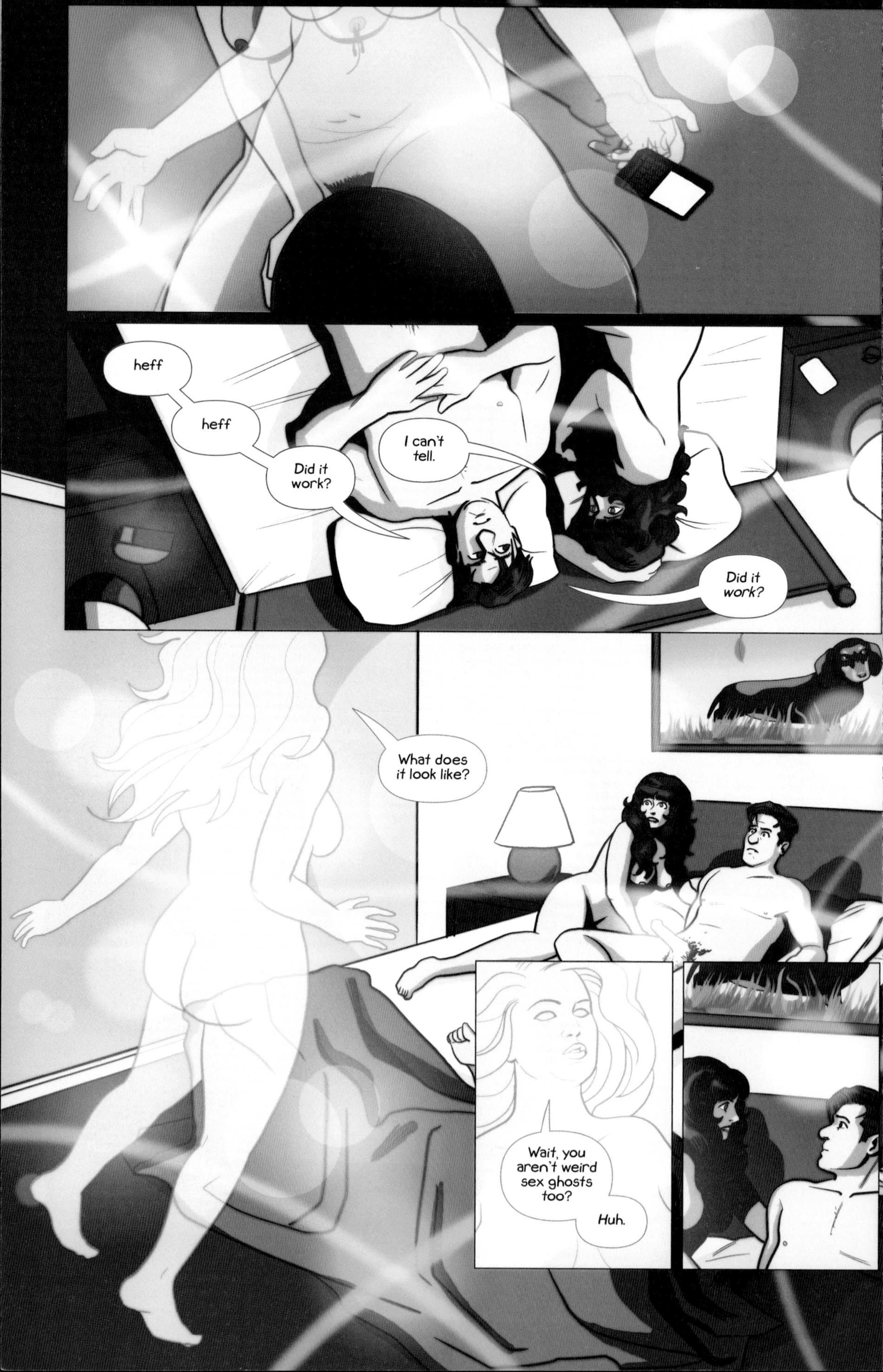
heff
heff
Did it work?
I can't tell.
Did it work?
What does it look like?
Wait, you aren't weird sex ghosts too?
Huh.

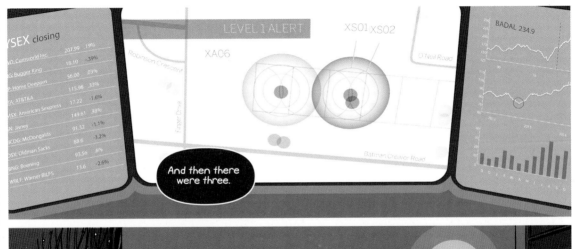

YSEX closing
WD: Cumworld Inc. 207.99 .19%
G: Bugger King 18.10 -.39%
P: Home Deeporn 56.00 .03%
TA: AT&T&A 115.98 .33%
MSX: American Sexpress 17.22 -1.6%
SN: Jisney 149.61 .38%
ICDG: McDongalds 91.32 -1.1%
DSX: Oldman Sacks 88.6 -3.2%
BNG: Boening 93.56 .6%
WBLF: Warner BILFS 13.6 -2.6%
LEVEL 1 ALERT
XS01 XS02
XA06
Robinson Crescent
O'Neil Road
Finger Drive
Batman Creator Road
BADAL 234.9
And then there were three.
What are—
—What are we gonna *do*? I mean—
What *can* we do? We are not actual officers of the *law*, we have no real authority.
And I can only buy and tear down so many *buildings*.
What next? Should I purchase and destroy their apartments? The homes of their *parents*, or—
Enough.
I will not let a couple of fuck-hungry asshole slackers get us all arrested and dissected and legislated just so she can save a few goddamn books.
The square world can never know about us.
And you're right, Badal. We *aren't* cops. And I'm glad.
Cops can't legally *do* what we're about to do...

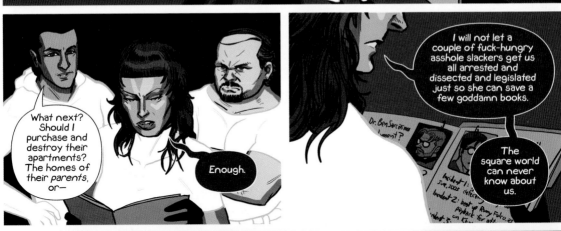

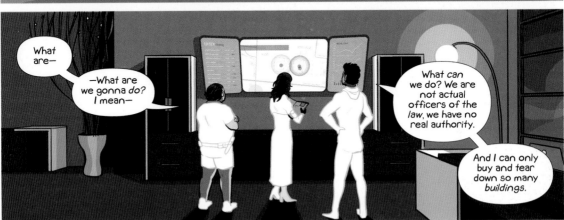

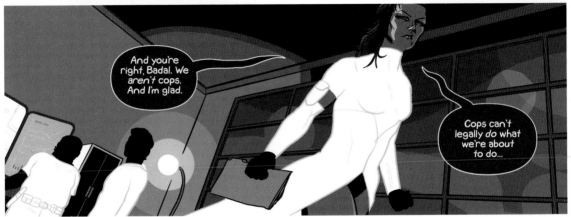

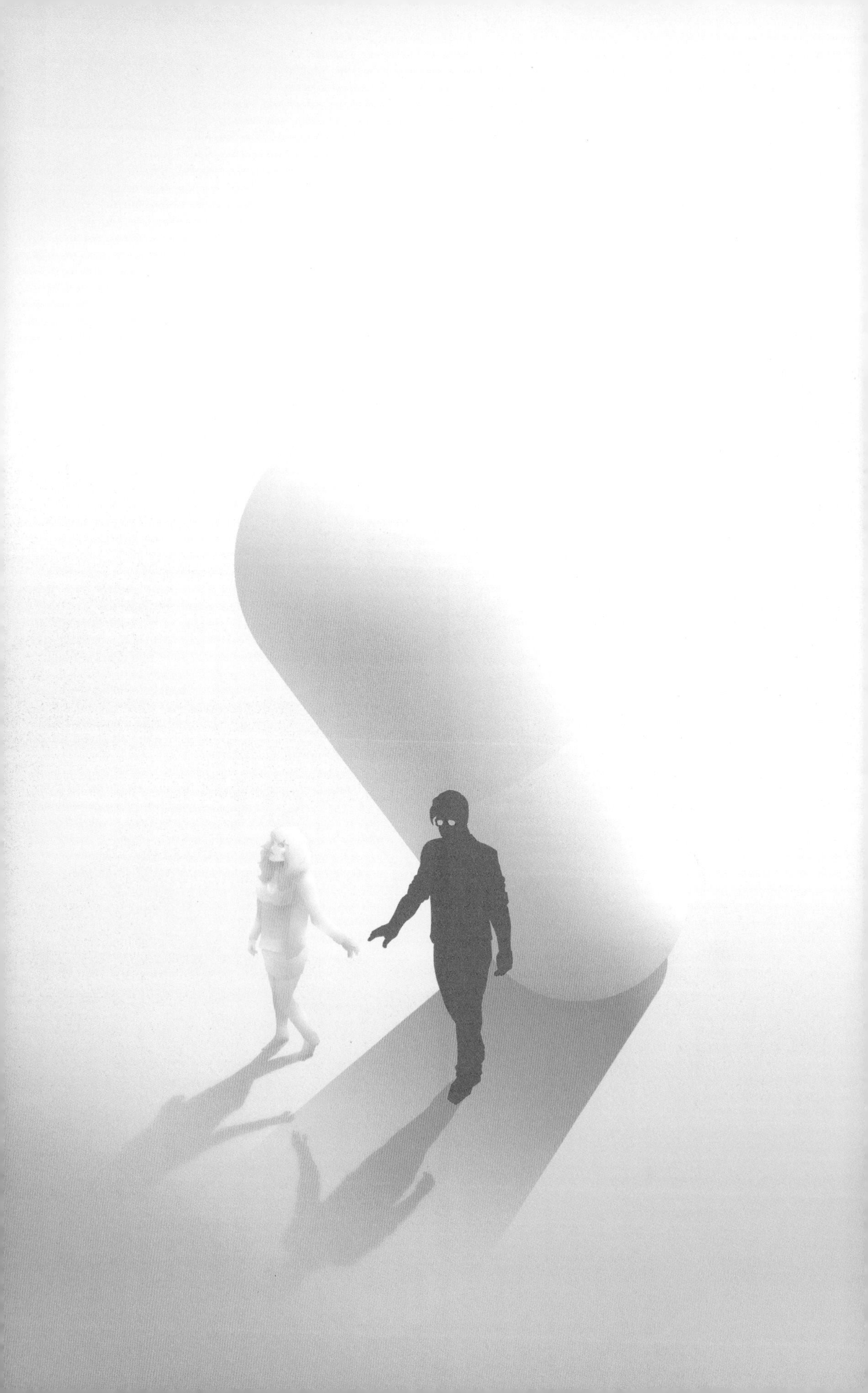

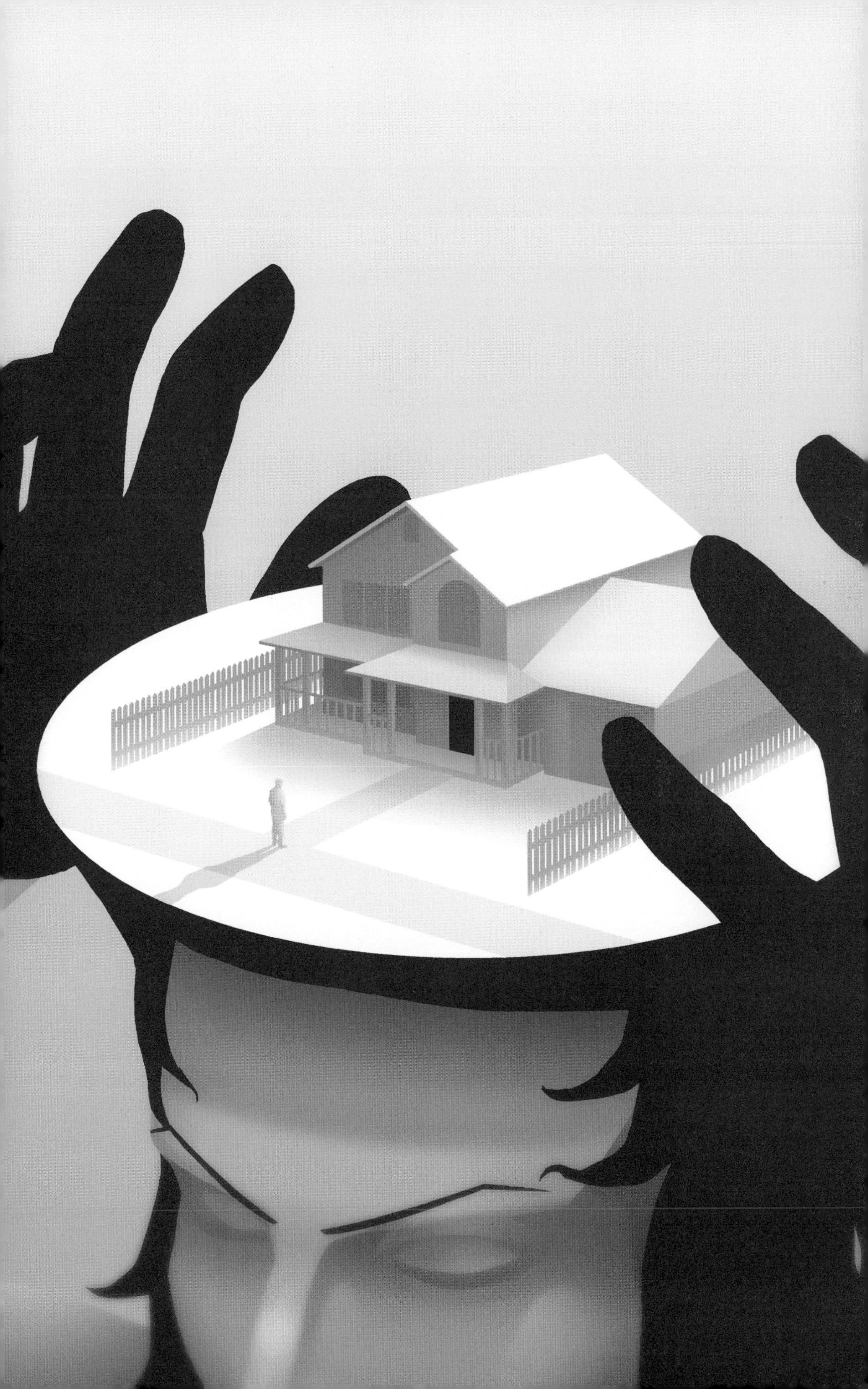

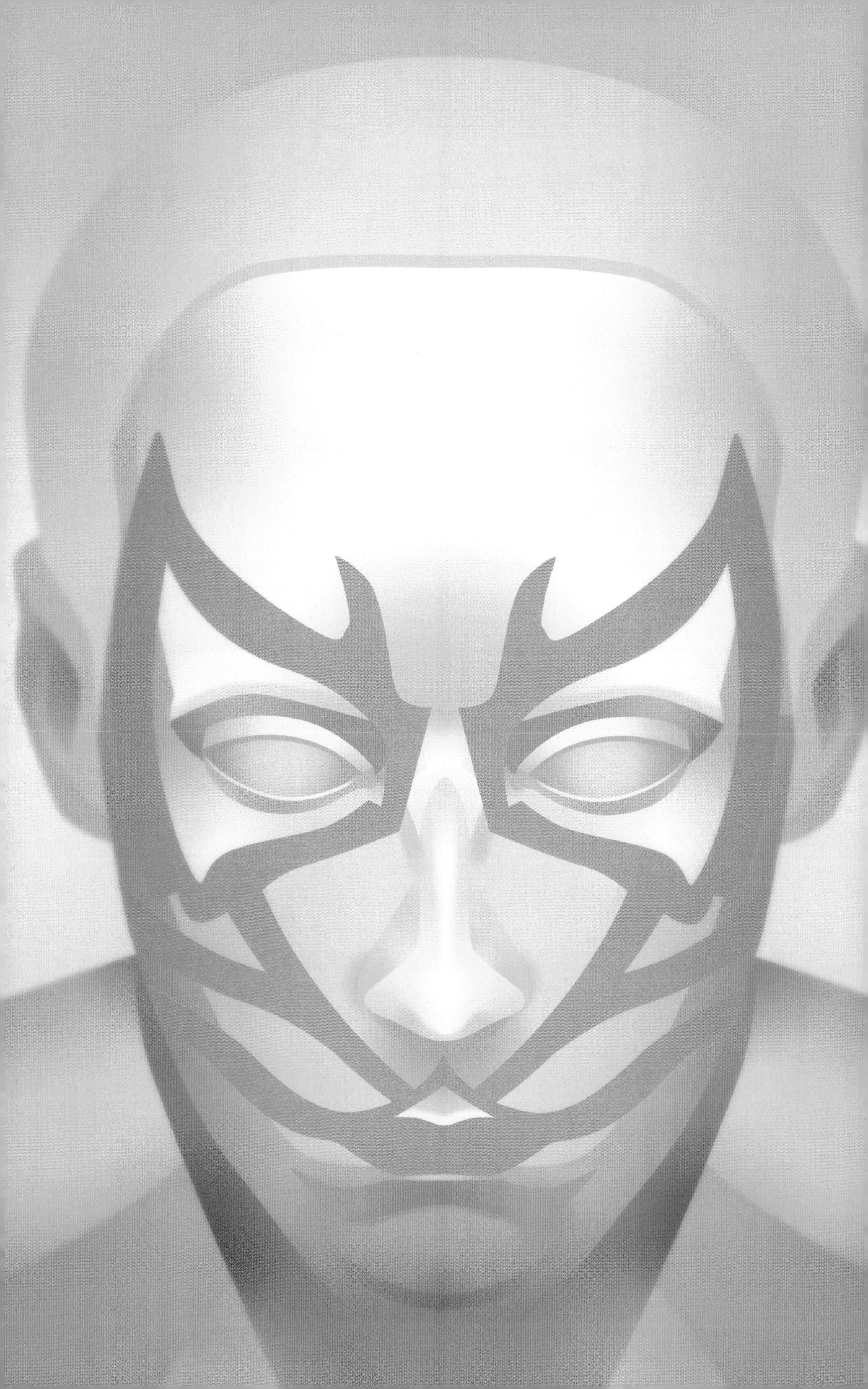

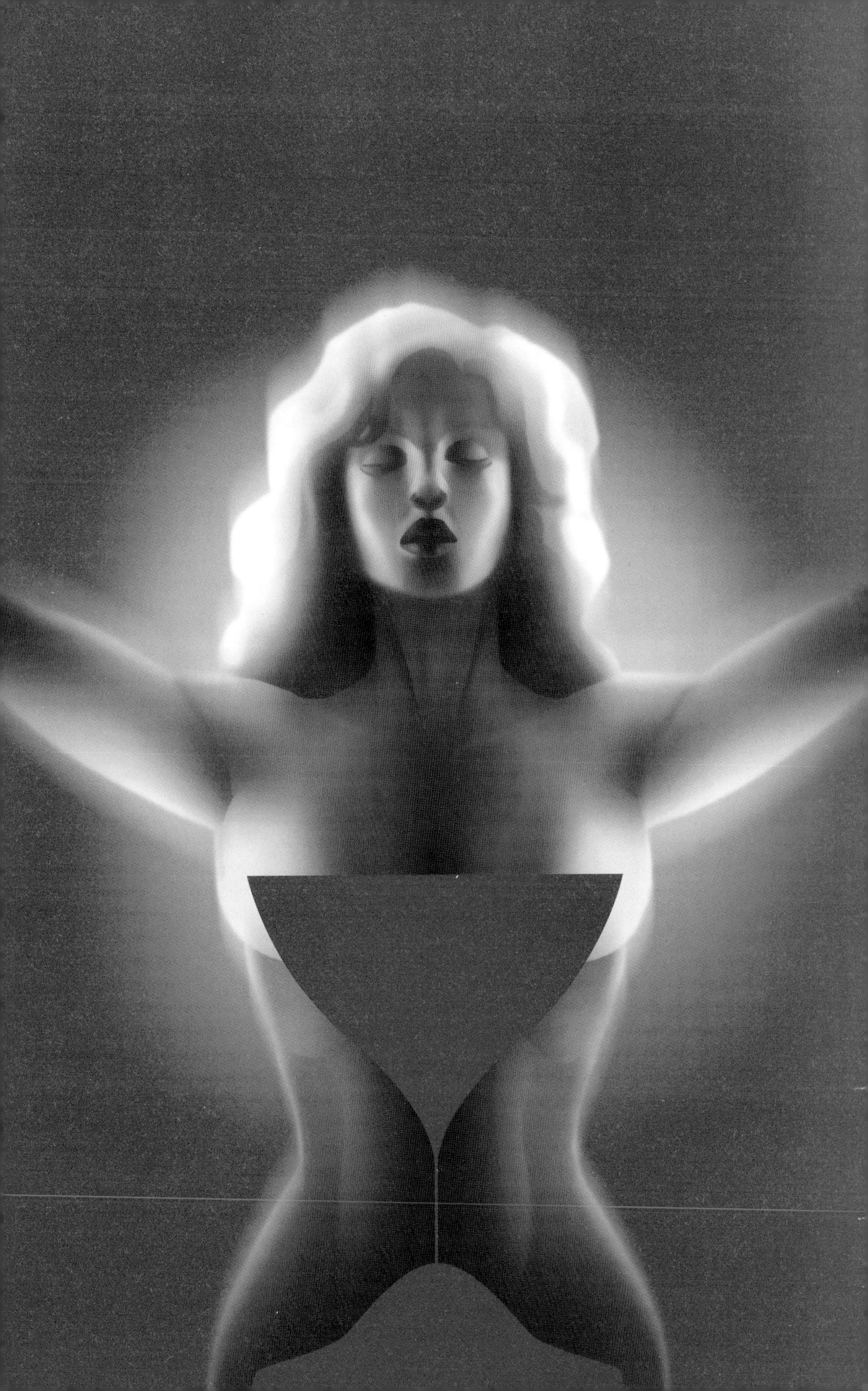

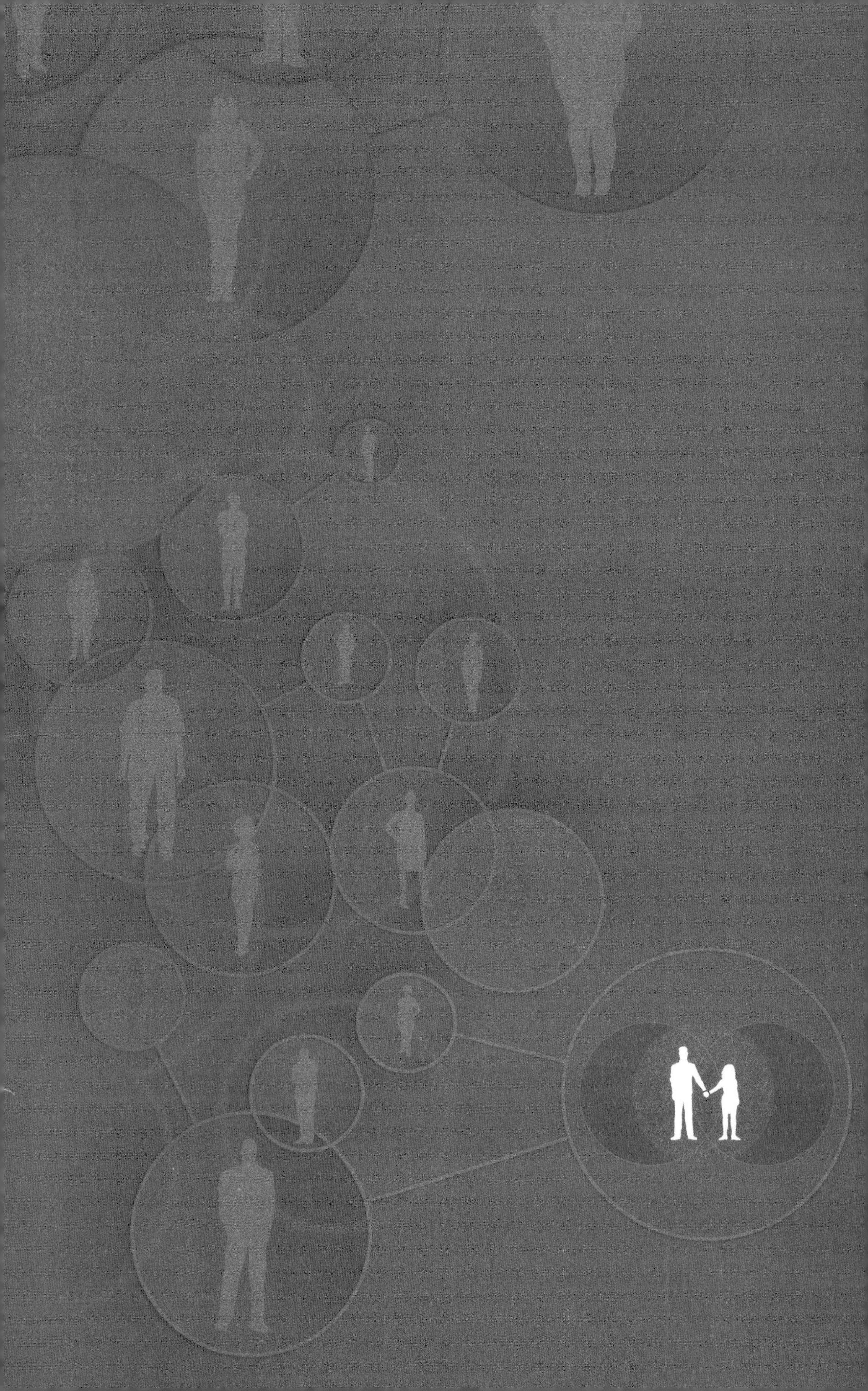

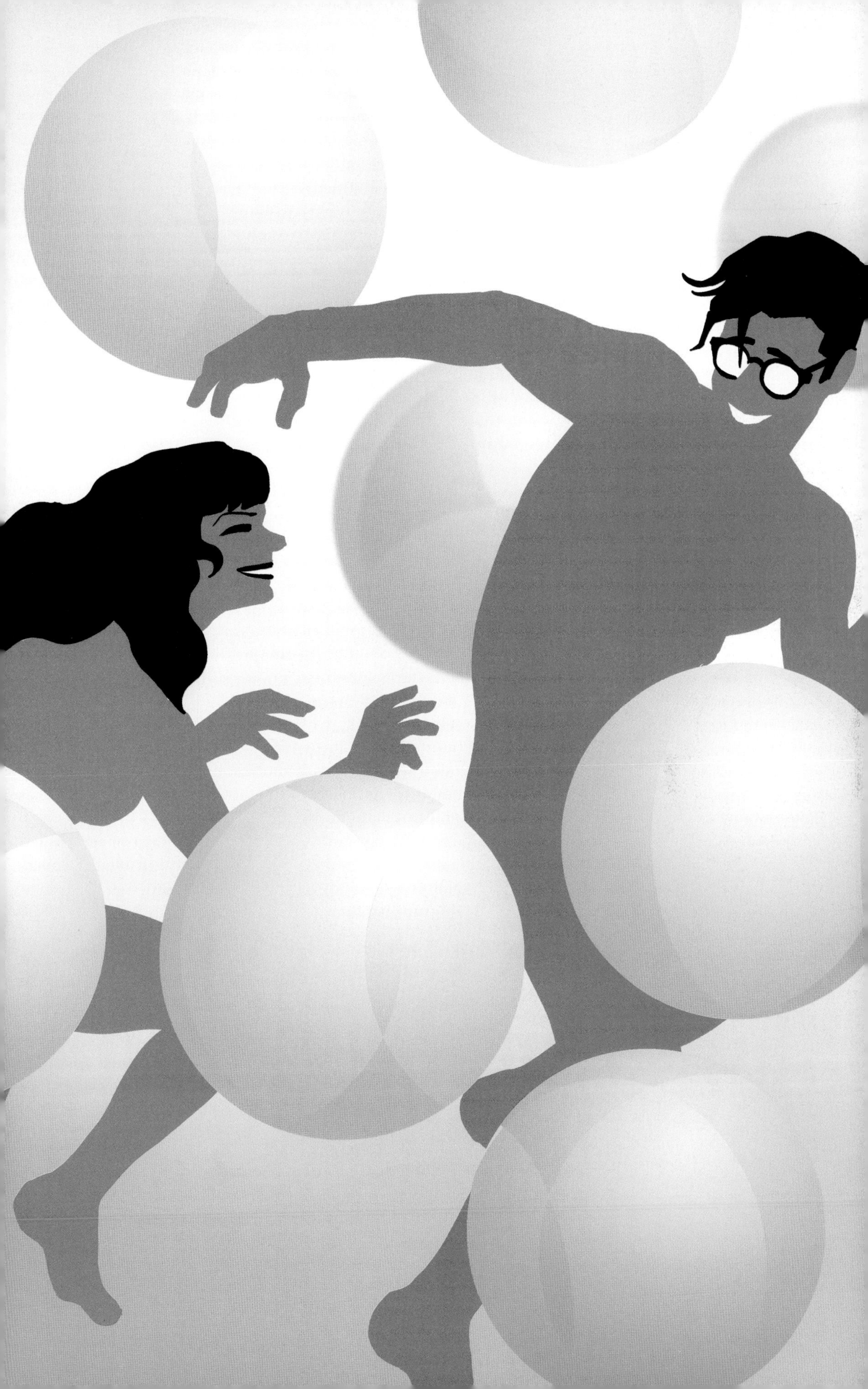

goshlondon.com

/200

Limited-edition bookplate for Gosh! Comics London

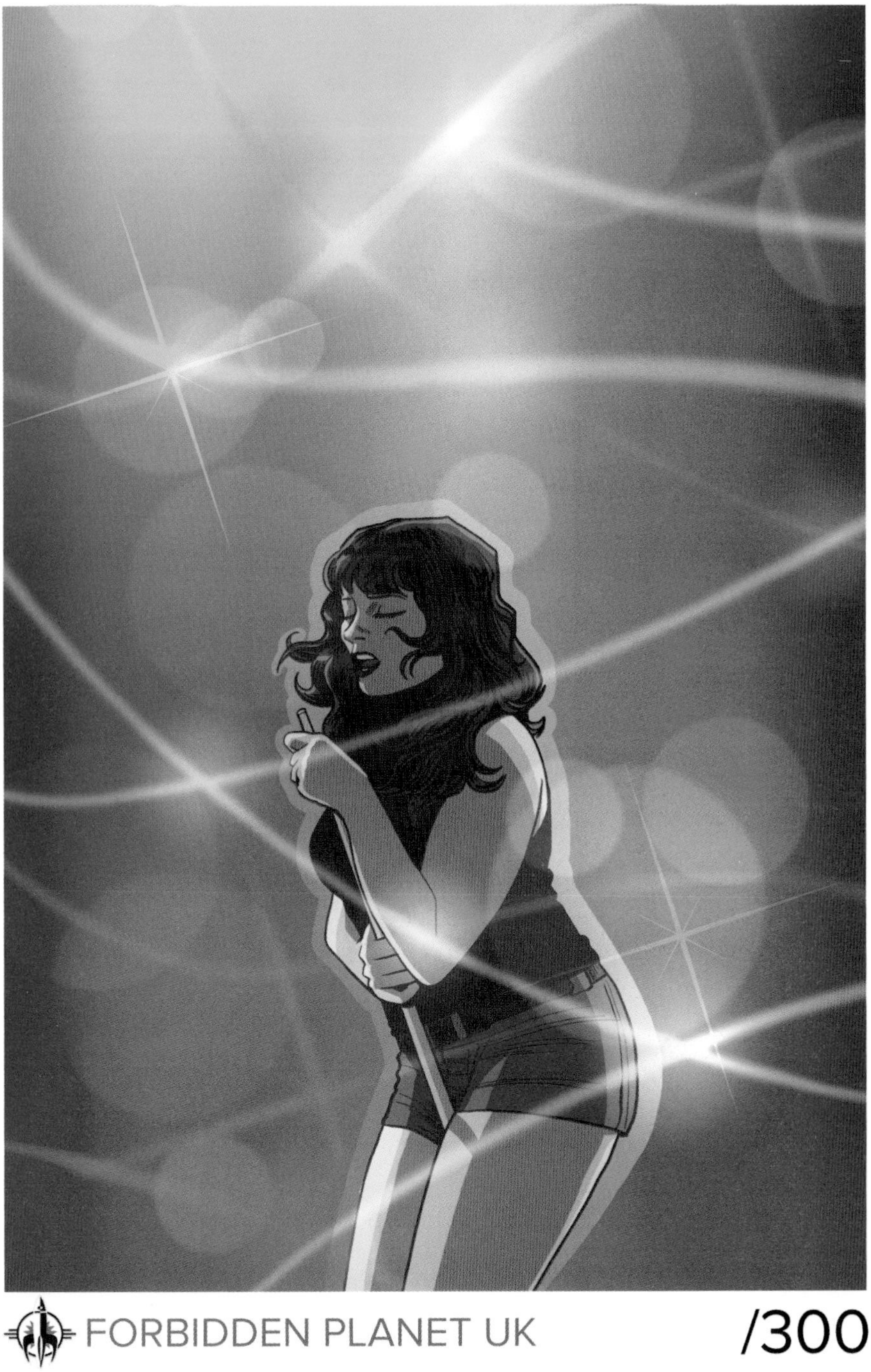

FORBIDDEN PLANET UK /300

Limited-edition bookplate for Forbidden Planet UK

SEX TIPS

Each and every issue, Matt and Chip dole out helpful sex tips! So many that they managed to fill a whole new book with them called JUST THE TIPS, featuring the ISBN number 978-1632151780! Here are the ones from issues 6-10! But be careful: don't try these at home! Try them at someone *else's* home!

Do not refer to your partner's vagina as: Baby Sleeve, The Good Sarlaac, Meat Vault, The Asshole's Companion, Downton Alley, The Uncanny Valley, Ms. Nasty's School For Boys, The Holistic Healer, The Matrimonial Hole, Sandra, Number 36, Vag of Honor, Boner Hotel, Mystic Pizza, Natural Fleshlight.

Do not refer to your partner's penis as: Hmm Interesting, Sexual Gary Jr., Tickle Stick, Mr. Nuisance, The Crying Noodle, Stinkpeen, Adorable, Wubby Nubby, Is It In, Discount Hot Dog, Non-Detachable Dildo, Non-Vibrating Dildo, Dildo That Suddenly Becomes Soft, Cute Li'l Thing, Ha Ha Ha.

Have sex while standing up (for the rights of gays & lesbians to marry their partners).

If she doesn't want to go down on you, try improving the taste of your semen by eating watermelon, celery, her pussy.

A fun, sexy tattoo for guys would be to make it look like your penis is a strap-on.

Pre-ejaculate is nature's lubricant, so feel free to drag your freshly erect penis along your bike chain every few months.

Remember, slow and steady wins the race. And it IS a race. Never forget that if you want to be a winner.

Feet are EXTREMELY sexy and should be paid attention to in bed. Oh, also, did you know Quentin Tarantino is a foot fetishist, I—wait, where are you

Denying your partner satisfaction can be a real turn-on for both of you. Blindfold your partner, tease them with light touches and then move to a new city.

Don't feel bad if your partner needs to touch themselves and your best friend in order to get off.

Having sex in new locations can be exciting, like when Neil Armstrong fucked the moon.

Shower sex is great because you can fantasize that you're having sex out in the rain, but the rain is hot because these are the End Times.

If you find you don't have time during your busy day for sex, then start having microsex while you go for coffee or fold laundry. Just super tiny sex.

Ladies! When faking your orgasms, don't forget to contrive a convincing backstory and family history for each, just in case he quizzes you later.

Try blindfolding and restraining your lover in bed so they can't come stab your eyes out when they hear you refer to them as your "lover."

Remember this simple mnemonic: "Stuck in a rut? Thumb in the butt. Need to slow down? Grab your cock and punch it as hard as you can."

Blow his mind in bed tonight! Tell him Shane is dead at the end of SHANE and that's why he didn't respond to the kid. He's slumped over in his saddle even.

"Crossing your fingers" has a 0% birth control effectiveness rate, but I don't know, maybe this time?...

Communication is key so you should probably learn sign language since that ball gag practically lives in your mouth.

Remember this simple mnemonic: "Feelin' kinky? Stick in a pinky! Feelin' romantic? Grab your cock and punch it as hard as you can."

For god's sake eating ass is not literal what are you doing Sandra

FELLAS! Want to drive her wild? Then learn how to fold a goddamn bath towel, Gerry, jesus FUCK

Blow his mind in bed tonight! Point out that if you hold an original pressing of WHITE LIGHT/WHITE HEAT by the Velvet Underground at the right angle you can make out the black-on-black image of a skull tattoo belonging to Warhol actor Joe Spencer.

BDSM stands for BONDAGE DISCIPLINE SPIDER-MAN.

Crtl-Alt-Delete your sexual shame away by practice-fucking the holes on old 5.25" floppy discs.

LADIES! Looking to blow his mind in bed? Invent a time machine in bed.

Are you into golden showers? Traveling on a Delta flight to Atlanta on 30 Dec? Reading this over my shoulder? Hm? Well?

Spice things up by using a vacuum cleaner during sex if your fetish is emergency rooms.

Fellas! Having problems because of the generous girth or length of your member? Yeah that must really fucking suck for you bro.

Blow her mind in bed tonight! Reveal your matching skull tattoo to that of Warhol actor Joe Spencer that appeared in black-on-black on the cover of original pressings of the Velvet Underground's WHITE LIGHT/WHITE HEAT. I mean, you've been married for 14 years. It's time.

Milk milk lemonade / round the corner / won't get pregnant

MATT FRACTION & CHIP ZDARSKY

The bad boys of comics reflect on their badness, a year of weirdness, their favourite backmatter, and why they gave themselves the nickname "the bad boys of comics"

PLAYBOYZ When was the first time you remember feeling ripped off by 'backmatter' in a comic or collection of comics?

CHORP ZDERSKY The Maus "how to draw mice" section felt super slapped together, imo.

MATT FRACTION It's gotta be, like, the typical, the stereotypical answer for lots of people of a certain age like me — it's WATCHMEN, right? Like, I don't know if I've, to this DAY, read the stupid pirate comic thing, even. What the shit WAS that? And then there's, there's, what, the fake memoir of the old man character so boring even Alan Moore kills him off halfway through, and, and, and like a fake PLAYBOY interview or whatever? Christ, how lame. How "meta." Whoop-dee-shit.

CZ I kind of want a Zack Snyder adaptation of just the backmatter stuff now.

Oh, there was a Sandman collection which had an entire script in the back and I was all, like, "uh, I just read this, motherfucker."

MF That actually would've been amazing on the DVD. If those were all the supplements.

PB Well, then, conversely, what's your favourite comics backmatter?

MF HATE used to have a letter column and backup strips so thick it was like a milkshake. HATE #27 is still, like, my personal high water mark for what single comics should be.

CZ This may not count, but I liked the million pages of annotations at the back of FROM HELL, because if I was reading it in public I could just flip to the annotations when someone would walk by so it seemed like I was reading a real book.

I never read HATE. I think it just scared me.

MF Did you ever read or see METAMAUS? It's backmatter to MAUS as its own book. It's no HOW TO DRAW COMIX THE ART SPIEGELMAN WAY but it's pretty amazing all the same.

CZ What? Really? Is it like Spiegelman's version of JUST THE TIPS?

MF More holocaust-y, nervous-breakdown-y, dysfunctional family as neurotic obsession-y, but about as many blow job jokes on the whole.

PB Speaking of blowjob jokes, you guys are ridiculously juvenile. Aren't you both 39? At what point will you stop making dumb dick jokes?

MF We aspire to make smart dick jokes.

CZ When I'm 58 years old and on my deathbed, I'd better see through my one good eye Matt drawing a donger on my forehead, cum doodles dripping down my face like life-giving tears.

PB Speaking of cum doodles dripping down the face, Chip, you seem like you're a pretty sexually interesting fellow. Are any of the events in SEX CRIMINALS torn from the torrid pages of your own personal fuck stories? Are there ribald tales of boinkery that you've lived that have NOT found their way in yet?

CZ All the great sex stuff in the book happened to Matt. The biggest "torn-from-Chip's-life" moment is the sadness of being dumped and going to see a matinee of SHROK, eyes black and blue from crying, surrounded by the laughter of children. Ha ha! Funny!

MF I've also shamelessly pillaged some of my friends' stories and I've just made a lot up too. Chip has a few amazing stories I want to work in and I hope we'll get to, too, and I think we'll find the space for it soon. I think that stuff gives the book a sense of verisimilitude, at least on the edges, and somehow that makes the ridiculous shit go down easier.

CZ When I fuck I stop time.

PB What other books do you find inspire the combination of "ridiculous shit" and genuine stories and emotions?

MF A big part of the SEXCRIMS origin story came from wanting to write a book I wanted to read because it didn't exist. So there's never... I have a lot of points of inspiration, but there weren't really any comics. I love nonfiction stuff about sex and human sexuality, and physics-y books about time. Ana is very much me in that regard. The rest is writing I guess; making stuff up and daydreaming about how to join all these things together. And just talking to Chip. That inspires the most.

CZ I guess, uh, The Bible? It's filled with some pretty ridiculous, fantastical stuff, but there's some genuine relatable stories as well. Like when Lot's wife (I want to say ... Mavis?) turns around to see Sodom despite the angels' protestations not to, and she becomes a pillar of delicious salt. A similar thing happened to my friend Gord. He actually cries now whenever he uses salt on his food! Which, as I like to point out, is pretty funny since his tears are filled with saltwater.

I like talking to Matt. I do NOT like finding out that Ana is "very much" him since she's the character I'm most attracted to.

PB Has the book caused any problems in your personal life?

CZ People seem to like me more, which I call "The Fraction Effect." My parents are ecstatic that I'm finally working on a sexual comic book, so, no problems there. I think my girlfriend is a little worried that I'm going to start mining our sexual activities for the book, but Matt wants the comic to still be "relatable" and "purchasable."

MF I sent the Eisner and Harvey awards - the physical things - to my mom and never heard a word about it. So that relationship is pretty much fucked.

CZ I love that if it was for SATELLITE SAM she'd probably go, "Oh! Matt's working on a fun science fiction kids comic!" And immediately put it on display. That book's so much filthier! Or at least it was until we hit, like, issues nine and ten.

Why are you so dirty, Matt?

MF The thing about SATELLITE SAM is the thing about Chaykin to me, and that's, FOR me, he was the first person I encountered making work that presented sex as something other than the thing that everybody in PORKY'S was so fucking fired up about. He showed sex as complicated, multi-layered, not-at-all-connected to love and marriage, and most of all, as an extension not of some magical holy joy that radiates from our purity within, but this kind of hot, kind of sexy, always complicated thing that could actually be acting as an extension of all sorts of emotions, including no emotions at all or even self-loathing. It was the first time I saw sex shown as something I could understand and relate to, even if I had questions about its mechanics. Anyway, I don't understand why more comics don't address sex, like, at all. I don't understand movies or books that don't address it either. I don't think I'm a particular horndog or particularly sexually overactive or anything like that — but, y'know, it's a thing I like and it's pretty important in the scheme of things that keep things happy and humming along. I suspect a lot of people feel like that in their lives; why don't our stories reflect that more? I know this is supposed to be a funny dumb thing where we pretend we're being interviewed by PLAYBOY or whatever and I'm suddenly getting all real and stuff, but I guess if I

was to get all real and stuff and honestly po-mo, the thing about SEX CRIMINALS that I'm proudest of is how the sex we portray is the least prurient thing in the book — like, it's not the sex that's arousing here, it's not the sex that's dirty. What, if anything, is arousing, is I hope two people so into trying to keep each other aroused. I like that our book is about people that like to have sex.

CZ Whenever someone talks to me about SEX CRIMINALS like it's the dirtiest thing in the world I kind of just scratch my head. Like, there's nothing in this book that most people haven't done or wanted to do or tried doing and got their donger stuck in something. But because it's written and drawn in a book it's somehow surprising. Sometimes I think that maybe I'm just too comfortable with sex. I mean, it's no secret that I'm a pervert, but I just kind of assume that everyone else is as well but they just don't like to talk about it for some reason.

I don't know why, but this reminds me of a thing I used to do when a relative would ask me when my girlfriend and I would have a baby. It's a funny question to ask, 'cause it's SO deeply personal. It's essentially asking me if we're going to start fucking without protection so my cum can get inside and possibly form life within my beloved. So I would always say that we're trying, but so far nothing! And then graphically describe the sex we're

having. All the filthy details. 'Cause for some reason people think they can ask these personal questions as if they're pure and adorable when they're actually about fucking and giant life decisions.

Let's just talk about the fucking and giant life decisions already.

MF I always try to respect people's decision that the book isn't for them; I'm not a hard seller (well) at all for... well pretty much the same reasons. It's a personal thing and there's not a 'right way' to respond to it. "I don't like this" or, "this makes me uncomfortable" or, "Matt what are you doing under my sink were you hiding?" all feel as valid to me as anything else. And it's kind of the point, or one of 'em anyway, of the whole dumb damn book I guess. Everybody's got their own response, and that we have it and it's ours personally and no one else's ties us together somehow.

PB Has SEX CRIMINALS changed your sex life at all?

CZ No, not really. You'd think working on a book like this would help me tear down some psychological barriers and be myself during sex, but no, Dr. Baron Von Plowman still makes an appearance.

I've been masturbating a lot more though. It's incredibly difficult researching and drawing sex scenes without summoning Li'l Von Plowman.

MF I think it's maybe changed my emotional life, somehow. I know it's grown my empathy and straight-up made me a better person, a better human, a kinder and more compassionate being. Always embarrassing when that happens in public but it's true; once the book stopped being just dick jokes, once I stopped laughing at the characters, a lot of stuff changed for me, in my head.

And in my pants too — during the production of SEXCRIMS I started really shaving the base of my dick

and that's given me an optical inch... of confidence.

CZ FOUR INCHES OF PURE CONFIDENCE.

Yeah, I'm with Matt on this one. I've never really worked on anything that's ... affected people? Besides making them laugh? So the response to the book has made me level up in a way to try and be a better person. I feel a tremendous amount of responsibility to the readers and to Matt, who have changed my life in so many ways. Oh god, I'm going to start crying.

PB Are you criers? Do you cry often? Are you two widdle babies?

MF When I drank I was a quiet, angry drunk trying hard to PREDATOR my way out of whatever room I was drinking in. Now when I get low, I just get real real low and quiet and not so angry anymore, I suppose. When I cry it tends to be day-long tantric tantrum kinds of things — epic, like, cathartic, awful, exhausting, multi-hour sobs that require silence and isolation, and when I'm done I'm exhausted and physically drained. Whatever the opposite of an amazing weekend sex binge with a new and fabulously exciting partner is. I cry like that.

CZ I'm an easy crier (and lover). I will cry at songs, fleeting thoughts, empty peanut butter jars, etc. If I'm at a funeral for someone I don't know, I won't be able to stop crying. I'd be more OK with it if I wasn't such an ugly crier. I look like my face is about to explode.

I totally welled up at a convention when a Jon cosplayer proposed to a Suzie cosplayer.

MF That was pretty special. I made a note to have feelings about that at a later juncture.

CZ NO FEELINGS AT THE CON.

PB Any tales of sexual humiliation or hilariousness you'd like to share that can't find a home in

SEX CRIMINALS?

CZ I once was going down on a lady (as one does), but it was that weird position where you're not quite off the bed, but not quite on it either, so you kind of tuck your legs in, head down, ass up, like a licking ball. Like a cunnilingist popple. Anyhoo, I'm delivering swift tongue justice when suddenly I have the best sensation occurring on and around my testicles. It takes me a second to figure out what it is and react accordingly: My girlfriend's pitbull is licking my testicles.

I cease and desist all activities and curl into a NON-sexual ball, wondering if I can ever recover from this. I did, and finished the tongue race a few minutes later. But it haunted me.

The same dog also had trouble pooping in the park one time. Would just squat and nothing. I went to see what was wrong and noticed that there was a condom stuck in his butt. The little asshole ate one of my used condoms from a recent lovemaking session, but it was now having trouble making its escape. I had to chase him around the park until I could pull the rubber out of his butt with a plastic bag. The whole time I was worried people thought I was fucking the dog safely in my off hours. Which WASN'T TRUE. I just let him lick my balls once.

MF I fucked Jeremy Piven once.

CZ Once?

MF Most of the time we 'made love.'

PB With this volume you moved the characters from just having sex to something more resembling a relationship. It's portrayed as something messy and fraught. Is there a 'sweet spot' for a relationship? Does that ever happen?

CZ I've been with my girlfriend for almost ten years and I'd say we finally hit that sweet spot a couple

of years ago. The beginning is such a rush of sex and emotions, so much of it getting in the way of deeper communication and really falling in love, not just falling in lust.

I like what's happening with Jon and Suzie. It's a testing time in a relationship and I think Matt is treating it with heart and smarts.

MF My wife points out that what Jon and Suzie are going through in this volume is what Chip and I have been going through with the book itself — the rush of passion and giddy first-timer's enthusiasm and verve gives way to a more resonant pool of energy that means you're in for a marathon and not a sprint. We thought we'd have four and be done, and now it's a book we can, y'know, settle down with some and grow with over time.

And I like messy and fraught. It gives one stuff to write about, it gives one stuff to read about. It's, y'know. Drama. Who wants to read about easy get-togethers, obstacle free? Well maybe a lot of people, I don't know, but I sure as shit don't want to write about it.

PB Did you really fuck Jeremy Piven?

MF No.

PB Then tell us a shitty sex story like how Chip shared his tale about **the time he and a dog made love to a young lady together.**

MF There was a girl I was crazy about, once upon a time, and we got together and it was great, then didn't see each other for a while because we both went to different colleges, then got back together on break and she tried to get a four-gy going between us and my best friend and his girlfriend at the time. And it ended weirdly and awkwardly with her calling her ex and saying, "They didn't go for it," and as I tried to get her to talk to me she said, "Get out of my way, you little shit," and that was the last time we spoke. It was the… it was unpleasant for any number of reasons, none of which had to do with anybody's predilections for group sex necessarily, but that line of hers, the 'little shit' line, like a shitty parent scolding a child, just devastated me. Like — like I didn't just feel embarrassed because I'd brought this girl into my friends' home who literally sat on everyone's lap while trying to kiss and/or grope them, but… well, not emasculated, but de-aged, tactically juvenile-d or something. I felt like a dumb kid, scared and uncool and unhip, I felt like I was caught playing dress-up. It was a weird Christmas.

Later that night, after she'd left and her ex picked her up, I went out for a drink and watched a man shit all over a gold Lexus. Like — like just cover this car in explosive feces.

Any of which feels like SEXCRIMS grist but requires such a different… that dynamic, the group sex that fails, that's awkward and tense and sexy and hilarious and embarrassing and all this stuff, all at once but it, like, I don't know how to get that kind of a thing onto the page with these characters. One day maybe.

We DO have people shitting on fancy cars all through the next storyline though.

PB Chip, who was "Sandra" and what did she do to you?

CZ The world is Sandra and Sandra won't stop stabbing me.

PB Matt, what's your favourite thing about working with Chip? And Chip, what's your favourite thing about working with Matt?

MF The best thing about working with Chip is how much better he makes this book, and that people almost always automatically assume his amazing contributions are my own, making me look like a far better, smarter, funnier writer. And then, the cherry on top, his innate Canadian politeness prevents him from rightfully claiming all of the praise and attention rightfully due to him. He's like human Human Growth Hormone. It's great.

CZ Can't answer cause we're out of roo

BRIMPCEPTION

It's like Inception, but better, and featuring more fleshed-out female characters.

Chip and I refuse to believe that people pay money for our dumb cum comic, and thus try our level best to pack every issue with as much content as we can manage — letters or small jokes or pictures of Matt's soft, shitty body or Chip's bare ass — including new, different, constantly changing covers.

Chip wanted to do a photo cover. He managed not only to put it together in, like, eight minutes, but somehow created a fourth printing that became a hotly-ordered item in its own right (in fact our fifth printing reprinted the fourth printing with just a small tweak to the text).

It also inspired brimpers to start mimicking the photo and sending theirs to us, or asking us to recreate the photo with them at shows. All of which we found fucking hilarious. And it started with Juliette and Heather. Thus began a kind-of live action Matryoshka convention game between the four of us.

Then Chip and I decided to take this shit nuclear, so we printed only one hundred copies of this: a secret "Brimpception" cover trump card to end all trump cards, sent only to their store.

Then we took a picture of ourselves holding the Brimpception cover. Then of course Juliette and Heather started it all over again, so we just went ahead and had them killed.

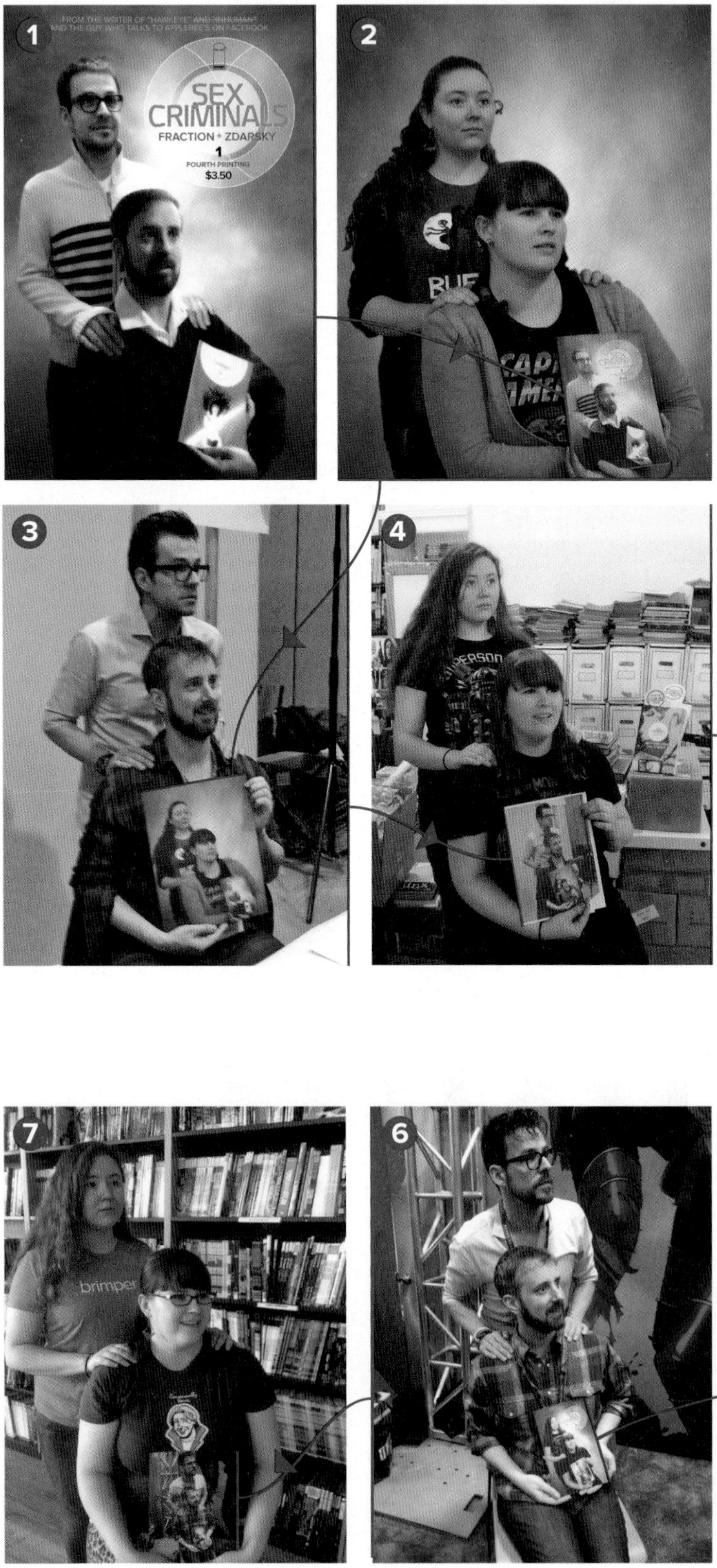
1
FROM THE WRITER OF "HAWKEYE" AND "INHUMAN"
AND THE GUY WHO TALKS TO APPLEBEE'S ON FACEBOOK
SEX CRIMINALS
FRACTION + ZDARSKY
1
FOURTH PRINTING
$3.50
2
3
4
7
brimper
6

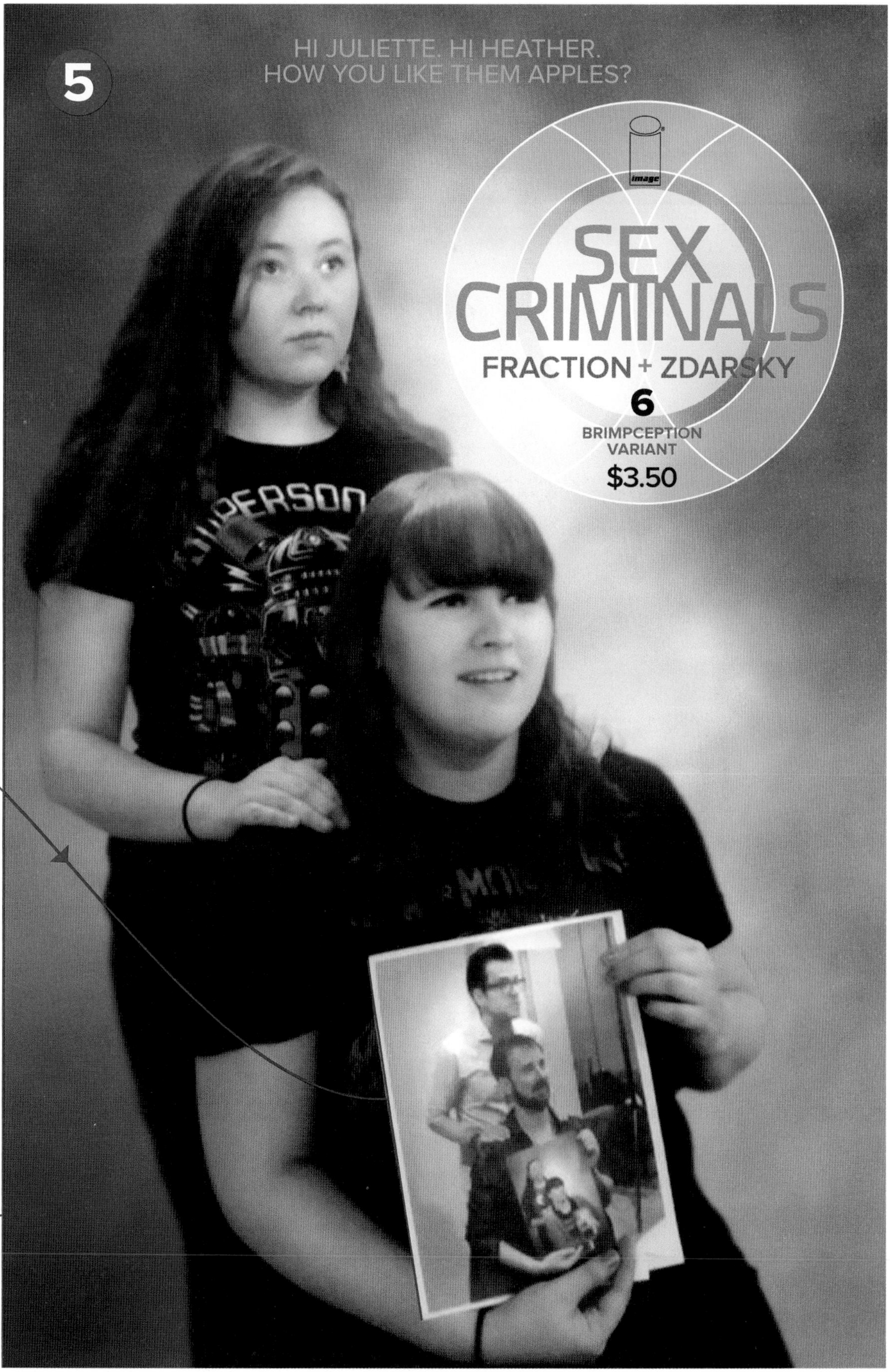
5
HI JULIETTE. HI HEATHER.
HOW YOU LIKE THEM APPLES?
image
SEX CRIMINALS
FRACTION + ZDARSKY
6
BRIMPCEPTION
VARIANT
$3.50

MATURE READERS

On the back of every issue is a warning, legally required by President Obama, against youngsters reading this trash. We take it very seriously. Here is every warning from the backs of our book, to date.

FOR MATURE READERS
DUH
DON'T SELL THIS TO A KID
WHAT ARE YOU, NUTS?
SERIOUSLY

#1 first printing, EH! variant, FP variant

FOR MATURE READERS
DUH
"SEX CRIMINALS IS AN IMAGINARY STORY ... AREN'T THEY ALL? ;) LOL"
CHIP ZDARSKY (SEX CRIMINALS)

#1 second printing

SECOND PRINTINGS ARE FOR CHUMPS. AND YOU, FRIEND, ARE NOT A CHUMP.

#1 third printing

THIS BOOK'S FOR MOMMIES & DADDIES WHO LOVE EACH OTHER VERY MUCH & MAYBE LOVE OTHER PEOPLE AS WELL IF THERE ARE SOME GROUND RULES, OK?

#1 fourth printing

COME FOR THE PALE, WHITE FACES ON THE COVER; STAY FOR THE HEARTWARMING STORY ABOUT LOVE AND SEX AND BUTT STUFF, I GUESS

#1 fifth printing (second printing of the fourth printing)

UNWHOLESOME COMICS ENTERTAINING

#1 sixth printing

IF YOU LOVE IMAGE COMICS SO MUCH WHY DON'T YOU MARRY THEM PFFT YOU PROBABLY CAN THANKS OBAMA

#1 Image Expo variant

THERE'S, LIKE, AN ENTIRE SCENE THAT TAKES PLACE IN A SEX SHOPPE

#2 first printing

WEIRD. AN OUTLINED YELLOW FONT ON BLACK ALWAYS LOOKS LIKE STAR WARS.

#2 second printing

REMEMBER: YOU CAN'T SPELL "IMATURE" WITHOUT "MATU—" WAIT. HOW DO YOU SPELL IMATURE AGAIN? HELLO?

#2 third printing

JUMP ON BOARD FOR THE SERIES CHIP'S MOM CALLED "VERY INTERESTING!"*
(*ZDARSKY FAMILY NEWSLETTER, XMAS 2013)

#2 fourth printing

I DON'T WANT MY KIDS LEARNING ABOUT LOVE FROM SOME FILTHY COMICAL BOOK

#3 first printing

FOR MATURE READERS DUH

TIME MAGAZINE'S BEST CAPTION ON THE BACK OF A FUNNY BOOK 2013

#3 second printing (TIME cover)

FOR MATURE READERS DUH

ALL TYPES OF BOTTOMED HUMANS ARE ALLOWED TO READ THIS PROVIDED THEY ARE ADULT HUMANS OF WHATEVER GENDER WHICH IS REALLY JUST A RELATIVE POINT ON A COMPLEX AND EVER-CHURNING CONTINUUM

#3 third printing (Queen cover)

DO NOT READ THIS COMIC UNLESS YOU'VE HAD "THE TALK" ABOUT STOPPING TIME & MAD PORK SESSIONS

#4 first printing

I LIKE TO THINK THAT THE GUY WHO MAKES FUNNY NOISES WITH HIS MOUTH WOULD STILL BE IN 'SEX POLICE ACADEMY'

#4 second printing

FOR A GOOD TIME, CALL OUT INTO THE WILD, "FOR MATURE READERS," AND JUST WAIT FOR ME

#5 first printing

From: **Chip Zdarsky**
Subject: Re: what if
Date: 31 March, 2012 11:39:37 AM EDT
To: Matt Fraction <mattfraction@gmail.com>

that is a romp i can get behind

#5 second printing

OR FOR EXTREMELY IMMATURE READERS, LIKE BABIES, WHO WILL JUST CHEW ON THIS PROBABLY

#6 first printing

OR FOR DISCERNING READERS WHO FREQUENT AUSTIN OGRE BALL COMICS

#6 retailer variant

DUH
FOR
MATURE
READERS
DUH

#6 Brimpception variant

BUT IT'S TOTALLY COOL IF SOMEONE'S JUST READING IT TO YOU I GUESS

#7 first printing

THAT WOULD ACTUALLY MAKE FOR A GREAT TATTOO ABOVE YOUR JUNK

#8 first printing

THIS COMIC CONTAINS GRAPHIC LANGUAGE, #BUTTS, #CHIP, #MATT, DOWNSTAIRS BUSINESS

#9 first printing

BUT MORE IMPORTANTLY IT'S FOR READERS WHO HAVE $3.50 CAUSE THIS AIN'T A LIBRARY, DUH.

#10 first printing

IT'S TOO LATE FOR YOU

This book right here, right now

Matt Fraction writes this, *SATELLITE SAM* (with Howard Chaykin), *ODY-C* (with Christian Ward), and *CASANOVA* (with Gabriel Bá, Fábio Moon, and Michael Chabon). He endeavors daily to put the 'criminal' into Milkfed Criminal Masterminds, the company he created with his wife, the writer Kelly Sue DeConnick, but is pretty much just a middle-age dad these days so blah blah.

Chip Zdarsky is the popular co-creator of *Sex Criminals Vol. 1* and will be the wildly unpopular co-creator of *Sex Criminals Vol. 3.* He won a Harvey Award in 2014 for "Most Promising New Talent," and died in 2015 from old age. As of press time he is writing *Howard The Duck* for Marvel Comics, but let's be honest, that could change at any second.

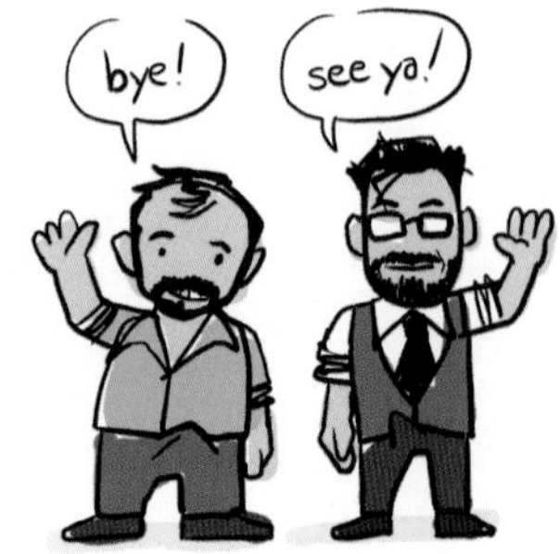
bye!
see ya!